Thinking Philosophically

Thinking Philosophically

An Introduction to the Great Debates

David Roochnik

WILEY Blackwell

This edition first published 2016
© 2016 John Wiley & Sons, Inc

Registered Office
John Wiley & Sons, Ltd, The Atrium, Southern Gate, Chichester, West Sussex, PO19 8SQ, UK

Editorial Offices
350 Main Street, Malden, MA 02148-5020, USA
9600 Garsington Road, Oxford, OX4 2DQ, UK
The Atrium, Southern Gate, Chichester, West Sussex, PO19 8SQ, UK

For details of our global editorial offices, for customer services, and for information about
how to apply for permission to reuse the copyright material in this book please see our
website at www.wiley.com/wiley-blackwell.

The right of David Roochnik to be identified as the author of this work has been asserted
in accordance with the UK Copyright, Designs and Patents Act 1988.

Library of Congress Cataloging-in-Publication data applied for

9781119067252 [hardback]
9781119067078 [paperback]

A catalogue record for this book is available from the British Library.

Cover image: Gettyimages/ktsimage

Set in 10/12.5pt Galliard by SPi Global, Pondicherry, India
Printed and bound in Malaysia by Vivar Printing Sdn Bhd

1 2016

Compete: From the Latin *com*, "together," and *petere*, "strive for, seek."

Brief Contents

Contents

Prologue

This book is largely about other books. Its list will include works by, among others, Plato, Rousseau, Nietzsche, and Augustine. One of its purposes is to help you, the reader, learn a bit about what is usually called "the history of philosophy." This phrase, however, is potenially misleading, for it suggests that Plato and company are now in the dustbin and that their books should be studied only because once they were influential. On this view, you should read them in order to become a well educated person who understands something about how the present emerged from the past. Of course, this is true. It is impossible to understand Western culture without having some background in the history of philosophy. But education in this sense is not the primary objective of this book. Instead, my task is convince you that these thinkers are as alive today as they were back then. For even in the age of the super-smartphone they have something to say. Their works articulate philosophical worldviews, rigorously connected trains of thought, that forge answers to the same questions that press us hard today. Even in the twenty-first century, a time convinced of its unique achievement, it is possible to recognize in a Rousseau or Augustine a kindred spirit.

This book has not been written for scholars. My assumption is that when you get to Chapter 1 you may well be picking up Plato's *The Apology of Socrates* for the first time. But pick it up and read it thoroughly you should, at least if you wish to participate fully in the project on which we will soon embark. If you don't, then you won't be able to judge whether what I'm saying holds water or not.

My chapters will discuss short selections from several great works of philosophy. The authors we will read, however, have each produced a vast corpus, and so the picture I present of them will be severely truncated. Chapter 2, for example, will discuss only a few passages from Rousseau's *Discourse on the Origin of Inequality*. But he also wrote the *Social Contract*. At first blush, these two books seem to express very different views.

It is the task of the Rousseau scholar to explain how they fit together, but not mine. Instead, I will concentrate only on a small chunk of the *Discourse* and extract from it Rousseau's remarkable analysis of what it means to be a social being. The result will surely be an oversimplification (albeit, I hope, a responsible one). You are, of course, encouraged to read more of his work, and of the other philosophers we will study, and thereby fill out the picture on your own.

The chapters to follow will not be arranged chronologically. Instead, they will be organized around a series of questions that have generated intense debate over the centuries. Chapter 2, for example, will feature Rousseau going head to head against Aristotle, even though they lived two thousand years apart. I have two reasons for structuring the book in this manner. First, to show that the ideas it will put into play are not specific to the particular moment of history in which they were written. Instead, they are basic intellectual options and thus are living possibilities even today. To emphasize this, I will consistently use the present tense when speaking about writers who lived long ago. Second, my goal is to generate *philosophical competition* between divergent views. I will explain why, and what this means, in Chapter 1. Suffice it to say here that the purpose of this book is to invite readers to enter the fray. As the etymology of "competition" suggests, I hope that "together" (*com*) we will "seek" (*petere*) answers to questions that have inspired thinkers of the past and continue to inspire today.

With the exception of the first, each chapter in this book will pit two thinkers who disagree on a specific topic against one another. The first section of these chapters will state what the question at issue is, and suggest why it matters. The next two sections will each concentrate on a single book written by one of the two philosophers being discussed. The fourth and final section will offer some recommendations on how you might begin the process of resolving the dispute. It will sketch the kinds of conceptual steps that need to be taken in order to think through the issue in a serious way. It will present positive and negative aspects of both views in the hope that this will help you determine, even if just provisionally, where *you* might stand in the debate. This is important. You have a stake in the outcome of these debates, and only by realizing this, only by having some skin in the game, will you go full steam ahead in philosophical pursuit.

A final few words on mechanics. This book will contain a great deal of quoted material. Some of it will be dense and difficult. In order to assist you in identifying key ideas, I will highlight words, phrases, and sentences that are both clear and reflective of the author's intentions. Think of my quotations as *pre-underlined* texts.

All the books we will read were written by men. When I discuss them I will typically use the male pronoun or the word "man." I will do this only in order to reflect the authors' sensibility, for they themselves largely conceived of their enterprise in masculine terms. By contrast, when I am speaking in my own voice – in particular, when I'm giving examples (and there will be many) – I will do what comes most naturally to me: use male and female pronouns. In thinking about philosophy, and imagining concrete cases and scenarios to illustrate the abstract ideas I struggle to explain, it never occurs to me that I am speaking exclusively about or to men.

All quotations will be followed (in parentheses) by the page numbers of the works I have cited. The relevant bibliographic information on them is contained in the "Works Cited" section found at the end of the book. It will also refer you to alternative translations, including ones available online. Some brief notes are included, the main purpose of which is to provide suggestions for further reading, as well as some ancillary comments that might be helpful in grappling with the material. This book is an introduction – better yet, it is an invitation – and the notes are meant to provide a resource for your future studies.

Good luck.

1

An Introduction to Philosophy

What Makes Philosophers Tick?

Philosophy is a peculiar enterprise, a strange form of conversation that began in Ancient Greece some 2500 years ago and continues today. The purpose of this book is to invite you to join in. But what is it you might be getting into?

On the one hand, philosophers are anything but unique. Like scientists, scholars, and students of every sort they are energized by an experience, or even a feeling: that of being bowled over – by curiosity, interest, amazement, fascination, perplexity, or wonder. This in turn sparks them to ask questions, usually ones that begin with "why." Philosophers want answers to their questions; that is, they want to explain why things are the way they are. In short, like other intellectuals they are driven by the desire to know.

Astronomers are amazed by the planets, and want to know why they move as they do. Biologists are fascinated by the intricate mechanisms of living organisms and they try to figure out why they work as well as they do. Mathematicians are captivated by the complexity of formal relations, which inspires them to summon ever more intensely their capacity for analytical reasoning. Historians spend their days in archives because they wonder about the when, where, and why of the past. They too want to know.

Philosophers are also seized by wonder and strive to answer questions that they experience as urgent. But what they (we) wonder about is different from what triggers the astronomer, biologist, mathematician, or historian. Natural scientists are amazed by things like bacteria, plants, animals, rocks, or stars. They are interested in the world outside of themselves and

Thinking Philosophically: An Introduction to the Great Debates, First Edition. David Roochnik.
© 2016 John Wiley & Sons, Inc. Published 2016 by John Wiley & Sons, Inc.

so they turn to the microscope or telescope to see it better. Philosophers, by contrast, are amazed at, and so they scope, themselves. Mathematicians are dedicated to solving problems in algebra or geometry. For philosophers the very life they are leading is the problem. Historians study the past. Philosophers wonder why they have a past in the first place and what role, if any, it should play in their lives.

A line from Plato's dialogue the *Phaedrus* makes this point sharply. Socrates – who is the inspiration for this book – is walking in the country-side with a companion who asks him whether he believes the stories about Boreas, the god to whom the Greeks assigned responsibility for the cold north wind. His companion's question implies that a scientific account, a little lecture in meteorology, would be far better than a silly old myth. Socrates responds by saying that while he admires the work of the scientists who debunk such stories, he himself has no time for such pursuits. He explains why:

> The reason, my friend, is this. I am still unable, as the Delphic inscription orders, *to know myself*, and it really seems to me ridiculous to look into extraneous matters before I have understood that. (*Phaedrus* 230a)[1]

The philosopher, at least according to Socrates, seeks *self-knowledge* rather than knowledge of the external world or of the mathematical structures that underlie it. But be careful. This does not mean that Socrates seeks to understand his uniquely personal self. He has no interest in probing the details of his childhood or learning how the traumatic events of his past made him into the person he became. Instead, his question is far more broad: What does it mean to be who I am; that is, a human being?

Another line, this one from the *Phaedo*, elaborates. Again, Socrates is contrasting himself with the natural scientists of his day. While he professes to admire their work, he describes himself as singularly unsuited for that kind of research. As he puts it, "I didn't have the nature" to study nature (96c). This statement implies that there are two senses of "nature." One is external: the world of wind, water, and stars. The second, to which Socrates devotes himself, is human nature, which somehow is different.

When I was in biology class as a kid in high school, I was struck by how eagerly other students were peering into their microscopes. They were amazed at all the little creatures that were swimming around in the drop of pond water that was on the slide. Me? I was more interested in why they were so interested … and why I was not.

The word "philosophy" is derived from two Greek words: *philia* (love) and *sophia* (wisdom). But to describe philosophy simply as "the love of wisdom" is far too vague. After all, the biologist is also impelled by a love of wisdom – about living organisms – and the historian seeks wisdom about the past. What, then, distinguishes philosophers? Again: the wisdom for which they (we) strive concerns the nature and meaning of human life.

The biologist might object: "I too want to understand human life. After all, we are animals with hearts and lungs and, most interesting of all, with genes, those molecular stretches of DNA and RNA that contain the information responsible for building and maintaining our cells. Like all other organisms the human animal is subject to the laws of natural selection and so in studying fruit flies in my laboratory I'm actually studying myself."

Where Socrates sees difference – there is human nature and then there are insects, plants, and cells – the biologist envisions an undivided realm of living organisms. Richard Dawkins, the renowned evangelist for Darwin's theory of natural selection, makes this point forcefully:

> An octopus is nothing like a mouse, and both are quite different from an oak tree. Yet in their fundamental chemistry they are rather uniform, and in particular the replicators that they bear, the genes, are basically the same kind of molecule in all of *us* – from bacteria to elephants. (*The Selfish Gene*, p. 21)

Note the word I have highlighted. For Dawkins "us" refers not only to himself, you and me, but also to the octopus and oak tree. "We" are all one.

Or consider what he says about natural selection: it is "the blind, unconscious, automatic process which Darwin discovered, and which we now know is the explanation for the existence … of *all* life" (*The Blind Watchmaker*, p. 5). Even more extravagantly, he says this:

> Darwinism encompasses all of life – human, animal, plant, bacterial … extraterrestrial. It provides the only satisfying explanation for why we all exist, *why we are the way that we are*. It is the bedrock on which rest all the disciplines known as the humanities. (*The Blind Watchmaker*, p. x)

Dawkins claims that the entire living world, including us (you and me), is of a single piece and that only Darwinism offers a satisfying explanation of "why we all exist." What is striking about this assertion is that it cannot itself be proven by the biological science he admires so greatly. For it is a totalizing claim that cannot possibly be verified by empirical evidence. No biologist, however assiduous, could actually study all of life. So, just as much as it is supported by his research, Dawkins's claim is also what initiates and shapes it. It tells him who he is as a thinker and as such is as much a presupposition as it is a conclusion.

This is not a criticism. Every science, like every proof, method, or research program, requires just such presuppositions. After all, you can't begin a search until you know what you're looking for, or an inquiry until you have a sense of what sort of answers you hope to find. But Dawkins's claim is so extravagant that we should at least raise the question: if he cannot prove that all living beings are essentially the same, that Darwinian natural selection is not just the bedrock of the humanities but the only satisfying explanation of why we all exist, then why should we believe him?

To paraphrase Dawkins, I too want to understand why I am the way I am. Part of who I am these days includes the fact that I ride a bicycle around the city of Boston. Why? Here are some scattershot answers.

I enjoy the convenience of using a bike rather than a car in a crowded city. It's easier and more efficient than struggling in traffic and trying to park. It gets me from door to door.

I enjoy the physical exertion a bicycle demands, which in a small city like Boston is typically not much. I'm probably healthier as a result of my many years on the bike.

When I'm on my bike, especially at night when I'm on the esplanade flanking the Charles River, I feel a bit like a kid doing something slightly dangerous and out of bounds. This is one of my favorite times to ride.

Because of my years of cycling around Boston I now have intimate knowledge of several neighborhoods in my city. I understand the traffic patterns at various intersections, which streets are crowded, which have bike lanes or give me a good view of the harbor. I know what kind of people to expect on the sidewalks, where the parks are, and the best routes to good restaurants that have outdoor seating and serve cold beer. I know what the town feels like in a visceral way.

When I'm in a car I typically have the windows closed and either the heat or the air-conditioning on, and I listen to the radio. I'm sealed off from the streets, ensconced in my own little world, and there's little chance of surprise. This is often quite pleasant and I still enjoy driving a great deal, especially on highways. But I prefer the bike in the city where chance interactions with cars, pedestrians, buildings, and other cyclists are the norm. On the bike I am plunged directly into the flow of public life. At the same time, I'm also more independent. I don't have to wait for a train or bus, don't have to worry about traffic. I can go door to door and do so when I want. Yes, sometimes it takes longer and it demands work from me. But that's a small price to pay.

My wife and I no longer own a car, although we do belong to a car-sharing service, which allows us to rent one for short periods. We're both delighted to be saving as much money as we are by not having a car.

According to one estimate, the average cost of maintaining a car in 2012 was nearly $8000 per year. (See http://www.autoblog.com/2012/05/04/average-cost-of-car-ownership-rises-to-8-946-per-year/.)

Because I can no longer simply jump into the car and go to the super-market to buy a quart of milk, I've become more deliberate about my shopping. I need to plan routes carefully and, because I can carry so little on my bike, shop frequently. Because my transportation requires effort, I am more mindful of where and when I travel.

The best months for biking here in Boston are in the summer and early fall when the weather is warm and farmers' markets are scattered all over town. Since my wife and I have been on our bikes, the geography of our lives has shrunk dramatically. We don't go to the big-box stores on the highway in order to save money. Our shopping is almost exclusively local and we buy directly from the farmers, cheese-makers, and bakers who are selling their goods. We hand them cash instead of a credit card, and talk to them far more than we would to the minimum wage clerks at the supermarket who have no stake in the multinational corporation that has employed them. We also talk to the other customers, with whom we often feel something of a bond.

There's always some risk in riding a bike on a busy city street. I've narrowly missed serious accidents and many cyclists tell stories of being "doored" or otherwise hit by a car. But the little jolt of adrenaline that comes with competing against traffic on Commonwealth Avenue is part of the attraction. I'm alert and ready to turn quickly or clutch the brakes hard. Unlike most of my ordinary day, during which I'm preoccupied with my worries and responsibilities, when I'm on the bicycle my focus narrows. I'm more concentrated and attentive. It's both relaxing and energizing at the same time.

Like a car, a bicycle is a machine, a device that changes the direction or augments the magnitude of a force. But the force of a car is generated by burning an energy source external to the driver, while that of a bicycle is generated by the energy provided by the rider. On the bike I am responsible for making myself move and so it's more like an extension of my body than is a car – which is another reason why I feel more actively alive on the bike.

I'm usually scrupulous about obeying the same rules that apply to the cars. I stop at red lights. By doing so I let the cars around me know that I too belong on the road and so deserve their respect. I am telling them that I am an equal partner in the social contract they've made to obey the rules. As a result, I feel safer when I obey the law.

Because I no longer own a car I'm something of an outlier in my circle of friends. I've been on the margins before and it's a region where I feel at home. On the other hand, there are now so many cyclists on the road that riding a bike is almost like being part of a movement. In taking to our bicycles we make a statement. In the last 60 years the automobile has decisively shaped the infrastructure, economy, and way of life in American cities and suburbs. By and large this has been a disaster. Instead of celebrating and affirming the importance of vibrant public space, and their own bodies, instead of living small and in the local, most Americans move from one large private place to another in their cars. Being on the bike makes me part of the city in a new and politically healthy way.

Being on a bike forces me to acknowledge my vulnerability; in particular, my incapacity to alter the weather. I enjoy the warm sunshine, but suffer when I get caught in an unexpected storm. The car, by contrast, affords me a predictably comfortable ride. But the bargain I've made seems to me a good one.

By riding a bike rather than driving a car I am responsible for a little less carbon being spewed into the atmosphere. If the predictions are correct, then global warming will cause people around the world a great deal of harm. I am doing my tiny bit to counteract this frightening process. Perhaps we all should.

A biologist like Richard Dawkins can surely explain much about what I have just described. He can teach me a great deal about how my muscles work as they propel the bicycle through space, or how my brain processes the visual stimuli flying past my eyes. He can supply me with an account of how the human organism has evolved such that it now receives positive feedback from physical exercise and motion. He would have something to say about the good feeling I have of being connected to my community, of being public, when I'm on my bike. He might argue that human animals have evolved such that they now have a natural desire to cooperate with one another, and that doing so has increased the survival prospects of the species.

A psychologist perhaps could explain why I relish being an outlier and reverting to an activity that was an important part of my childhood. Maybe I've retained some remnant of my adolescent rebellion. And the social scientists can supply data that would verify my hunch that riding bicycles contributes to the well-being of a city. Researchers in Copenhagen, for example, have calculated that some $30 million a year is saved by the reduction in air pollution, accidents, and wear and tear on the infrastructure that is due to the enormous number of people there who use bicycles instead of cars. (An extensive discussion of this can be found at http://www.forbes.com/sites/justingerdes/ 2012/01/23/copenhagens-green-sheen-its-not-just-about-the-bikes/.)

This statistic, whose accuracy I have no way of verifying, appeals to me. But neither it nor any other scientific account fully addresses the questions sparked by my own reflections on riding a bike.

What does it mean to feel more alive on the bicycle, when I'm powering a machine with my own muscles, than when I'm the passive beneficiary of the effortless motion of a fuel-burning car? Is being alive equivalent to the expression of power? In turn, is this equivalent to being physically active? If so, what would that say about my mind? Might I not be even more alive, more powerful, if I spent more time in my office thinking or working on my computer? Perhaps rather than augmenting my life I'm actually sacrificing precious time by giving so much of it to crude physical exertion instead of intellectual activity.

There are obvious health benefits to riding a bike. But what exactly is health? These days I feel pretty good. But is this fleeting sensation the best way to measure health? Perhaps a better assessment would be to methodically compare the life spans of cyclists to those of automobile drivers. The question would then become, am I tacking years onto my life by riding a bike? We won't know until I'm done, but I can ask this question now: is longer life equivalent to better life? Indeed, is good health something that can be measured quantitatively? Even more generally: is there a significant difference between merely staying alive and having a good life? If so, what is it?

In a similar vein: why deliberately put myself at some risk of injury by riding a bike rather than driving a car? Does the value of bike riding somehow trump the risks associated with it? This question leads to a more general one: is the value of any activity determined only by its future benefits? I'm saving money by not owning a car. Is having the extra cash what makes bike riding valuable? Or are some activities, even dangerous ones, valuable just because they are what they are? Are they good simply in and of themselves?

A related question: if we assess the value of our activities by their consequences and possible benefits, does this imply that our orientation to the future is paramount in our lives? We are animated by our plans, expectations, hopes, and worries. What, then, are we to make of our engagement with the present? Why can't we simply be here now? Perhaps we should try. Or is the attempt to be in the present finally a fool's errand? Perhaps the present is no more than a vanishing moment, a gateway between past and present with no duration of its own. If so, there is no "now" for us to be in at all. Whatever the answer, we are forced to reflect on the fact that we are irrevocably implicated in the flow of time from the future through the present and into the past. And to ask, what is the best and healthiest stance we can adopt to this overwhelming fact of our lives?

Why, since it's possible to protect ourselves from inclement weather inside of a car, might it be preferable for us willingly to put ourselves at the mercy of nature's unpredictable force? If it is possible to minimize contingencies with ever more powerful technologies, why not do so?

And that feeling of childhood joy, of playfulness, that comes with riding at night? I'm amazed and delighted that at my age I still enjoy this. But what's that all about? Is play merely a frivolous abdication of adult responsibility?

And that sense of being physically present in the city, in the public realm? Why is this good? What's positive about public space and cooperating with others? My bike riding represents a tiny protest against a culture that isolates us from one another. Or is that nonsense? If you think something's gone wrong in your own community, shouldn't you do more about it than ride a bike in silent protest? Perhaps I should run for office or become a political activist.

Farmers' markets are attractive because they are small, local, and personal. But the goods they sell are more expensive than what's available in the supermarket. Is it worth it to pay the higher price? Why is a small enterprise better than a huge one, especially when the latter, as we are so often told, is vastly more efficient in bringing goods to the market? What is so alluring about the local?

Should I obey the law simply because it's the law? Or should I do so only when I am benefited by doing so?

I take a small bit of pride in my membership in the biking community when most of my agemates are stuck in their cars. They know Boston hardly at all. I, by contrast, know much of it well. Or is this merely the voice of stubborn vanity? Am I just showing off?

I know what Boston looks like, how it feels, and how it moves because I interact with it physically. But does this really qualify as knowledge in any serious sense? I have some experience with the city's streets, but maybe that's all. What is knowledge?

Are people morally obligated to take the small measures we can in order to protect the fragile atmosphere on which our lives on earth depend?

These are a few of the questions that occur to me in thinking about bike riding, and they are not directly or fruitfully addressed by scientists whose basic task is to understand how things work or the brain has evolved. By contrast, this book is animated by the conviction that the philosophers to be studied in the chapters to follow will provide resources for seriously grappling with them. A third line uttered by Socrates, again from the *Phaedo*, helps clarify. He imagines a natural scientist responding to the simple question, "Why am I sitting here now?"

> the reason that I am sitting here [says the imaginary scientist] is because my body consists of bones and sinews, because the bones are hard and are separated by joints, that the sinews are such as to contract and relax,

that they surround the bones along with flesh and skin which hold them together, then as the bones are hanging in their sockets, the relaxation and contraction of the sinews enable me to bend my limbs, and that is the cause of my sitting here with my limbs bent. (*Phaedo* 98d)

Socrates finds this answer unsatisfying. By his lights "the true cause [of my sitting here] ... is that *it seemed best* for me to sit here" (*Phaedo* 98e).

There are any number of ways of answering the question, why am I sitting here now? The physiologist will do so by explaining the mechanics of my body that put me in this chair. The evolutionary psychologist will explain how the human brain has evolved such that it can read and write, as I am now doing as I sit. The economist can explain why some people, like me, have enough free time to enjoy this kind of leisurely and perhaps pointless activity, while others work day and night just to put food on the table. Different kinds of explanations satisfy different kinds of inquiry. Dawkins, for one, believes that only Darwin's theory of natural selection provides a satisfying answer to the *why* question. But this is because that's what interests him. He is fascinated by the history and mechanisms of animal behavior and so, like Socrates' imaginary scientist, would explain how my "bones and sinews," which themselves are the result of millions of years of evolutionary development, brought me into this chair now.

Socrates admires such intellectual work. But he doesn't find it satisfying, and not because the science of his day was primitive. No, other questions demanding different sorts of answers call out to him. As he puts it, he is sitting here now because it "seemed best" for him to do so. After all, had he wished to he could have stood up and walked away. But he didn't. Why? And did he make the right decision? Again, a mechanical or evolutionary answer to such questions would, to Socrates at least, miss the target. As he said in the *Phaedrus*, it would provide only "extraneous" information. What he wants to understand instead is the *meaning* of his own action.

"Meaning" is a word with some pizazz. It has two senses. The first is linguistic: "to signify" or "have import." So, for example, the word "table" means a piece of furniture with vertical supports and a flat top on which to place objects. The second is "have as one's purpose" or "intend," as in "I have been meaning to call you but I forgot." Put these two senses together and the familiar phrase, "the meaning of life," suggests that life has a purpose that can be intelligibly signified and articulated. It is to this project, broadly construed, that Socrates is committed.

Whether you will continue reading this book or not will depend on what questions you find compelling. Would a lecture in anatomy or neuroscience slake your thirst for knowledge? Would an evolutionary theory provide you with a satisfying answer to Dawkins's question, "why we all exist, why we are the way that we are?" If so, read no further. By contrast, if Socrates' comments about the natural scientists of his own day ring true, if his demand that our attention be focused on the meaning of our lives as we actually experience them has some pull, then perhaps you should continue.

Five Questions

This book will be organized around five broad questions that can be extracted from my reflections about riding a bike. To state them briefly:

1   *Are we social-political beings?*   I enjoy shopping in a local farmers' market with my wife, riding my bicycle on the crowded streets of my city, and spending time in public places. I read the newspapers and care a great deal about what is happening in my country. I hold those people who are consumed by self-interest in contempt. But my doing so raises a question: are we by nature social-political beings? Are we more ourselves when we're involved and concerned with our community than when we're on our own? Or is it somehow only in solitude, far from the judgmental gaze of others, that we can be fully ourselves? Is being part of a community an abdication of our responsibility to be authentic individuals?
2   *What should we do?*   Burning fossil fuels will likely harm other people, probably poor ones, by contributing to global warming. Are we therefore obligated to do our bit to lessen the impact? Is my eschewing of a car, then, a morally admirable act? But how do we determine when an act is genuinely moral? Realistically, riding my bike rather than driving a car will make no appreciable difference to the chemical composition of the atmosphere. Is an action's morality determined only by what it accomplishes? Or are some actions, regardless of their consequences, simply the right ones to take?
3   *Whom should we emulate?*   This question is obviously similar to the previous one, but it is also significantly different. Rather than asking about the morality of specific actions – should I do X or refrain from doing Y? – it demands that we take a step back and examine our lives as a whole. What is the most excellent and fulfilling, what is the most truly human life available to us? Is there a specific type of person who can function as a model to emulate? If so, can he or she provide concrete guidance on how to conduct ourselves on a daily basis?

4   *What do we know and how do we know it?* I claim to have knowledge of Boston because I am familiar with its streets. But should this sort of accumulated experience really count as knowledge? Perhaps knowing is a far more demanding enterprise and is strictly an act of the mind. Perhaps the researchers in Copenhagen who have measured the economic impact of bicycle riding can, with quantitative precision, claim to know something. But me? What do I know? And if I do know something, how did I come to know it?

5   *What is it to be-in-time?* I'm restless and often preoccupied by future possibilities. I'm almost always slightly ahead of myself and so my morning writing sessions are often interrupted when I remind myself of what's on tap in the afternoon. My wife, by contrast, is better able to pay attention to what's before her eyes. She knows how to linger and enjoy, and she rarely worries – which is why she is often late for appointments. And yet at night she is often consumed by the past. Her regrets keep her awake.

We are inescapably temporal beings and how we orient ourselves to the future–present–past flow of time shapes who we are. Some of us aim relentlessly toward what might be tomorrow, others drift into what was yesterday, while some seem more comfortable in the present. But the big question is this: what is time? What reality does it have? After all, the past is gone, the future is not yet, and the present may be no more than a vanishing moment through which the future flies into the past. Here today, gone tomorrow: is that it? If so, then perhaps we should seek elsewhere – that is, to what is timeless – for solace. But what if nothing is exempt from the annihilating flow of time?

Perhaps one reason I like riding my bicycle on city streets, where the action is often fast and furious, is that it forces me to concentrate and be more fully engaged in the present than I usually am. I can't afford to worry about tomorrow while I'm riding. Instead, I have to pay attention to the parked cars in order to make sure a door doesn't open in my path. Perhaps riding a bike under these conditions is rewarding because it affords me a temporary refuge from the unyielding passage from future into past.

Reading Great Books

As with everything else in this introductory chapter, these five questions have been briefly sketched with an eye toward giving you some inkling of what the philosophical enterprise, inspired by Socrates, might be like.

By myself, however, using language of my own and drawing on my personal experiences and capacity for analyzing them, I cannot go very far in answering them. I'm just not that smart.

Fortunately, I'm not on my own. Throughout my adult life I've been a student of those old books typically labeled as "great" or "classic." If I have made any progress whatsoever in addressing, or even articulating, the questions just posed, it is because I have read them. Therefore, my own book will largely be about them. Authors to be discussed will include Plato, Rousseau, Aristotle, Saint Augustine, Nietzsche, Mill, Kant, Descartes and Hume ... great thinkers all. (There will also be a brief chapter on two great Chinese thinkers: Confucius and Lao-Tzu.)

What makes a philosophical work great is that in it the author has generated a comprehensive answer to a question sparked by wonder. Since great thinkers wonder about everything and their minds are so powerful, they develop an enormous train of thought, one that stretches from beginning to end. They understand that no question, not even the broad ones sketched above, can be answered in isolation from all the others. For example, how we should act morally (2) and what sort of life we should aspire to (3), depends on how we are or should be oriented in time (5) and whether we are by nature social/political beings (1). Understanding how we know (4) underlies any response we might make to the other questions. A serious philosopher conceives a big picture and aspires to give a consistent account. Unless you're a genius, it's a bad idea to try this on your own. There is, then, no better way for most of us to learn how to think philosophically than by carefully working through all the many steps a great thinker has laid down in a book.

I could try to explain more of what I'm talking about, but that would not be wise. A far better way to illustrate what I mean is to do what I've been doing for 30 years in classrooms: open a book and work my way through it; try to retrace or reconstruct the author's thought process as he develops his account and do so as clearly as I can; and invite others to do the same. This is precisely what the chapters to follow will do.

A potential obstacle looms. A striking fact about these putatively great philosophers is that they *disagree* with one another. Aristotle, for example, believes that human beings are by nature political. This implies that to conceive of oneself as primarily an individual rather than a citizen, which is what most people in America do today, is to be less than fully human. Rousseau, by contrast, argues that by nature we are solitary beings. In society, he thinks, we continually compare ourselves to, and thus see ourselves through the eyes of, others. As such, in society we are invariably lost to ourselves. For him, then, Aristotle is dead wrong.

John Stuart Mill believes that a moral act is defined by the positive consequences it has on other people's lives. If riding a bike and thereby depositing a little less carbon into the atmosphere makes the world a better place, then perhaps it is moral to ride a bike. Kant, by contrast, argues that a moral act is not dependent on its consequences, but only on the principle that guides it. If, as he believes, we ought to keep our promises, then we ought not to break them under any circumstances.

In keeping with his commitment to the political nature of human being, Aristotle thinks that the best life is led by a mature, serious, fully rational adult, who accepts the responsibility of providing sound leadership to others. Nietzsche, by contrast, finds the paradigm of human flourishing in a child at play. As we will see in our one chapter on non-Western philosophy, Confucius and Lao-Tzu similarly disagree. The former finds some common ground with Aristotle, while the latter is closer in spirit to Nietzsche.

Descartes argues that some ideas are so clear and distinct that by utilizing them alone we can attain certain knowledge. Such knowledge is a priori; that is, it is independent of sensible reality and so neither can nor needs to be empirically verified. By his lights, my claim to have gained some sort of experiential knowledge of the city of Boston through bike riding is muddled nonsense. Hume, by contrast, believes that all our ideas, and thus the very possibility of knowledge, arise from our experiences. For him no purely cognitive capacity can discover the truth about the world in isolation from sensible reality.

Saint Augustine believes that everything that exists in time – everything we can see with our eyes or touch with our hands – is insubstantial and necessarily unsatisfying. For him what is here today and gone tomorrow is not fully real. He offers a brilliant analysis of what is now known as "time consciousness" and argues that a life implicated in the past–present–future flow of time is, by itself, no more than a disappearing wisp of smoke. As a result he thinks it is altogether reasonable for us to orient ourselves toward what is immune to the flow of time; to, in other words, the Eternal; to God. By contrast, Nietzsche finds Augustine's denigration of temporal flow despicable. For him, to deny the reality and goodness of the passage of time is a kind of self-hatred. Yes, time flies, but that's all we've got, and so Nietzsche challenges us to have the courage to affirm our lives for what they are rather than to escape into an imaginary and lifeless beyond.

In short, the history of philosophy is a series of disagreements and disputes, of competing ideas, in which an uncontested winner has never emerged. Unlike contemporary chemists, who would agree on how many elements are on the periodic table, or the overwhelming number of biologists who affirm the theory of natural selection, philosophers contest the most basic issues even today. Unlike their colleagues in the natural sciences or in economics, philosophers do not share a single theoretical framework by means of which they can join others in order to make cumulative progress. Instead, their job is to determine what the foundations and frameworks are. And on these issues they disagree. The competition goes on.

But here's the problem. If the authors just mentioned above disagree with each other so radically, how can they all be "great?" With views so thoroughly opposed, don't some of them simply have to be wrong?

One philosopher was so repelled by the endless disputation and lack of progress in his own discipline that he decided to chuck it all. Descartes wrote the following:

> Concerning philosophy, I will say only that, seeing that it has been culti-
> vated for many centuries by the most excellent minds that have ever lived
> and that, nevertheless, there still is nothing in it about which there is not
> some ***dispute***, and consequently nothing that is not ***doubtful***, I was not at
> all so presumptuous as to hope to fare any better. (Descartes, *Discourse on
> Method*, p. 5)

Descartes's apparent humility is bogus, for he was determined not only to junk traditional Western philosophy but to start from scratch and come up with something better; namely, a theoretical position that, unlike his predecessors', was not "doubtful." Of course, his attempt has also been disputed ever since he presented it some four hundred years ago. In other words, Descartes himself became part of the very tradition he held in contempt.

Even if within the history of philosophy there is no topic about which there has been full agreement, this need not be reason for despair. Descartes may have thought it was, but this is because (as we will see in Chapter 6) he was a thinker with a very specific intellectual temperament and consequent agenda. Most tellingly, he loved the clarity and certainty he found in his study of mathematics, which became for him the standard against which all other claims to knowledge had to be measured. As such, he recoiled at any whiff of ambiguity or doubt. But surely it is possible to conceive of philosophical disagreement in a more positive way. Regardless of how beautiful and powerful it may be, mathematics is not always the best example of knowledge. If that's true, then the competition between philosophers of the past need not be construed as a depressing litany of failure. Instead, it can be understood as a vibrant and ongoing conversation into which, even today, we are not only welcome to enter but would benefit from doing so. To clarify, consider this example.

Rousseau must have read Aristotle's book *The Politics* for he uses the following line from it as the epigraph of his own work, *The Discourse on the Origin of Inequality*: "It is in things whose condition is according to nature that one ought particularly to investigate what is by nature, not in things that are defective."

In the passage to which Rousseau refers, Aristotle proposes a methodological principle: in order to understand any natural being – say an animal species – we should study the best representatives of that species, those whose condition is, as he puts it, "according to nature." To understand what it is to be an eagle, study a healthy adult in the prime of life who is fierce, flies high, and has powerful vision. Doing so will disclose "eagleness" or what it means to be an eagle. In a parallel fashion, to understand human nature study those people whom Aristotle would call "excellent." These are the ones who have actualized their natural capacities and maximally fulfilled their human potential. It is by looking to them rather than to those who "are defective" that we best learn what it means to be a human being.

In a sense Rousseau agrees, and his book is devoted to precisely the task of examining the most fully natural of human beings. But he disagrees entirely on who such individuals might be. In short, Aristotle gave Rousseau his question – what is human nature? – and a method for responding to it, but then Rousseau, entering the competition, thought it through for himself. As we will see in some detail in Chapter 2, he then forged an answer that, even while being indebted to Aristotle's, was radically opposed to it.

Once again, Descartes's challenge must be raised. If these two putatively "great" philosophers disagreed with one another so thoroughly, how could any of us adjudicate the competition between them? And why should we even try? Perhaps because both Aristotle and Rousseau were ignorant of recent discoveries in neuroscience and evolutionary psychology neither had a legitimate shot at answering the question in the first place. If so, why bother with them at all?

When I was a graduate student and would visit my parents on holidays, my father, an engineer and amateur mathematician, would tease me. "Any breakthroughs lately?" he'd ask. Deep down he was a generous and supportive man, but his question was meant to bite. He simply couldn't understand why I had decided to study philosophy. Why plunge into a useless discipline, which seems to go nowhere?

To develop a response I again turn to Socrates for assistance.

An Introduction to Socrates

 Plato, *The Apology of Socrates*

The Greek word *apologia*, translated as "apology," did not mean saying you're sorry or regretfully acknowledging a fault. Instead, it was a legal term referring to a defense speech. Socrates had been accused by the authorities of a crime: "corrupting the young and not believing in the gods in whom the city believes" (24b). He was charged with subversion, which in turn was tied to his (alleged) rejection of traditional religion. In his "apology" he attempts to convince the jury that he is innocent.

He begins by recounting a story. His friend Chaerophon had consulted the Delphic Oracle and asked if anyone was wiser than Socrates. The answer: "no one was" (21a). Socrates took this to mean that he was "the wisest" (21b) of men. This puzzled him because, as he puts it, "I am very conscious that I am not wise at all" (21b). Presumably Socrates still finds the world a puzzling place. In any case, he explains to the jury that in order to fathom the meaning of the Oracle he attempted to find someone wiser than himself. To this end he sought out three kinds of people who, at least in the eyes of public opinion (and themselves), were counted as wise. In other words, he sought out the intellectual celebrities of his day, the ones who, were they living now, would appear on talk shows. These were the politicians, poets, and technical experts. Surely, he reasoned, a representative from one of these groups must be wiser than he.

First, let's get clear on why Socrates singled out these three groups. Politicians, whether in ancient Athens or contemporary America, are inevitably and relentlessly assertive, for in order to compel their audience they must project a sense of authority. They are putative leaders who have to make quick decisions, some of them genuinely consequential, and they cannot be seen to falter. As a result, it's hard to imagine a successful politician, having been asked a question, answering with, "You know, I'm really not sure. Let's talk about it." Instead, they invariably make pronouncements with the highest level of confidence in their own wisdom, and ask the rest of us to follow along.

"Poets" too had a reputation for wisdom. The meaning of this word in Greek is broader than it is in English. It refers to those who "make" (*poiein*) something, and so actually comes close to our own word "artist." The contemporary equivalent of the ancient "poet" would thus include not only literary lights such as Robert Pinsky, but also playwrights, storytellers, video-makers, painters, and web site designers. These are the people who shape a culture, give it a voice, an image, and a sense of itself. Like the politicians, the "makers" are so sure they understand the way things are that they eagerly sell their views to the public. Through the dissemination of their artwork they tell us – sometimes explicitly, more often implicitly – how we should look and talk, what we should do, think, feel, wear, and watch. They exert great influence over their audience, especially the young. Just like the politicians, then, their very activity implies a confident claim to know how things really are.

The third sort of notable Socrates interrogates are the ancient versions of today's engineers; those who have some form of technical expertise. These are people who figure out how to construct devices that the rest of us use to make life easier. The ancient potter knew how to make jars that could efficiently store olive oil and wine for long periods of time. The carpenter could build houses. And today's software engineer writes the code that provides user-friendly access to vast amounts of information. Socrates acknowledges that these are very smart people. As he puts it, "they had knowledge of many fine things ... they knew things I did not know" (22d). But, like the politicians and the poets, they overreach. Because they are good at what they do, and the results of their work are often both powerful and useful, "they thought themselves very wise in other ***most important*** pursuits" (22d). Socrates doesn't specify what these are, but we can guess. What is most important – at least to him – are questions like, is it best for me to be sitting here now? Or, by being so preoccupied with the future am I squandering the little time allotted to me here on earth? Why is having dinner with friends a vital ingredient in leading a meaningful life? What's good about riding a bike in Boston? Why should I care about the impact of my actions on other people? What should I do when things are going badly in my country? Do I really know anything, and if so how did I manage that? In short, his questions all concentrated on the goal of, broadly construed, self-knowledge.

Politicians continually harangue us with their declarations of how things should be, but they rarely stop to ask themselves what counts as genuinely good, beautiful, or just. Poets may tell terrific stories, their characters may spring to life off the page or on screen, but they can't explain what their artwork means. And, regardless of how rigorous his training has been, the expertise of the engineer confers no knowledge as to how technological innovations should be put to good use in the human world. By itself this is no failing. Instead, where techies go wrong is in thinking "they know something when they do not" (21d). Merely having technical knowledge isn't enough for them. Instead, they think they know that the latest device is good and that it should be used. They believe that technical knowledge is the be-all and end-all of the human intellect, and that those who possess it should run the show.

Socrates exposes the fraudulence of such blowhards by rigorously testing their assertions. How exactly he does this is a long story. Suffice it to say here that by his lights – and of course his own lights need to be thoroughly scrutinized – those who are most famous for being wise don't measure up at all.

So far, this brief description of Socrates' philosophical activity seems entirely negative. He knocks top dogs off their pedestals by showing them that they don't know what they think they do. But there's a positive side to his story as well. After interrogating one of the politicians and revealing the emptiness of his claims, he concludes that,

> I am wiser than this man; it is likely that neither of us knows anything worthwhile, but he thinks he knows something when he does not, whereas when I do not know, neither do I think I know; so I am likely to be wiser than he to this small extent, that I do not think I know what I do not know. (21d)

Socrates claims to possess what he calls "*human wisdom*" (20d). He recognizes his limitations, but precisely by doing so he becomes wiser than anyone else. His wisdom, then, is simultaneously negative and positive. To clarify, consider the following example.

When I woke up this morning, I got dressed, made coffee and then opened the newspaper to the sports page to find out who won the baseball game last night. I did so because I knew that (1) there was a game; (2) since a baseball game cannot end in a draw there was a victor; (3) I did not know the outcome of the game; (4) I wanted to know the outcome of the game; (5) the newspaper would contain the answer to my question.

Just like Socrates, asking questions is simultaneously negative and positive. It's an admission that answers are lacking, but it also requires the possession of background knowledge that makes it possible to ask questions in the first place. I did not know the outcome of the game. But I did know the five items listed above, and that's why I opened the newspaper in order to discover the answer to my question.

Of those five items, the first two are simple facts of which I was knowledgeable: there was a game last night and, given the rules of baseball, it could not have ended in a draw. The third item – I knew that I did not know the outcome of the game – presupposed that I already knew the first two facts but required something additional: some introspection. I recalled that I went to bed early last night and so did not stay up to watch the whole game. As a result, I was aware of my own ignorance this morning. The fourth item – I knew that I wanted to know the outcome – also required a tiny bit of self-knowledge. I am a life-long sports fan who, for better or worse, cares about boxscores. As a result, I know what to do when I see a newspaper: open it to the sports page. I was conscious not only of the knowledge I lacked but of its significance to me, and so I strove to overcome my ignorance. For this reason I asked a question (of the newspaper): "Who won the game last night?"

Finally, I knew where to find the answer to my question: the sports page. After all, I've been reading newspapers my whole life and am familiar with what sort of information they contain. When we ask questions – or at least when we do so with intelligence and seriousness of purpose – we already have in mind what the answer might look like and how it might be found. Had I not already known a great deal about baseball, simply seeing the headline, "Red Sox Lose to Orioles," would have been meaningless to me.

To sum up so far: asking questions has both a negative and a positive side, and this helps us understand the peculiarity of Socrates' self-description in the *Apology*. On the one hand, with apparent modesty he denies having wisdom and claims that his only advantage over the intellectual celebrities of his day is his cognizance of his own deficiency. On the other, he claims to possess a kind of wisdom. And about this he can be remarkably arrogant. At one point, for example, he compares himself to a famous athlete. (The Greeks were as mad for sports as we are today.) Because he achieves victory for the home team and makes the fans watching him from their seats in the stadium scream for joy, the athlete "makes you think yourself happy." But Socrates claims that this momentary elation is illusory. After all, the fan does no more than bask in the glow of someone else's achievement. By contrast, Socrates says, "I make you be really happy" (36e).

This is strange. How can Socrates, who aggressively unmasks ignorance, make people happy? Because he propels them into a state of questioning. And this requires him to do more than make them cognizant of their deficiencies. He must inculcate in them a positive desire to know. He must make them hungry. As items (3) and (4) above suggest, you don't ask a question unless you realize not only that you lack knowledge but that you want to overcome this lack. If the first stage of Socratic examination is to show people they are ignorant of "the most important matters," the second is to convince them that this should bother them, and they should do something to remedy the situation. For this reason, he exhorts people to ask the most pressing of questions – such as, why is it best for me to be sitting here now? – and to try to find answers. By doing so, he claims, they will become genuinely happy.

Again, this is strange. You might rather think that having answers would make you happy. No, says Socrates, it's the asking of questions. He expresses this point emphatically:

> I say it is the greatest good for a human being to discuss *virtue* every day and those other things about which you hear me conversing and testing myself and others, for *the unexamined life is not worth living for men.* (38a)

The best life is one of self-examination in which we enter into philosophical conversation. And our topic should be "virtue" or, as the Greek word (*aretê*) is also translated, "excellence." In other words, the "greatest good" available to human beings is discussing what the greatest good might be. To this question we should pose possible answers and then test them against competitors. Together we should strive for understanding. Indeed, so paramount is this activity that Socrates declares that "the unexamined life," the one spent in unreflective assurance that you know what's really going on, is not worth living. At this moment of the *Apology*, Socrates is no longer Mr. Humility who is aware only of his own ignorance. He is more like a Hebrew prophet who thunders that his fellow human beings, especially the intellectual celebrities who pontificate on talk shows, might as well be dead.

How could this outrageous statement possibly be true? Perhaps only if the following is true: at the core, the human being is a questionable animal. Because of who we are and the world in which we live, because of the nature of both our intellects and the objects of our inquiries, rather than being fixed and settled we are in-between and on-the-way. Our nature is ever to strive. To think – and worse, to act as if – we possess definitive answers to our most pressing questions is to distort our very being.

To clarify, recall my simple example. To ask (of the newspaper) who won the game last night is to locate myself in between knowledge and ignorance. For asking it requires me not only to understand a couple of simple facts, but also to know both what I lack and that trying to overcome this lack is a meaningful task. Finally, I must know what an answer to my question would look like and have an intuition about where to find it. What if this kind of being-in-between, this mingling of lack and desire, of negative and positive, constitutes human nature itself? If so, then asking a question would express and fulfill, would do justice to, our nature. Asking the right questions, and being willing to test our answers by engaging in philosophical competition, would itself be a kind of answer.

No doubt, at this point Descartes is rolling his eyes in disbelief. For how could a question be an answer, and why should anyone ask "what is excellence?" if, as Socrates seems to believe, definitive resolution is not readily, if ever, forthcoming? Furthermore, while it's obvious that the sports page contains the answer to my question about the game last night, do we have even the slightest clue about where to find answers to such questions as "what is goodness?" or "what is beauty?" or "what is the meaning of our lives?" How, then, do we heed Socrates' exhortation and begin our inquiry?

Socrates suggests a sort of solution: use him as a "model" or "paradigm" (23b) of the philosophical life. Watch him as he converses with others and as he relentlessly examines their assertions and beliefs. To begin, pay attention to the way in which his questions are specifically tailored to the person with whom he is conversing.

In the dialogue titled the *Euthyphro* Socrates interrogates a very religious young man by this name who is deeply convinced of his own piety. And so the question he forces Euthyphro to confront is, "what is piety?" This is typical. In his conversations, Socrates begins by addressing what matters the most to the person with whom he's talking. He does not pummel Euthyphro with puzzles, paradoxes, or what contemporary philosophers call "thought experiments." Instead, he begins with what the human being standing in front of him cares about. Answers to the questions Socrates asks, which most people (falsely) think they already possess, are what give shape and direction, give meaning, to one's life.

In the *Laches* Socrates converses with two generals. He asks them, "what is courage?" After all, this is what such leaders demand of both their soldiers and themselves. They must, therefore, believe they can recognize it when they see it, that they know what it is. In the *Republic* the main interlocutor is a young man animated by political ambition. To him Socrates asks, "what is justice?" In the *Theaetetus* he conducts a dialogue with two mathematicians, the topic being, "what is knowledge?" When, in the *Lysis*, he meets two boys who are close friends, he asks them, "what is friendship?" In each case, his questions are meant to invite people to wonder about the core principles on which they, however unreflectively, have staked their lives. Socratic philosophy is designed to force us to look into ourselves.

Consider another, somewhat complicated example. In the *Apology* Socrates cross-examines Meletus, the man who has charged him with subversion or "corrupting the young"; that is, with making them worse. He begins by asking him this: since you accuse me of corrupting the young, you obviously believe that older people should make younger people better, right? Meletus agrees. Okay, Socrates says next, since you identify me as someone who fails to fulfill this obligation, are you also able to identify those men who succeed? When Meletus says yes, Socrates asks, who are they? Meletus falls silent, and so Socrates pushes him. Finally, Meletus answers: it is "the laws" that make people better. Socrates disqualifies this response, for he wants the name of a person. Again, Meletus hesitates, but then he says that the members of the jury (there were 501) and the audience at the trial make the young better. Indeed, by his lights, all Athenians "make the young into fine good men" (25a). All except Socrates.

To attack this assertion, and thereby to defend himself, Socrates offers an analogy. When it comes to young horses, no one would say, as Meletus has just said about Socrates in his relationship to the young men of Athens, that everybody makes them better and only one person makes them worse. For in this case there is a recognizable expert who can manage the task far better than the rest of us: the professional horse trainer. If everyone, especially non-experts, were allowed to suggest ways of improving young horses – if, for example, a vote were taken about what sort of diet they should have – the animals would certainly be damaged. When it comes to making horses better, it's clear that we require knowledge possessed by only a few people. Surely, Socrates seems to suggest, it must be similar when it comes to young men. The majority can't improve them, as Meletus said they could. Only someone with real knowledge can. Such a person, whom Socrates does not identify, would be an expert in human excellence. Once again, Meletus falls silent.

Socrates has succeeded in showing the jury that Meletus hasn't thought very much about how young people are actually made better. By itself this doesn't prove that his accusation of Socrates is false. It only shows that he is thoughtless. That this is indeed the case is revealed when he fails to challenge the most striking element of Socrates' cross-examination: the analogy between the horse trainer and horses, and the virtue-expert and human beings. Meletus *should* have challenged this, for it is certainly problematic. When it comes to horses, expert trainers can be readily identified (and then hired), but it is not obvious that there are analogously identifiable experts when it comes to making young people into excellent citizens. Properly trained horses will take the bit and bridle, and allow their movement to be controlled by a human master who holds the reins. People are far more complex than horses and rarely are willing to be so thoroughly subordinated to someone else. Therefore, making a young person better is a vastly more difficult, and less obvious, enterprise than training a horse.

Think, for example, of all the many parents who would love their children to become good people. While they may be confident that the school to which they send their kids will teach them to read and write, it is far harder to identify a teacher-of-virtue. Would it be the local clergyman? The baseball coach? While there may be institutions that teach and then certify horse trainers, there does not seem to be a viable analogue when it comes to human excellence.

It is of course possible that Socrates takes himself to be one of the few virtue-experts. But this is unlikely. After all, he claims to possess only "human wisdom," which entails his recognition that he is not wise. By his lights the greatest good for human beings is not giving expert advice to others – which is what the politicians, poets, and technocrats do – but examining one's own life.

The purpose of this little exchange between Socrates and Meletus – and here I am speaking about Plato-the-author's purpose – is to invite the reader into a dialogue. He wants us to question the notion of the virtue-expert that the analogy implies. If such a person exists, what does he know and how does he teach? And if such a person can be identified should he, like the horse trainer, be put in charge of the young? If there is no recognizable expert – and Plato surely wants us to consider this possibility – then perhaps Meletus' answer, however thoughtless it may be, isn't entirely wrong. After all, when he says that all the Athenians make the young people better he might be referring to the familiar procedures by which a democracy makes decisions. In countries like the United States, when an important question about human excellence comes up – such as, should physician-assisted suicide be allowed or gay marriage legalized? – people are unwilling to submit to the authoritative judgment of a virtue-expert. Instead, all citizens get to vote. And if the vote doesn't go their way they are obligated to follow the judgment of the majority and be good losers. If there are no virtue-experts, no analogues to the horse trainer, then democratic decision making makes real sense. It is likely that a commitment to democracy, whose Greek roots mean "rule" (*cratos*) of the "people" (*demos*), is for Meletus a deeply held, even if poorly understood, conviction.

Is Socrates, then, anti-democratic? To the extent that he actually affirms the analogy between the horse trainer and the virtue-expert, perhaps he is. But, to ask again, who are the virtue-experts and what sort of knowledge could they possibly possess? Would they know what virtue itself really is?

By carefully tracking Socrates' conversation with Meletus, by considering the unstated presuppositions that lie behind his response, the reader learns what her task is: to do what Meletus doesn't; that is, to think hard about what human excellence is. As such, even if it doesn't result in definitive answers, a Socratic examination can still teach us something. It can help us understand not only what a bad answer is like, but what a good one might be like.

Consider the *Euthyphro*, where, as mentioned above, Socrates is interrogating a self-righteous young man confident that he is wise in matters concerning the gods. To show him that he is deluding himself Socrates asks, "what is piety?" After all, if Euthyphro is the expert he thinks he is, he should be able to answer this question. He tries. Piety, he offers, is what is loved by the gods. Socrates then attacks by asking him whether the gods love someone who is pious because he is pious, or is someone pious because the gods love him? If Euthyphro says the latter, then he runs the risk of admitting that the pious person – and of course he thinks himself to be one – doesn't really deserve any credit. For on this account, a person is pious only because the gods love him, which they may do for reasons that have nothing to do with the person himself, or for no reason at all. It may seem more likely, then, that a person is pious because he is a certain kind of human being who merits the love of the gods. But Euthyphro cannot identify what qualities the pious person might have. He can only repeat that piety is what is loved by all the gods.

Socrates' interrogation is meant to convince Euthyphro that he should ask himself whether, when the gods love someone, they do so for a reason. If not, do they love arbitrarily? If that's the case and the gods love for no discernible reason, then there really isn't much to talk about when it comes to piety, nor can there be any real wisdom concerning it. But perhaps the gods are more rational than that. If so, and if they love certain people for good reasons, then it should be possible to specify why they do so. Defining piety as that which is loved by the gods is therefore inadequate. Because he is so full of religious enthusiasm and intellectual bravado, Euthyphro hasn't thought the issue through. And he is dangerously self-righteous as a result.

Socratic examination, as we have briefly seen in the cases of both Meletus and Euthyphro, demands that people think "backwards" toward the fundamental *presuppositions* that lie behind their assertions. Before confidently posing an answer to Socrates' question, Meletus should have investigated the issue, what is human excellence and how is it attained? Before making his impassioned speeches, Euthyphro should have thought harder about whether the divine is rational or not. By exposing the weakness of such opponents Socrates reveals what a better answer to one of his questions would be like. It must be able to trace its origin to first principles, to basic assumptions, that are fully exposed to the light of day for rational inspection and can then be defended.

Another example: in Book I of the *Republic* Socrates questions Thrasymachus who claims justice is "the advantage of the stronger" (338c). By the "stronger" he means the ruling body. On his account, justice depends on who is in power. It therefore varies from regime to regime. Justice in China is what is advantageous to the Communist Party, which is the ruling body. By contrast, justice in a democracy such as the United States is what is advantageous to the "people" (*demos*). Thrasymachus, then, implicitly denies that there is an "absolute" justice that exists independently of any given regime. Instead, he's a *relativist*. For him the many different conceptions of justice – authoritarian rule in China, monarchy in Saudi Arabia, democratic rule in Great Britain – are all equally valid in their local context. There is no "justice itself," only justice according to the Chinese, justice according to the Saudis, and so on.

Socrates attacks this definition. If justice is the advantage of the stronger, if those who are in power act justly simply because they are in power, then it follows that it must be just for the subjects of the ruling body to obey all the edicts their leaders stipulate. They must, in other words, obey all the laws. Now, since even the smartest rulers occasionally make mistakes, at some point they will enact laws that are actually disadvantageous to them-selves. A ruler may, for example, impose an onerous income tax on his subjects because he believes that this will increase his wealth and so be to his advantage. According to Thrasymachus, subjects are required by the demands of justice to obey this and every other law. In reality, however, it may turn out that the tax ends up bankrupting first the subjects and then the ruler himself. As a result, Thrasymachus' definition of justice contains a fatal, if hidden, flaw. Subjects are required to obey all laws, even ones that are ultimately disadvantageous to the ruling body. But this means that Thrasymachus has contradicted himself. Justice both is and is not doing what is advantageous to the ruler.

What counts as a good answer to a Socratic question is beginning to emerge. It must be what the Greeks called a *logos*, a rational account, that articulates and defends both its *presuppositions* and its *consequences*, and does so without contradiction. It must be both consistent and comprehen-sive; that is, a logical whole, a rigorously connected body of well-defended propositions. That's a tall order, and so it's no wonder that the people with whom Socrates converses regularly fall short. Indeed, Socrates himself never supplies us with such a *logos*, such a theory. But he has, at least, given us some idea of what to strive for.

Socrates, whose conversations often seem to be frustratingly negative, actually teaches us much that is positive. Most basically, that we should be energetically thoughtful about "the most important matters"; those core principles that give shape to our lives. He shows us that far too often about these matters the vast majority of people, especially celebrated intellectu-als, have thought least. In other words, he shows us that most people, and we ourselves, are not wise. But equally importantly, he tries to convince us that this should bother us. Without philosophical self-examination we will operate unreflectively and, as Socrates so stridently puts it, "the unexamined life is not worth living for men." And so he exhorts us to overcome this lack and gives us some indication of what doing so would be like. Ours should be lives of rational examination, of conversation and competition, wherein we discuss virtue every day. We should be hungry for genuine wisdom, for a complete account whose first principles and their consequences are clear. In short, Socrates tries to convince us to become philosophers.

The best way to flesh out what has only been briefly sketched above – that is, to begin to grasp the nature of the philosophical enterprise – is to plunge into the activity itself. That we will do in the chapters to follow. Each of the philosophers we will discuss tries to forge a comprehensive and consistent answer to a basic question. By following their thinking as well as we can, we will enter the conversation. With them we will seek and strive; that is, we will compete.

Note

1   Visitors to Apollo's temple at Delphi were greeted by two inscriptions: "Know thyself" and "Nothing in excess." When I mention Socrates in this book I am referring only to the Socrates who appears in Plato's dialogues. Whether Plato's picture is an accurate depiction of the historical figure himself, who lived from 469 to 399 BCE, is another story altogether. For a general introduction to both Socrates and Plato, as well as to other figures in Greek philosophy, you might consider David Roochnik, *Retrieving the Ancients: An Introduction to Greek Philosophy* (London: Blackwell, 2004).

2

Alone or With Others?

The Question

At 11 years old I discovered solitude. I was attending a summer camp and for some reason decided to take a walk by myself on a path that circled the lake. In my memory it was a bucolic, remote place. In reality, it was probably no more than a pond not far from a highway. For the camp was in New Jersey, only a few miles outside of New York City. But to me it was the country.

Walking alone in such a place was new to me, for I lived in an urban area and, more important, was a kid who spent almost all of his time either in school or playing ball with friends. I liked my camp so much because it was entirely devoted to competitive sports. The campers were divided into two teams, Army and Navy, and everything we did, from playing softball and basketball to making our beds in the morning, was a matter of winning points for the team. I was a good ballplayer and so I flourished there.

I don't know why I ended up alone by the lake that day. But I do remember the feeling. It was good. A burden I didn't know existed had been lifted and I felt lighter. No one was looking at me, telling me what to do, or what I had failed to do, and I felt no need to measure myself against the achievements of others. My thoughts flowed more smoothly, free from a stress so routine that it was unnoticeable. Like never before I felt calm. No parents, friends, or teachers, no need to impress. I was alone.

In the 50 some years that have followed my little walk, I have returned again and again to such solitude, and often have felt myself to be more at home there than anywhere else.

But what could this possibly mean? Can solitude actually be a home? Was that feeling of freedom real? Or was I just a shy kid, inept in all

Thinking Philosophically: An Introduction to the Great Debates, First Edition. David Roochnik.
© 2016 John Wiley & Sons, Inc. Published 2016 by John Wiley & Sons, Inc.

things social, who was glad to have momentarily escaped from the judgmental gaze of others?

Years ago I was on a beach in Mexico with my family. My older daughter, then a teenager, was swimming alone in the ocean. Her back was to the shore and she stayed there, bobbing up and down in the warm waves, for nearly an hour. I couldn't take my eyes off her as I imagined what she was feeling. Like most teenage girls her life was highly pressurized by the social reality into which she had recently plunged. Concern for her grades, appearance, and friends were the foundation of her shaky world. This was why, I guessed, she stayed in the water so long, facing the empty horizon of the Pacific Ocean. She was free from all that.

So much, however, countervails. I'm a husband and a father, and for a long time was a son, and I have spent vast numbers of good hours with my family. We have always spent a lot of time eating together, which is something we all do well. I'm a teacher and like nothing more than being in a room with young people talking about books. I have friends with whom I watch football on Sundays. And I'm a citizen. I vote, read the newspapers, and do my best to study the political world. I stay engaged, not least by teaching and writing books such as this one.

Nonetheless, solitude beckons. These days I swim for exercise. Several times a week I spend nearly an hour in the pool going back and forth, back and forth, back and forth. I don't keep careful track of my laps but instead lose myself in the mindlessly repetitive motion of my body and the free flow of unencumbered thought that rises to the surface. Because swimming is not a sport in which I have been competitive I don't care whether the woman in the lane next to mine goes faster than I do. In fact, I barely notice she is there. For I am reduced to my body at work, moving steadily if awkwardly, oblivious to my position relative to others. It's refreshing in a way that I cherish.

The question, then, is this: when are you most yourself? Alone, perhaps while exercising or walking silently in the secluded woods? Or together with others, in conversation, cooperation, and competition? Connected on Facebook or in solitary drift?

Rousseau's Answer

 Jean-Jacques Rousseau, *Discourse on the Origin of Inequality*

In 1753 the Academy of Dijon sponsored an essay competition. Contestants were to respond to the question, "What is the Origin of Inequality Among Men, and is it authorized by natural law?"

The inequality at issue was not of the physical sort. When it comes to their bodies human beings obviously vary in height, strength, speed, and coordination. There are also easily discernible differences when it comes to innate mental ability. Some people have a powerful memory or analytical ability. Others do not. The judges in Dijon were not interested in these kinds of differences. Instead, their question concerned political, social, and economic inequality. Some people have lots of power, money, and fame. Others do not. Is this sort of inequality natural? In other words, is social stratification and the unequal distribution of goods built into the unchangeable order of human things? Is inequality hardwired into our DNA? Is it natural?

The question has significant consequences. If its answer is "yes," then it would be foolish for politicians to attempt to make society a community of equals. On this view the poor and powerless will always be with us. If the answer is "no," then it would be reasonable – indeed, it might be obligatory – to figure out why social and economic inequality is so great and then to propose remedies for it. Declaring a war against poverty or fighting for equal access to education would then make good sense.

Jean-Jacques Rousseau submitted an essay. He did not win the competition but he published it anyway, and it is now counted as a key text in the history of philosophy.

The State of Nature

Rousseau begins with a simple thought. In order to know whether the inequality that we see in the world originates in natural differences or is socially constructed (and therefore remediable), one must first understand human nature as it is, or was, before society began to shape it. He calls this pre-social condition "the state of nature," and the task of Part I of the *Discourse* is to explain what it is.

Rousseau understands that his project is intractably difficult:

> And how will man be successful in seeing himself as nature formed him ... and in *separating* what he derives from his own wherewithal from what circumstances and progress have added to or changed in his primitive state? (10)

How can the influence of nature be separated from that of nurture when we, who are making the inquiry, have already been nurtured? Consider, for example, the relationship you have with your parents. Whatever it is, it probably feels natural. But is it? You were, after all, raised by these people. They shaped you, no doubt decisively. But what if you had grown up in a commune in which there were no families? Would you have the same feelings? Or think of this. Many of us are highly competitive. When we see people similar to ourselves – in the same profession, say, or on the playing field – our first impulse is to outshine them in some fashion. Is this feeling natural? It certainly may seem so. But what if we had been raised in a society where cooperation is supremely valued? How, having been born and bred here, can we figure out what we would have been if we hadn't?

The difficulty, perhaps the impossibility, of distinguishing the influence of nature and nurture becomes ever greater the more advanced a society is:

> What is even more cruel is that, since all the progress of the human species continually moves away from this primitive state, the more we accumulate new knowledge, the more we deprive ourselves of the means of acquiring the most important knowledge of all. Thus, in a sense, *it is by dint of studying man that we have rendered ourselves incapable of knowing him.* (11)

In a highly technological society such as our own – in reality, however, in any society whatsoever – "new knowledge" constitutes the fabric of our daily lives and stands in the way of genuine self-knowledge. Think of the spectacular advances made in the field of neuroscience. We know a great deal about how specific regions of the brain are responsible for different cognitive abilities. If your frontal lobe gets banged, your emotional life might well be significantly altered. We're infatuated with such discoveries for they seem to promise us insight into ourselves. What they reveal, however, is no more than mechanical infrastructure. This is valuable information to be sure, especially if repairs have to be made. But such new knowledge teaches us only how the brain works, and tells us nothing about what our cognitive and emotional lives actually mean to us. The neuroscientist is thus like an engineer who understands the working parts of a bicycle. Knowing how a derailleur works is necessary in order to build the machine and then to fix it, but it provides no insight into why we might love riding so. In fact, a subject like neuroscience may, just as Rousseau suggests, render us less able to know ourselves. For the images of the brain on a screen are so impressive that it's easy to convince ourselves that they tell us who we really are. But such knowledge, however powerful, is no more than what Socrates called an "extraneous matter."

Or think of the role that super-smartphones play in our lives. They have decisively influenced the way we relate to others and transact our daily business. Especially to those who grew up with them, using such phones certainly seems natural. In fact, to many people they feel more like an extension of the hand than a foreign object. Not only our behavior, then, but our very conception of ourselves is anchored in what we can do with such devices. How, given the impact of such "progress," can we ever determine who we are simply in ourselves? How can we isolate what is natural; what has not, in other words, been infiltrated by culture or shaped by technological society?

Now consider social inequality. It certainly appears to be natural for it both is, and seems always to have been, ubiquitous. But might it be the result of historical forces that have created the conditions in which we live today? Rousseau thinks this question will typically be answered incorrectly, and for one reason. People readily assume that what is most familiar to them is natural. As he says of other philosophers who developed their own theories about the state of nature, "they wrongly injected into the savage man ... a multitude of passions which are the product of society" (35).[1] This is hardly surprising since the investigation of human nature untouched by social force can only be conducted by a social being.

Rousseau is honest about this dilemma and he adjusts his own aspirations accordingly:

GOOGLE

Let my readers not imagine, then, that I dare flatter myself with having seen what appears to me so difficult to see. I have begun some lines of reasoning; *I have hazarded some guesses, less in the hope of resolving the question than with the intention of clarifying it.* (11)

Like Socrates, Rousseau acknowledges that he is not wise and cannot do what cannot be done; that is, not be the social being he already is. The best he can offer, then, is "some guesses" about what we were like in the primitive or "savage" condition. His work, he insists, is merely "hypothetical" (17) and he urges us to "begin by putting aside all the facts" (17). As a result, his *Discourse* is far more like a story than an anthropological theory. Rousseau hopes that by telling it, by describing the state of nature and then the process through which human beings left it in order to enter society, he will force his readers to confront the question of this chapter: who are we? Beings who need others in order to be ourselves, or beings by nature solitary?

To begin, Rousseau asks us to imagine a human animal who is anatomically the same as we are today; that is, "walking on two feet, using his hands as we use ours" (19), and so on. That's easy. The next move is this:

When I strip that being ... of all the artificial faculties he could have acquired only through long progress; when I consider him, in a word, as he must have left the hands of nature, I see an animal less strong than some, less agile than others, but all in all, the most advantageously organized of all. I see him satisfying his hunger under an oak tree, *quenching his thirst at the first stream, finding his bed at the foot of the same tree that supplied his meal*; and thus all his needs are satisfied. (19)

The image Rousseau conjures here is of a simple but successful animal who met his physical needs rather easily and in an almost haphazard fashion. Our savage ancestor did not engage in agriculture or live in a built structure. Instead, he ate whatever was available in the forest, drank water from "the first stream" he happened upon, and "bedded down in some random spot and only for one night" (29).

Clearly, then, Rousseau presupposes that the resources needed to satisfy basic needs were, prior to the advent of technological society, abundant and readily accessible to the savage:

> When the earth is left to its natural fertility and covered with immense forests that were *never mutilated by the axe*, it offers storehouses and shelters at every step to animals of every species (19).

Remember Rousseau's instructions on how to read his book: put aside all the facts! Who cares what the world of primitive *Homo sapiens* was really like! (Figuring that out is a job for archaeologists and anthropologists, for scientists not philosophers.) To reiterate, the *Discourse* is more a story than a theory. In fact, it clearly echoes a familiar one: that of the Garden of Eden. Needing only the fruit of trees, water, and some leaves (all of which were abundant), natural man was self-sufficient. As a result, and because of the complete absence of technology – note that in the primitive forest there wasn't even an ax – in the state of nature he was strong:

> Since the savage man's body is the only instrument he knows, he employs it for a variety of purposes that, for lack of practice, ours are incapable of serving. And *our industry deprives us of the force and agility that necessity obliges him to acquire*. If he had had an axe, would his wrists break such strong branches? If he had had a sling, would he throw a stone with so much force? (20)

The highlighted phrase exemplifies the real purpose of the *Discourse*. Yes, it's a story about the hypothetical state of pre-technological, pre-social nature that existed long ago. More important, though, it reveals a basic dynamic at work in society. Technology provides us with power. In doing so, however, it also takes away. Our wrists will weaken if we use an ax rather than just our wrists to break branches. The automobile allows us to travel great distances with ease, but our legs become soft when we don't walk. Our phones have a contact list and so we don't have to exercise our memory to call our friends. As our technological power expands, other capacities diminish. It follows, then, that in the state of nature, bereft of all devices and with only himself to rely upon, savage man was very strong.

More important for the story than his strength was another feature of the savage: he was *spontaneous*. Operating with no preconceived notions of health, propriety, or success, he ate when he was hungry and slept when he was tired. In general, because "his desires do not go beyond his physical needs" (26) his life was concentrated in the present and extremely short-term future. He took pleasure in food when he found some, and suffered hunger pangs when he was caught in a storm and could not forage. His life was the simplest imaginable. As a result, savage man did not experience something that we in society never seem to be without: *stress*. He was so thoroughly engaged in the tasks at hand, so attuned to his immediate needs and desires, that he did not worry about what might occur later. More specifically, he could not imagine things being other than they were. As Rousseau puts it, "*his imagination depicts nothing to him*" (27). He elaborates:

> *Imagination, which wreaks so much havoc among us, does not speak to savage hearts*; each man peacefully awaits the impetus of nature, gives himself over to it without choice and with more pleasure than frenzy; and once the need is satisfied, all desire is snuffed out. (40)

Once again, far more significant than the historical accuracy of this observation is Rousseau's identification of a psychological dynamic that we in society know all too well. Human unhappiness is by and large fueled by the imagination, which projects a panoply of (more or less realistic) possibilities, some of them rather threatening. Expectation of future events makes us uneasy. By contrast, "the only evils savage man fears are pain and hunger" (26). When he was hungry he either worked to alleviate it or, if conditions did not allow him to do this, he simply suffered. If he bumped into an angry bear in the forest he felt an immediate spasm of alarm and then ran away. Other than that, he did not worry about bears. What he didn't do is what we in society invariably do: plan for the future and concern ourselves with (imagine) problems that have not yet arrived. For savage man was largely unaffected by what was not present before him.

The following passage makes it clear that, once again, the real purpose of Rousseau's story is not to propose a scientific theory about human origins, but to force his readers to reflect on their current condition. He does so by making the shocking pronouncement that in crucial ways the state of nature, however primitive, was superior to life led in society:

> Although a sick savage, abandoned to himself, has nothing to hope for except from nature, on the other hand, he has nothing to fear except his illness. ***This frequently makes his situation preferable to ours.*** (23)

When natural man was feeling good, he simply felt good. He didn't worry about how he would feel tomorrow. When he was sick, he just hunkered down and endured the pain. By contrast, consider what happens to us today when we get a headache. We go straight to the medicine cabinet and look for a pill. Is this a tylenol headache or would ibuprofen do the trick? Or maybe even old-fashioned aspirin? But what if it's a migraine? For us pain is rarely felt straightforwardly on its own. Instead, because we have such a vast array of tools to diagnose and then combat it, it is experienced as a problem that needs to be eliminated. If a headache persists we might start to worry. Is it a brain tumor? We know that there are machines in the hospital that can detect brain tumors and, precisely because such technology is available, we consider this possibility. We are, as a result, on edge.

Think here about the outsized role that testing has come to play in medicine. Men, for example, are regularly screened for indicators of prostate cancer, and women for breast cancer. On the one hand, such procedures seem unambiguously positive. After all, no one wants to die young from such diseases, and early detection promises a better chance of survival. On the other hand, the availability of such information can lead to an unhealthy preoccupation with future health. A test may show that my prostate gland is fine, but what about my lungs or my colon or pancreas? Aren't they also subject to fatal illness? Why not test them as well? After all, if the doctors discover a growing cancer they might save me from future pain and an early death. Such reasoning, however attractive, can easily become a trap, or even an addiction. Maybe I should have a full body scan in order to examine every internal organ. Why not a thorough genetic examination to see if I am predisposed to developing cancer? Why not implant microchips and sensors to detect any deviation from the physiological norm? In short, living in a society dominated by hospital technology poses a risk: namely, the medicalization of our minds and the consequent inability simply to enjoy our health during those short periods that we have it.

Even if medicine in eighteenth-century France was primitive compared to our own, Rousseau understood this dynamic well. As more tools become available to battle illness, the more pain becomes unacceptable. Of course, when the doctors succeed in alleviating our pain we are terribly grateful to them for doing so. But, Rousseau thinks, medicine brings with it a significant cost. For what, he asks, is worse? Straightforwardly suffering a pain or endlessly worrying about our health and attempting to ward off a future sure to come? Technology gives, but it also takes away. It has transformed life into a fool's errand; a perpetual battle against inevitable death.

Rousseau observes what happens as people become increasingly dependent upon their devices:

> For in addition to their continuing thus to soften body and mind (those conveniences having through habit lost almost all their pleasure, and being at the same time degenerated into true needs), *being deprived of them became much more cruel than possessing them was sweet*, and they were unhappy about losing them without being happy about possessing them. (48)

When you get a new computer you are, at first, delighted by what it can do. But after a few weeks using it becomes a routine on which you rely to get through the day. Instead of a pleasure it has become a need. As a result, if the power goes out or the thing breaks, you feel lost. Precisely as Rousseau puts it, being deprived of the computer is far worse than having it was sweet. So too is the worry that the machine, even when it is working, will fail.

And then there's this scenario: a few months after purchasing your super-smartphone you see a new and faster one in the store, and your own starts to feel like a clunker. At that point you may well feel a bit of envy for those who possess the latest model. In sum, a steady even if inaudible buzz of anxiety accompanies our technological dependency.

A decisive feature of the state of nature, one that follows directly from the reflections above, is that savage man did not fear death. After all, to do this requires the ability to imagine nothingness, a future condition unlike anything we actually experience. Because savage man has so little by way of the imagination, he cannot do this. As Rousseau puts it,

> *An animal will never know what it is to die; and knowledge of death and its terrors is one of the first acquisitions that man has made in withdrawing from the animal condition.* (26)

It is arguable that fear of death is a primary constituent of life as we (who are socialized) know it, and it may well be the source of other forms of anxiety. By contrast, natural man, with no imagination to propel him into the future, did not worry about his own demise. Rousseau proposes that this difference is fundamental. Those of us who at the onset of a headache fear a brain tumor and run to the doctor are evidence that "*most of our ills are of our own making*" (22). Although he may suffer when he is hungry or cold, savage man does not make himself unnecessarily miserable.

There is one desire that has as yet gone unmentioned: the "ardent, impetuous ... terrible" passion that "renders one sex necessary to the other" (39). About this Rousseau is emphatic:

> In that primitive state, since nobody had houses or huts or property of any kind, each one bedded down in some random spot and often for only one night. Males and females came together fortuitously as a result of chance encounters, occasion, and desire, without there being any great need for words to express what they had to say to one another. *They left one another with same nonchalance.* (29–30)

In the state of nature there were no relationships, only hook-ups. Just as savage man drank when thirsty from the "first stream" he found, and instinctively ran away from the angry bear he encountered in the forest, so too did he have sex when he was feeling the urge and happened to bump into a woman. For both partners it was a "purely animal act" (45) that generated no lasting connection. "Once this need had been satisfied, the two sexes no longer took cognizance of one another" (45). This was true, Rousseau says, even if a child resulted from the union. The mother nurtured her offspring, but only until the child could walk off on his own. The children "did not hesitate to leave the mother" (30) and "the child no longer meant anything to the mother once it could do without her" (45).

Rousseau's story here may be both implausible and objectionable, but he insists on it nonetheless in order to bring into sharp focus the condition of socialized man. In society sexual desire is (more or less) channeled toward one other person and it entails a set of mutual commitments and shared projects. It becomes love. What Rousseau emphasizes, however, is the dark side of what we normally take to be our most precious gift. For love, he argues, invariably generates possessiveness, and it causes us to compare ourselves to, and to concern ourselves with, others. Your girlfriend, you think, is more beautiful than other women. This is why you want her to be yours. But possession generates the fear of loss. You're on edge because you wonder if your girlfriend will like me more than you. In short, as Rousseau so harshly puts it, "*jealousy awakens with love; discord triumphs, and the sweetest passion receives sacrifices of human blood*" (49).

In the state of nature, sexual desire propelled savage man to conjoin with a woman for a few minutes of pleasurable friction, and that was it. He lived alone and without possessions. Most important, he did not measure himself against others. Because he had no imagination, he did not wonder what people were thinking about him, or how he stacked up. If he was hungry and food was available, he ate. If he felt sexual desire and the opportunity presented itself, he acted on this impulse. If he felt no love, he also felt no jealousy.

So far it is clear that for Rousseau human beings are by nature solitary. Indeed, as with all other animals, our most "natural sentiment" is "love of oneself" and the impulse "to be vigilant in [our] own preservation" (90). Nonetheless, Rousseau thinks that even in the state of nature we were not entirely bereft of feeling for others. For latent in our nature (in our DNA) is the capacity for what he calls "*pity*" (36), which he defines as a "*natural repugnance to seeing any sentient being, especially our fellow man, perish or suffer*" (14). What he has in mind here is what we would call "empathy." It is a "pure movement of nature prior to all reflection" (37) – that is, an instinct – that moves us "without reflection to the aid of those we see suffering" (38). If savage man saw another human being fall and hurt his leg, he would feel a sympathetic spasm. He would feel the pain of the other, and thus might go over to help him up. But he wouldn't do more than this, and he certainly would form no attachment.

Animated by this primal feeling of pity, man in the state of nature did not harm other animals (unless his own immediate survival depended upon his doing so.) The terrible suffering that human beings inflict upon each other, and on other animals, in society is thus anything but natural. In fact, it results precisely from the weakening of the natural sentiment of pity. And what causes that weakening is moral reasoning:

> *The most decent people learned to consider it one of their duties to kill their fellow men.* Finally, men were seen massacring one another by the thousands without knowing why. More murders were committed in a single day of combat and more horrors in the capture of a single city than were committed in the state of nature during entire centuries over the entire face of the earth. (57–58)

People must *learn* to inflict pain on others. A simple example: a child will not obey the rules of the house. The father takes it to be his duty to punish him. So even though he hates the thought of doing so, he forces himself to spank the child. When he mutters to himself, "this hurts me more than it hurts you," he may well be speaking the truth. To inflict suffering on a child requires the adult to repress his natural instinct to pity for the sake of a higher goal: moral education and the future well-being of the child. The father reasons himself into doing what is unnatural.

At the more grievous level of warfare this same dynamic is at work. It is called "collateral damage." The enemy threatens us and to safeguard the interests of the country the citizens must go to war. Yes, dropping bombs from high altitudes will kill innocent people. But future benefits are measured against present costs and the decision is made. This is unfortunate but necessary. For the cause is just and so the heart must harden in order to prevent an even worse outcome. In warfare reason trumps natural sentiment and society will inevitably be soaked in blood. By contrast, in the state of nature savage man never harmed another animal, unless his own life was immediately at risk.

To sum up, in the state of nature human beings, bereft of technology as well as imagination, were innocent and at ease with themselves. Life was simple, peaceful, and spontaneous. Nonetheless, the transition was made to society.

Society

The momentous passage from the natural to the social occurred because, however similar savages were to other animals, they nonetheless differed in one decisive respect. They were free. While non-human animals cannot deviate from their instincts, our species can. A pigeon, Rousseau says, "would die of hunger near a bowl filled with choice meats" (25). By contrast, human beings are able to resist the pull of instinct. Even in the state of nature we possessed something that pigeons did not: freedom and "*the faculty of self-perfection*" (25).

A lightning bolt hit a tree and happened to fry a squirrel who was taking shelter in its branches. The squirrel fell at the feet of a savage who smelled the aroma of burning meat. Never having eaten such food before he nonetheless gave it a try. Discovering that it was tastier and easier to consume than his customary diet of fruit and nuts, he went on the look-out for similar occurrences during the next storm. Or more massively yet, he attempted to reproduce the fire whose effect he has just witnessed. Pigeons, slaves as they are to instinct, can't do this.

Note two things about this crucial move in Rousseau's story. First, it is problematic. The capacity for self-perfection seems to require some ability to imagine a better future, which Rousseau eliminates from the state of nature. Second, he characterizes this unique capacity of the human animal, the one which makes progress inevitable, in negative terms: "*this distinctive and almost unlimited faculty is the source of all man's misfortunes*" (26).

It was freedom that allowed human beings in the state of nature to respond to the vagaries of the forest in innovative ways and thereby to begin the long process of evolution that brought us into technological society. The single most important moment in that development has already been mentioned: "lightning, a volcano, or some fortuitous chance happening acquainted them with fire" (45). This was not only the onset of all subsequent technological progress but also of the demise of the natural. For Rousseau that spelled disaster. As he puts it, "*it is iron and wheat that have civilized men and ruined the human race*" (51). For with the development of fire, tools, and agriculture human beings became conscious of their unique status among the animals:

> The new enlightenment which results from this development increased his superiority over the other animals by making him aware of it. He trained himself to set traps for them; he tricked them in a thousand different ways ... Thus the first glance he directed upon himself produced within him the first stirring of *pride*. (46)

The emergence of technology caused savage man not only to recognize his superiority to other animals, but also to become aware of his kinship with beings like himself. As a result, "he concluded that their way of thinking and feeling was in complete conformity with his own" (46). Eventually – and especially if through a flood or an earthquake an island was created and several people were put in unavoidably close proximity to one another – human beings began to speak to one another: "a common idiom must have been formed" (48). Now adept in speech, they began to live together in primitive villages or tribes. Society has begun.

Before continuing, note how Rousseau's story, even if hardly scientific, is nonetheless strikingly similar to the Darwinian theory of natural selection that would emerge a century later. There too chance plays a pivotal role in evolution. On this account, the human species adapted to changes in the environment far more quickly than other animals and so moved vastly beyond its primitive condition. The use of tools, the building of shelters, the invention of agriculture, and language itself were all steps toward bringing us into the world as we know it today. In other words, for both Rousseau and Darwin human beings are essentially historical animals whose evolution is a response to the contingent alterations in the environment. In Rousseau's words, "the human race of one age is not the human race of another age ... the soul and human passions are imperceptibly altered and, as it were, *change their nature*" (69). Part of our nature, it seems, is its propensity to change.

Rousseau's story, however, differs radically from Darwin's and not only because it's not scientific. He is emphatically judgmental about the transition from the state of nature to society, and for one decisive reason. However brutish and at times painful the former was, in it there was neither evil nor unhappiness. Only with the advent of society did such demons arrive. He explains in the form of a story.

In the earliest manifestations of social life, people gathered in front of their ramshackle huts or the fire they shared at night. They amused themselves by song and dance. And this led to competition:

> *Each one began to look at the others and to want to be looked at himself*, and public esteem had a value. The one who sang or danced the best, the handsomest, the strongest, the most adroit or eloquent became the most highly regarded. And *this was the first step towards inequality and, at the same time, towards vice* (49).

In the state of nature we were animated by "love of oneself" (*amour de soi*), the instinctual drive for self-preservation that pushes all animals to nourish and protect themselves. In society this metamorphosed and became what one translator renders as "egocentrism." The original French, however, is *amour propre*, a different kind of self-love:

> We must not confuse egocentrism [*amour propre*] with love of oneself [*amour de soi*] ... Love of oneself is a natural sentiment which moves every animal to be vigilant in its own preservation and which, directed in man by reason and modified by pity, produces humanity and virtue. Egocentrism is merely a sentiment that is relative, artificial and born in society, which moves each individual to value himself more than anyone else, which inspired in men all the evils they cause one another, and which is the true source of honor ... *in the veritable state of nature, egocentrism does not exist; for each particular man regards himself as the only spectator who observes him, as the only being in the universe that takes an interest in him* ... it is impossible that a sentiment that has its source in comparisons that he is not in a position to make could germinate in his soul. (90)

In society we invariably see ourselves through the eyes of others to whom we compare ourselves. As such, we lose direct connection to our own desires and impulses. We cease to be spontaneous. Instead, what we want, or think we want, is based on how we imagine we will look. Such is the power of egocentrism, *amour propre*, and it is the pivot of Rousseau's rewriting of the biblical Fall. First, because of the power we slowly began to accumulate through our development of primitive technology we became aware of ourselves as superior to other animals. Then, animated by such self-consciousness, we began to compare ourselves to our fellow human beings. And thus was taken the fateful step. What came to matter most is not what someone is, but how he appears. *"Being something and appearing to be something became two completely different things"* (54). From this distinction arose hypocrisy, ostentation, deception, cunning, and all the vices that follow in their wake. What counts in society is who others think we are. Appearances trump reality. Or rather, appearances become reality.

It is precisely here that Rousseau presents the greatest challenge to his reader, and it is a Socratic one: *do you know what you really want?* Or is what you think you want shaped for you by someone else (like your parents or friends)? Do you do what you do only to look good in the eyes of others? Is that why you want to go to law school or make a lot of money? Rousseau's answer is emphatic and grim. In society, which is where all of us reside, a human being *"is always outside himself and knows how to live only in the opinion of others"* (81).

Amour propre fuels the continual drive to compare oneself against the apparent achievements of others. It is what prevents us from ever simply appreciating what we have. For us the cliché is spot on: the grass is always greener on the other side. Savage man, by contrast, did not waste time imagining the other side. If he happened to find some grass, regardless of how green it was, he was grateful and so lay down and took a nap. By contrast, our lives are filled with restless anxiety. What if someone sees us napping on a crappy lawn? For us nothing can be taken just for what it is.[2]

To sum up: Rousseau proclaims that *"man is naturally good"* (76). By this he means that in the state of nature we were simple, peaceful, and innocent. Unless our survival depended on it, we harmed no one. Except when propelled by the occasional stab of pity or sexual desire we kept to ourselves. We were oblivious to what others might have thought of us, and so were immune to envy or spite. We spontaneously acted upon desires that were truly ours. In society, by terrible contrast, we are consumed by *amour propre* and so work relentlessly to upgrade our status. Nothing we have will ever be good enough, for someone out there will always have more. Ours is a life of perpetual disquiet, and we are forever outside of ourselves.

Do not, however, think for a moment that the *Discourse on the Origin of Inequality* recommends that people attempt to return to the state of nature. For this is surely impossible. Once fallen there's no going back. Furthermore, the seeds of the fall – freedom and the faculty of self-perfection – were present from the beginning and only needed a chance event such as a lightning strike to germinate. Within human nature itself, therefore, lies the impulse to leave the state of nature. It is intrinsic to our nature to become non-natural.

And thus to become unhappy. In short, Rousseau's story about human origins is a tragedy. We are fractured beings who live in society and can never return to nature. We cannot make ourselves whole or happy.

And yet when I'm swimming alone in the pool, oblivious to those around me, indifferent to how long it takes to complete a lap, unencumbered by the relentless demands of *amour propre*, I feel a reassuring sense of calm. When I'm walking alone on the beach, or even anonymously on the crowded streets of New York, when the cellphone is turned off and I'm not thinking about where I stand in the latest rankings of philosophy professors, I feel the possibility of simply being myself and thinking thoughts that might somehow belong to me. When I'm riding my bike and have to concentrate hard in order to dodge car doors and pedestrians, I am more concentrated in the present and act more spontaneously than almost anywhere else. Most other times, I'm just playing for the numbers and the approval of the crowd. Perhaps, then, during these isolated moments even socialized man can glimpse the state of nature. But, Rousseau thinks, invariably the judgmental gaze of others will fracture this vision and return him to his all too familiar anxieties.

Aristotle's Answer

 Aristotle, *Politics*

For an answer to our question – are we by nature social or solitary? – radically at odds with Rousseau's, we turn to Aristotle's *Politics*. As mentioned in Chapter 1, Rousseau borrowed a line from this book as the epigraph for his *Discourse on the Origin of Inequality*: "It is in things whose condition is *according to nature* that one ought particularly to investigate what is *by nature*, not in things that are *defective*." Why would Rousseau, who disagrees with the teaching of the *Politics*, have found this line attractive enough to use in his own work? Before tackling that question, let us first examine what it means. In the *Physics*, his study of "nature" (the Greek word is *physis*), Aristotle explains.

Things that are "by nature" – or more simply are "natural" – have "in themselves the source of motion and of rest." By contrast, something like a bed "has no natural tendency in itself for changing" (*Physics* 192b). In other words, a bed would not have become what it is without the craftsman who made it. It is dependent on an external source for its being, and therefore is not natural. By contrast, no one crafted the moon or the stars. They exist and move on their own. In a more complicated way so too do animals. In one sense, of course, they are produced by something outside of themselves, for they need biological parents in order to come into being. But since the offspring belong to the same species (have the same DNA) as their parents, animals can also be said to have the origin of their being in themselves. In fact, biological reproduction is quintessentially natural, for an animal gives rise to itself in the form of its offspring.

With one stroke, then, Aristotle divides the world into two categories: what is by nature and what is artificial. From the outset this distinction should feel suspect. What would Aristotle make of genetically modified plants or those domesticated former wolves now known as dogs? And what would he make of the most peculiar animal of them all, human beings, whose nature includes the capacity to produce that which is non-natural?

Whatever the answer to these questions, we can already see why Rousseau, who surely would have shared the suspicions just mentioned, was nonetheless attracted to this line from the *Politics*. For the *Discourse on the Origin of Inequality* depends on the distinction between man "by nature" – that is, before the advent of technology and society – and socialized or artificial man. Furthermore, he would agree with Aristotle that we must study a human being who is "according to nature" – that is, one who fulfills, exhibits, actualizes, or lives up to his nature – in order to understand the species of which he is a member.

Here is an example to explain what this means: a seed is placed into fertile soil and for weeks receives plenty of sun and water. Soon it sprouts and then grows into a flourishing plant. The mature plant is "according to nature." It has fully expressed the potentiality latent in the seed. By contrast, another seed was placed in similar soil but during the spring there was a drought. Without enough water the plant that emerges is puny, pale, and unable to reproduce itself. It is "defective."

Aristotle's point, which Rousseau seconds, is that if we want to understand the plant – or better, the species of which the particular plant is a member – then we should study the robust one that is "according to nature" rather than the shriveled one. Only it will disclose all the fully developed aspects of the plant's being, and thereby tell us what it is. For Rousseau this means that to grasp human nature, and thereby attain self-knowledge, we should investigate man before technology weakened him, and society ruined him. As we saw earlier, however, he doubts that anyone can actually do this. The savage in the state of nature would have no inclination even to try, while socialized man is unable to separate the influence of nature from that of nurture, his true or natural self from the artificial one manufactured in society. The best Rousseau can offer, then, is "some guesses" and a story. As we will now see, Aristotle does not share these worries. If nothing else, he does not lack confidence.

Community Is Natural

Aristotle's *Politics* (written some time around 350 BCE) begins:

> Since we see that every city [*polis*] is some sort of community and every community is constituted for the sake of some good (*for everyone does everything for the sake of what is held to be good*), it is clear that all communities aim at some good, and that the community that is most authoritative of all and embraces all the others ... aims at the most authoritative good of all. This is what is called the city or the political community. (1252a1–5)

Note the "we see" highlighted in the first sentence. Aristotle begins by looking around. He is focused on the world that appears before his eyes. By contrast, the *Discourse on the Origin of Inequality* begins with an act of the imagination: namely, the story of a hypothetical state of nature, which likely never existed. The implications of this difference, as we will gradually see, are huge.

Second, reread the clause "everyone does everything for the sake of what is held to be good." People do things for a reason and to achieve some purpose. Broadly speaking, they do what they do because they think it will lead to something good. You're reading this book. No one forced you to open it nor are you a machine programmed to study the collected works of Roochnik. Instead, you're reading it for a reason; for the sake of what you hold to be some good, whatever that happens to be. In sum, human activity is *purposive*.

So far Aristotle seems to be offering no more than commonsensical observation. But he then generalizes sharply. Communities too, he says, operate purposively. A family aims for the well-being of each of its members, a baseball team for victory, a school for learning. And the most "authoritative" community of them all, which is the "city" (*polis*) or political community, aims for the most authoritative good of them all. He doesn't tell us what this is here, but he will soon.

(I will translate *polis* as "city," but bear in mind that the more relevant term for us would be "state." The *polis* of Ancient Greece was a "city-state." There was no nation or country called Greece back then, only small, independent political entities such as Athens, Sparta, and Thebes.)

Aristotle's next task is to explain what a city is, and he does so by following this procedure: "now in these matters as in other subjects it is by looking at how things develop naturally from the beginning that one may best study them" (1252a25).

Aristotle studies the city using the same method he deploys in "other subjects," particularly the biological sciences (which he invented): he observes its natural development. Be clear: the *Politics* begins by asserting that the political community is natural. In other words, from the outset Aristotle disagrees with Rousseau. This shouldn't be too surprising. After all, the *Politics* begins with "we see" and by making an observation about the actual world standing before his eyes. And we are all born into and then surrounded by a community. Unlike Rousseau, however, he claims that what is here now is natural. This is precisely the mistake that Rousseau accuses his predecessors (especially Hobbes) of making. They looked at the world around them and thought it was natural. But they were wrong, for they were doing no more than projecting their own familiar sensibility, which is socially constructed, onto the screen of nature where, according to Rousseau at least, it has no place. Aristotle, by contrast, claims that the political community in which we are now thoroughly embedded is natural. Therefore, we should study it just as we would any other living organism; by dissecting it and studying its component parts:

> First, then, there must of necessity be a conjunction of persons who cannot exist without each other: on the one hand, male and female, for the sake of reproduction, which occurs not from intentional choice but – as is also the case with the other animals and plants – from *a natural striving* to leave behind another that is like oneself. (1252a25–3)

Impelled by sexual desire and the urge to reproduce, men and women couple and then stay together in order to raise the offspring. The family is thus for Aristotle the result of an entirely natural impulse. Far from being by nature solitary and self-sufficient, human beings cannot exist without each other. We live together in families and for a reason: to have children and thereby propel our offspring, versions of ourselves, into the future.

That's not all, for the primitive community that he calls a "household" has other members as well. These are,

> ... *the naturally ruling and ruled* ... for that which can foresee with the mind is the naturally ruling and naturally mastering element, while that which can do these things with the body is the naturally ruled and the slave. (1252a30–33)

Again in stark contrast with Rousseau, for whom inequality is strictly a social rather than a natural phenomenon, Aristotle finds inequality present at the beginning of the human story. Some are natural rulers, while others are naturally ruled. There are, in short, masters and slaves. The mental capacities of the former are more powerful than the latter. They have forethought and can plan ahead. Slaves, by contrast, lack this ability and so they are best suited simply to obey orders. Joined together with an extended family they comprise the household, which like all communities has a purpose: to "meet the needs of daily life" (1252b14); that is, to keep its members alive.

To reiterate, for Rousseau, Aristotle went terribly wrong on this point because he began his analysis with "*we see.*" The Athens in which he lived was filled with slaves. In the ancient world it was not uncommon for one city to go to war against another and, if victorious, kill its men and take the women and children back home as plunder. Looking around, then, Aristotle would have seen families, somewhat like our own, accompanied by slaves. And then he made the fateful mistake. He called what he saw, particularly the rank inequality of human beings, natural. He was blinded by what was before his eyes.

Aristotle's developmental account continues. Households combine to form villages. These, he says, are for the sake of meeting "nondaily needs" (1252b16). Like the family and household, the village is for the sake of survival, albeit with an eye to a more distant future:

Finally, villages conglomerate in order to form a city.

> The community arising from the union of several villages that is complete is the city. It reaches a level of full self-sufficiency, so to speak, and while coming into being for the sake of living, it exists for the sake of living well. Every city, therefore, exists by nature, if such also are the first communities. For the city is their end and *nature is an end*; what each thing is – for example, a human being, a horse, or a household – when its coming into being is complete is, we assert, the nature of that thing. (1252b26-32)

The household and the village are able to sustain human life. That's their job. But they cannot provide the conditions that allow human beings to lead a full and excellent life, one according to nature. Only the city can do that. For the city is the goal or purpose – in Greek the word is *telos* – of the household and the village. It is the natural end or completion of the developmental sequence Aristotle has sketched. And the "end," goal, or purpose of the city, unlike its smaller and more primitive components, is not just survival but living well.

Notice the four words highlighted above: *nature is an end*. (In Greek, the word is *telos*, the root of our "teleological.") For Aristotle nature itself, and not just human action, is purposive or teleological. This notion is so basic to his thinking that we must briefly digress in order to explain it.

Teleology

In the *Physics*, Aristotle says this: "our inquiry is for the sake of under-standing, and we think that we do not understand a thing until we have acquired the 'why' of it" (194b19–20). The job of the "physicist" – a term that refers to anyone who studies what is natural – is to answer the question "why?" So, for example, to explain why when a match is struck it ignites, the chemical composition of the matchhead and the mechanics of friction must be explained. So far, so good. The cause of the fire is now known. What makes Aristotle distinctive is that he thinks that there isn't just one way of explaining natural things. Instead, there are four. He calls these "causes" or "explanations." Each has a traditional title, ones Aristotle himself does not use but are helpful nonetheless:

1 The *material cause* answers the question "what is its stuff?" or "what is it made of?" Why is the statue hard? Because it is made of bronze, which is the material cause of the statue.
2 The *efficient cause* is the "first origin of a change or rest" of a thing. Why did the cup move across the table? Because my hand pushed it. The efficient cause is what produces an effect. As such, it corresponds most closely to the modern conception of a cause.
3 The *formal cause* answers the question "what is it?" It explains the essence of a thing. Knowing what a house is will ultimately explain why it is constructed in the way it is.
4 The *final cause* is something's goal, purpose, or end (*telos*). It answers the question "for the sake of what?" Why did I take a walk after din-ner? Because it's good for my digestion. Health, then, is the *telos* of that sort of walk.

As Aristotle himself acknowledges, the *telos* or final cause – that is, the teleological conception of nature that underlies so much of his thinking – is controversial. In fact, in *Physics* II.8 he presents, in order to refute, the position of a potential critic who would dispute its very existence. (He is likely thinking here of the fifth-century thinker Empedocles.) This critic takes his bearings from a process like the falling of rain. This is a purpose-less or mechanical event that occurs only because of the contact-actions between various elements. When water is heated it evaporates and is drawn upward in the atmosphere where it is then cooled. Becoming heavier, it falls to the ground. Nothing purposive goes on at all. Furthermore, the fact that rain makes it possible for human beings to plant and then harvest nutritious grains does not reveal any purposiveness. Yes, rain causes the grain to grow, but it does not fall for the sake of doing so. (Nor is it the result of a benevolent deity who arranged for rain to fall just where and when we need it to.) Instead, agriculture is a coincidental, a lucky (for us) by-product of an otherwise mechanical (efficient) set of events.

When Aristotle criticizes his opponent it is not because of the way he analyzes how rain works – in fact, he would agree with it – but for conceiving of all nature as modeled on this sort of causal event. A thinker like Empedocles would, for example, explain the sharpness of our front teeth in just such terms. By his lights, the shape of our teeth is the result of a chance event – we would say a genetic mutation – that occurred in our ancestors millennia ago. Because it enhanced their ability to survive it was then transmitted to future generations. There was no purposiveness at work in the front teeth becoming sharp, only random events that happened to work out well for the human animals who then passed on this trait to their offspring. Aristotle objects:

> It is impossible for things to be like this. For [the front and back teeth] and *everything that is by nature either always or for the most part comes to be in this fashion*, while nothing that occurs because of luck or chance happens this way. (*Physics* 198b33)

If something happens "always or for the most part," if it is recognizably orderly, it cannot, thinks Aristotle, be the result of chance. If it were to rain in Greece during the summer, this would be recognized as a fluke, for normally, or naturally, it is hot in the summer. In generation after generation of human beings the teeth do good work as they tear food and prepare it for digestion. They fulfill a purpose that contributes to the well-being of the entire animal. Chance cannot account for organisms that consistently reproduce themselves such that their parts effectively maintain their integrity as living beings. Teleology (or final causality), he argues, is required to explain the stable and non-random character of natural processes, especially the orderly reproduction of the parts of animals. The front teeth, then, are shaped the way they are for the sake of, to achieve the goal of, tearing food. By Aristotle's lights, then, Empedocles was quite wrong. Worse than that, thinkers like him who deny teleology "destroy what is by nature and indeed nature itself. For those things that are by nature, being moved continuously by some principle in themselves, arrive at some *telos*" (199b15). Deny teleology, Aristotle believes, and you deny nature itself.

Clearly, another name, however anachronistic, must be added to the list of Aristotle's critics: Darwin. For Empedocles' inchoate notions of adaptation and survival prefigured, however dimly, the theory of natural selection. Darwin himself says as much when he comments on this very passage from the *Physics*: "we here [in Aristotle's reconstruction of Empedocles' position] see the principle of natural selection shadowed forth, but how little Aristotle fully comprehended this principle, is shown by his remarks on the formation of the teeth."

According to Darwin, had Aristotle but followed Empedocles' lead in accounting for the sharpness of the front teeth he would not have fallen into the conceptual abyss of teleology. Unfortunately, by insisting that efficient causality and chance, coupled with the drive to survive, are not sufficient to explain the organic structure of animals and the regularity of biological reproduction Aristotle wrongly attributed purposiveness to nature itself.

Today, of course, an overwhelming number of biologists would not only agree with Empedocles and Darwin that Aristotle was wrong, but would offer the same explanation of how he went wrong. He was seduced by appearances, by the way the world that shows itself in ordinary, naked-eye experience. For at first blush the natural world, the parts of animals in particular, does seem to be purposively ordered. Our front teeth do seem to be shaped as they are for the sake of tearing food. After all, they do this effectively. But to infer from this that the world is purposively structured is to succumb to intellectual laziness. For such a generalization is no more than a projection of what "we see" onto a non-human screen where it does not belong. Teleology may well seem to explain what things look like at a casual glance. It may well conform to the immediacy of lived experience, but according to the vast majority of post-Darwinian biologists – remember Richard Dawkins – it is really bad science.[3]

As mentioned earlier, Rousseau's *Discourse on the Origin of Inequality* also prefigures, however non-scientifically, Darwin's theory of natural selection. For his story is also stripped of teleology. In it savage man, more complex but not essentially different from other animals, evolves through a series of adaptations to chance events. A lightning bolt struck a tree and he managed to figure out how to make fires. A flood isolated a piece of the forest, turning it into an island, and so people started talking to each other. As Rousseau puts it, our evolution into social beings would never have occurred without "the *chance* coming together of several unconnected causes" (43). As he tells the story, once we lived in the state of nature, solitary and content. Then, we became social and political and thereby lost to ourselves. Our very nature, always adapting to new circumstances, is malleable. Aristotle would disagree.

A fundamental debate is looming here, having to do not only with politics but with the very project of coming to understand ourselves and the world in which we live. What should we count as relevant evidence in trying to figure out the way things are? Should we, like Aristotle, take our bearings from what "we see" around us? If so, we may conclude that living in communities is natural, and that our front teeth have a purpose. Or should we begin with the suspicion that what we take for granted in our everyday lives is misleading, and that an entirely different perspective is needed in order to proceed as responsible scientists?

An easy example: we are accustomed to saying that the sun "rises" in the east and "sets" in the west at the end of the day. For it certainly *seems* that the sun is moving across the sky. In fact, however, the earth is orbiting the sun, and not the other way around. Relying on ordinary, naked-eye observation of the world, then, can easily wreck us as scientists. On the other hand, no human being, regardless of how sophisticated their knowledge of astronomy may be, will ever cease to describe the sun as rising and setting, or feel the earth as anything other than the stable center of their own existence; as, in other words, their home.

By Nature Political

Because families, households, and villages are the constituents of the city, and because they are natural, so too is the city, which as the *telos* of all other communities is required for human beings to live well. Aristotle summarizes this line of thought: "from these things it is evident that the city belongs among the things that exist by nature, and that *human being is by nature a political animal*" (1253a1).

Being political is essential to who we are. Therefore, those who do not live in a city, or even those who do but are thoroughly disengaged from political activity, lead stunted lives. They are "defective" and do not exist "according to" their own natures. Yes, they can survive as individual animals, but as Aristotle strikingly puts it, a non-political life is fitting only for "*either a beast or a god*" (1253a9); that is, for a non-human being.

Imagine Aristotle were time-machined into the Boston of today. He'd be mightily impressed by the people he'd meet on the streets. Most would be well fed and healthy, and a surprising number highly educated. He'd be fascinated by the electronic devices they were holding in their hands, the tall buildings in the distance and the cars whizzing by. He would certainly want a tour of the laboratories that dot the landscape. But when he got to know the people a little better he'd also be struck by how indifferent so many of them were to what their own government was doing. Many would not have bothered to vote and some would not even know who their elected representatives in Congress were. Few would have served in the military, and a good number would be shockingly ignorant about the wars their country has been fighting for most of the twenty-first century. The Bostonians he would encounter would have their eyes fixed on small screens, their phones pressed hard to their head, their ears wired to listen to their playlists. In short, they would be preoccupied by their private concerns. Many, of course, would feel connected to their families and co-workers and Facebook friends. But what they wouldn't do is precisely what Aristotle thinks is most natural for members of our species: identify themselves as citizens. In his eyes, such Bostonians would be "defective." He makes this point emphatically in the next passage:

> *The city is thus prior by nature to the household and to the individual.* For the whole must of necessity be prior to the part; for if the whole body is destroyed there will not be a foot or a hand. (1253a20)

The political community is more basic or important than the individual. It is the whole of which an individual is merely a part. And any given part is what it is only because it is part of a whole. A hand is a hand only because it belongs to a living body, to a functioning animal. If it were removed from the arm and placed on a table it might still look like or be called a hand, but in reality it no longer would actually be one. Instead, it would be no more than a chunk of soon-to-decompose matter. The relationship between city and individual is, he thinks, analogous. An individual human being is what he is insofar as he is part of a larger community; insofar as he is a citizen.

Rousseau, at least in the *Discourse on the Origin of Inequality*, would disagree. For him the city is anything but natural. Instead, like an ax or an automobile it is an artifact and a tool. And like all tools, while it augments our power it also robs us of strength and takes us further away from who we are by nature.

There may be good reasons for siding with Rousseau, and celebrating contemporary culture, in this dispute. For Aristotle's declaration of the priority of the city – his teleological argument – can lead to awful consequences. If the city is an organic whole of which a citizen is merely a part, then citizens should subordinate their very selves to its maintenance. They should entirely identify their interests with those of the political community. But do we really owe the city our deepest attachment? At one point in the *Politics* Aristotle suggests we do. He tells us that just as the job of the sailor is to preserve the ship and help it sail, so too the job of the citizen is "preservation of the political community" (1276a27). In words, the individual exists for the sake of the city, rather than the other way around. Does this raise the specter of the state becoming a totalizing whole, a monstrosity, that swallows every aspect of human life?

By contrast, a city like contemporary Boston, in which people identify themselves as free agents animated by private concerns, may seem terrifically attractive. Liberation from the demand to be political allows people to pursue idiosyncratic projects and dreams. Constraints – be they political, geographical, technical, physiological, or religious – are construed as obstacles that can and should be overcome. In such a city creativity is unleashed to an unparalleled degree, and diversity seems to flourish. In such a place, the role of government is minimal. It should provide security by protecting the rights of the individual, and other than that should stay out of the citizens' way as they pursue happiness as they see fit.

But might such depoliticization, wherein people are more like atoms than molecules, have its own dark side? Might it lead to rootlessness, alienation, apathy, and even despair? It will if Aristotle is right that we are communal beings whose very nature is to enter into cooperative relationships with others. For him the sort of individualism so familiar to contemporary Americans is a kind of disease.

When are we truly ourselves? With others or alone? In the city or outside of it? And how can this fundamental question be decided?

Animals with Logos

Aristotle backs up his claim that we are by nature political with the following argument. It focuses on the Greek word *logos*, which means "speech" or "language," but also "reason," "rationality," or "rational explanation."

> That human being is much more a political animal than any kind of bee or any herd animal is clear. For, as we assert, **_nature does nothing in vain_**, **_and human being alone among the animals has logos_**. The voice indeed indicates the painful or the pleasant, and hence is present in other animals as well; for their nature has come this far, that they have a perception of the painful and pleasant and indicate these things to each other. But *logos* serves to reveal the advantageous and the harmful, and hence also the just and the unjust. For it is peculiar to human being as compared to the other animals that he alone has a perception of good and bad and just and unjust ... and partnership in these is what makes a household and a city. (1253a8–19)

Aristotle's approach here is not so different from that a zoologist might take in her study of an animal she has never seen before. She might, for example, observe that something is beating regularly inside its chest. She doesn't know what it is but she will assume that, because an animal is an organic unity, this part must contribute toward the maintenance of the whole. She will proceed in her research as if "nature does nothing in vain." So too does Aristotle bring this sensibility to his investigation of human beings. He observes that (apparently) unlike other animals, we have *logos*. While chimps and whales have "voice" and can effectively communicate with one another, they do not have *logos*; that is, they do not discuss what is good and bad, right and wrong, advantageous and harmful. They do not reform their lives based upon the outcome of their discussions.

Should we go to the movies tonight or stay home and play cards? Should we have burgers for dinner or shift to a vegetarian diet? Should we abort the fetus or raise taxes on the rich? Should you major in philosophy or take a more sensible course? We debate such questions, disclose to one another our commitments and hopes for the future, and thereby articulate the values that bind our communities together. The observable fact of *logos* is evidence – for Aristotle at least – that by nature we need to live and talk together in order to be what we are. Recall that at the outset of the *Politics* he declared that communities operate purposively. A family aims for the well-being of each of its members, a baseball team for victory, a school for learning. Such values are the organizing principles of these communities, and only through *logos* do they become public and shared; do they become activated.

Throughout the *Politics* Aristotle emphasizes the prominent role *logos* plays in the political community. A nice example comes from his discussion of what today is called "collective intelligence." As he puts it, "the majority of people, of whom none is individually an excellent person ... can when joined together be better even than those [who are best]" (1281a42). Each individual may possess only a small bit of "wisdom," but just as in a pot-luck dinner, the sum of all the contributions to a discussion or debate will be greater than any single one. Having many people weigh in on an issue is like "having many senses" (1281b6). With more people talking, more perspectives on a subject will be introduced into the conversation and so, at least if the others are listening, more information and insight will accrue. Citizens talking with one another has an "epistemic" benefit; that is, it helps them gain knowledge. (*Epistémé* is the Greek word for "knowledge.") If they deliberate and converse with one another about an issue or question they'll have a better chance of getting it right.

Helene Landemore uses a great example to illustrate this point: the old movie, *Twelve Angry Men*:

> In order to illustrate such alleged effects of deliberation, let me consider two stylized situations of what occurs in a deliberative process. I borrow the first example from the film "Twelve Angry Men." The beauty of that example, among other things, is that it easily lends itself to an epistemic reading, since the jury deliberation assumes a procedure-independent standard of truth to be figured out: the defendant is either guilty or not guilty.
>
> In the film, one brave dissenting jury member – number 8, played by the actor Henry Fonda – manages to persuade the other 11 jurors to reconsider the guilty sentence they are about to pass on a young man charged with murder. Asking the other jurors to "talk it out" before making up their mind, juror number 8 takes the group on a long deliberative journey, which ultimately ends in unanimous acquittal. "Twelve Angry Men" can be seen, in my view, as illustrating the phenomenon of collective intelligence emerging from deliberation. Juror number 8, left to his own devices, would have been unable to demonstrate that the sentence was beyond reasonable doubt. Only by harnessing the intelligence of the other members, including against their own passions and prejudice, does the group ultimately reach the truth.
>
> The contributions vary and complement each other: juror number 5, a young man from a violent slum, notices that the suspect could not possibly have stabbed his victim with a switch-blade. The perspective of juror number 5 is not only unique (no other juror was acquainted with the proper way to use a switch-blade), it is crucial to the progress of the group's reasoning, putting in doubt the validity of a key eye-witness report. Juror number 9, an old man, then questions the plausibility of the time it took another key witness (an invalid) to limp across his room and reach the door just in time to cross the murderer's path as he fled the building. He too contributes to changing the collective perspective on the way the crime took place.

Only by talking with one another, by allowing each individual's unique perspective to enter the discussion, did this group of 12 men reach the right verdict. For by the end of the movie, their robust and often heated conversation led them to reverse their initial appraisal of the situation. They vote to acquit the defendant.

Aristotle also highlights the role of *logos* when he considers the ideal size of a well-managed city. It can't be too small, for tiny cities will be overly dependent on their neighbors and so will fail to achieve the self-sufficiency that he identifies as a hallmark of political well-being. As he puts it, "too small a number is inadequate for a good or beautiful arrangement" (1326a33). On the other hand, the good city can't be too big either because "an overly excessive number is incapable of sharing in order" (1326b31). It will be unable to generate a sense of communal identity among the citizens, and so will be badly governed. The best of cities, then, will be just the right size: not too big and not too small. He doesn't present us with a specific population target or an ideal number of square miles. But he does say this:

> There is a certain measure of size in a city, just as in all other things – animals, plants, instruments. None of these things will be able to fully actualize its own capacity if it is either overly small or excessive with respect to size ... A ship that is a foot long, for example, will not be a ship at all, nor one of twelve hundred feet. (1326a35–43)

Here he is operating with a model that, as he so often does, he borrows from zoology. Animals of a given species can't get too big or small without compromising their biological integrity. A human being who suffers from giantism, for example, and is over eight feet tall will suffer circulatory problems. His heart is simply too small for his body. Similarly, a ship that is but a foot long is no longer a ship. What something is, its essence and proper function, determines its appropriate "measure." Only by achieving that will the being in question be able to maximize its potential and fulfill its nature.

What, then, is the appropriate size of a well-functioning city? Again, Aristotle does not offer a specific number, but he does give us a clue:

> With a view to judgment concerning what is just, and with a view to distributing positions of leadership and authority on the basis of merit, *the citizens must necessarily be familiar with one another's qualities*, where this does not occur, what is connected with the offices and with judging must necessarily be carried on poorly. (1326b16)

In order for a city to be governed well, the citizens must be "familiar" with one another, and thoroughly engaged in the local. If Bob is running for treasurer then you and I, in order to vote intelligently and well, must know something about him. Is he responsible and honest and good at math? We can make these judgments only if our community is small enough so that we actually do know something about both it and Bob. Clearly, then, what Aristotle has in mind in this passage is something like a town, rather than a giant nation. The ancient Athens in which he lived had about 25,000 citizens. But even in a city of this rather modest population no one would know everyone else intimately. Nonetheless, in a place of this size individuals would have reputations and there would be a lot of *gossip*.

Gossip is a form of *logos* whose very name sounds pejorative. People love to talk about their neighbors, relatives, co-workers, celebrities, and friends. Such conversations have an almost magnetic attraction and often such talk is fueled by envy. Nonetheless, despite its tendency to become shabby, gossip doesn't have to be all bad. In fact, it can benefit a community.

It is common in my department for faculty members to talk about the president of our university. Usually our chitchat is critical, occasionally it is spiteful and unbecoming. Nonetheless, however clumsy and unprofessional it may sometimes be, such gossip is animated by a desire to figure out what a good leader should be and do. We are grappling with the question of excellence, even if at times we are not quite aware of doing so.

Students gossip all the time about their professors. They no doubt do it about me. Aristotle would approve. Gossip can function as a filter through which our opinions of others are distilled into a concrete value judgment that we agree upon. What is a good teacher, anyway?

Rousseau would find all this rather terrible. For him, gossip is no more than *amour propre* unleashed. Fueled by the desire to compare ourselves with others, it takes us outside of ourselves. Even more fundamentally, Rousseau is suspicious about *logos* itself. Recall that in his view language, which was not present in the state of nature, was a late development in the evolution of the human species. As he puts it, there was an "immense space ... between the pure state of nature and the need for languages" (30). Language allows us to communicate, share, and implement our values in communities. For Rousseau, however, this means that it is a tool for deception and alienation.

We can now reformulate the dispute raised in this chapter: are we most ourselves when we are talking with others, and thereby forging some connection with them, or when we are silent and by ourselves, free from the annoying bustle? But when we are alone, aren't we usually talking to ourselves? Isn't this what thinking is? If so, then perhaps Aristotle was right. Discourse and the urge to communicate with others, and even with ourselves, is basic to who we are. Or is it the other way around? Perhaps the conception of thinking as talking-to-oneself is evidence of the degeneration that comes with being a member of a community. How would we tell?

By Nature Unequal

Back to the *Politics* and an uncomfortable topic: Aristotle's assertion that some people are by nature inferior to others, so much so that they deserve to be slaves. To us, imbued as we are with the spirit of **egalitarianism** that pervades our culture (even if it is inconsistently put into practice), his position seems monstrous. In fact, however, Aristotle's position is more nuanced than it may seem. For he does not defend or justify all forms of slavery, only that which he calls "natural." As mentioned earlier, in Ancient Greece slavery was an institution. If one city conquered another it would kill the men and enslave the women and children. This is *not* what Aristotle is defending. For the slavery of his day was the result of military force and thus was completely indifferent to the qualities of the people enslaved. By contrast, the defining feature of Aristotle's natural slave is precisely his unique quality. He is mentally deficient and capable only of understanding and executing the orders of others. As a result, he is actually benefited by being a slave:

> For being able to use thought to see ahead is characteristic of one who rules and is master by nature, while being able to labor with the body is characteristic of the one who is ruled and is by nature a slave. In this way, *the interests of both master and slave are served*. (1252a31–33)

Since, as Aristotle understands full well, the overwhelming majority of the human race would in fact be harmed by becoming slaves, there is no justification for enslaving them. In a similar vein, he offers this analogy: the natural slave is "as different [from other human beings] as the soul is from the body or humans from beasts" (1254b18). The "soul" – we would be more comfortable with the word "mind" – of a normal adult can rule the body. So, for example, even if you are very hungry you may choose not to eat if you think there is something more important to do. You can, when you're healthy, order your body around. As the soul/mind is to the body, so too is the normal adult to the slave. According to this analogy, then, the natural slave is more like a mere body than a full human being. His relationship to normal people is thus like the one that obtains between normal people and beasts.

The implication of these passages is clear: natural slaves are so deficient that they are few and far between. As a result, and perhaps surprisingly, Aristotle's defense of natural slavery can be translated into a critique of institutionalized slavery, in which people are indiscriminately forced into bondage. Consider the following passage:

> There is both advantage and affection between the master and the slave when both are worthy of these designations *by nature*. When master–slave are not determined in this way, when the relationship exists *by convention and has been instituted by force*, the opposite is the case. (1255b13–15)

To be counted as natural, a slave must not only be objectively benefited by his master, but must also feel some affection for him. By contrast, in the conventional practices of actual Greek cities, slaves were those conquered in war and so no doubt were typically neither benefited by nor felt affection for their masters. As such, their bondage would have been neither natural nor just. In fact, the strict conditions Aristotle imposes on natural slavery may virtually define it out of existence. After all, he insists that the rational capacity of the putative natural slave be so limited as to preclude any sort of deliberation about the future. But every human being, with the exception of those whose brains are damaged, can do at least a little bit of that.

Even if Aristotle's defense of natural slavery can be transformed into a critique of the Greek institution of slavery, his position may still be far from agreeable. For by his lights, it remains the case that people, simply by virtue of being human, are not politically or morally equal. Instead, some are better than others, and this stratification is built into the nature of things. Rousseau, for whom all were equal in the state of nature, would disagree. Who's right?

In many areas of life we are quick to agree that inequality is not only real but is also a good thing. So, for example, we surely expect our beloved sports teams and symphony orchestras to be staffed by the most talented people available. But when it comes to personal dignity or basic human rights we claim that all are equal. This is enshrined in the famous words of the Declaration of Independence:

> We hold these truths to be self-evident, that ***all men are created equal***, that they are endowed by their Creator with certain unalienable Rights, that among these are Life, Liberty and the pursuit of Happiness.

Not worrying for the moment about how the "Creator" entered the picture, or the fact that the word "men" as used in the original text referred only to white males, most Americans have a strong attachment to Jefferson's words. But why is the equality of human beings so self-evidently true?

Aristotle states that "the free person rules the slave, the male the female, and the adult the child" (1260a10). Today we certainly disagree about the first two items on this list. But presumably most of us would allow that adults should rule children. After all, kids can't take proper care of themselves, and so have to be told what to do for their own good. Children are clearly not the equals of adults and so do not have the same set of rights. But what about those adults who are more like children than mature human beings? They are incapable of resisting the pleasure of the moment and, as a result, regularly get into trouble and make a mess of things. What about people who are just really dumb or pathologically self-absorbed? Are they truly equal to those pillars of the community who make life better for the rest of us?

At the time of the invasion of Iraq in 2003, many Americans believed that Saddam Hussein was responsible for bombing the World Trade Center in New York City. This war, which arguably has been catastrophic for the United States, was thus ratified by a large group of uneducated citizens (and perhaps legislators) who hadn't taken the time to do the minimal research required for finding out who, in fact, the bombers were. Do we really want such people voting in elections?

My nephew is a smart kid, but wild. He hated high school, for he couldn't sit still. He spent an enormous amount of time playing video games. In his senior year he was starting to get into some serious trouble. Then, to my delight, he decided to join the Marines. This is just what he needed. Only by being forced to was he able to wake up early in the morning and resist the urge to dress like a thug and get the attention that comes with doing so. Guns, whether real or cyber, have long attracted him, and at least now he is being trained to use one properly and in the service of his country. Without the Marines I imagine his life would not have been a happy story. Some people need forceful constraint in order to organize their lives well. Others can do it on their own. Some people should give orders, others follow them.

A 92-year-old man, unable to walk, hear very much, or see well enough to read, and who is in chronic pain, is in a nursing home. As his son knows well, were this man to be allowed to die tomorrow he would surely agree to do so. For the old man, who has led an active and generous life, and on whom many people have depended over the decades, believes that his present circumstances are so thoroughly degraded that his life is no longer worth living. He is appalled that his health care costs so much money. He would much prefer that these resources were directed at younger people who could put them to good use. It simply doesn't make sense to him that the doctors are keeping him alive longer. Maybe he's right.

A deteriorated old man and a healthy young woman are, in one sense, perfectly equal: they are both human beings. Does this make them of equal worth? Or is there a fundamental difference, as Aristotle thinks, between being alive and living well? Between life and a good life? No such distinction is allowed in the hospital. The doctors, simply insofar as they are doctors, are radical egalitarians for they have one job only: to keep people, regardless of who they are, alive.

Perhaps there is no distinction between life and a good life. If so, then God bless the doctors. If there is, however, it would provide the basis for just the kind of stratification that Aristotle would affirm. Some lives would be worth living; others not.

Aristotle believes that a woman's place is in the home. Most of us now find this notion to be offensive. To pigeonhole someone into a place, especially one low on the totem pole, is to limit their freedom, and this is unacceptable. In the age of globalization, a woman's place is thus surely not in the home. It's wherever she wants it to be. By our lights, all people should have the right to choose their homes, jobs, level of education, sexual partners, nationality, even their genders. The question remains, however, whether such placelessness actually fosters well-being. Can the free range of possibility nourish the human soul?

Today millions of people around the globe are voting "no" on this question with their feet by flocking to fundamentalist religion, and thereby voluntarily putting themselves under the yoke of tradition. They want a place precisely because it constrains them. Muslim women in France often choose, despite the opposition of the secular state, to wear the hijab. Orthodox Jewish women in the United States, despite the freedom to walk the streets half-naked, choose to wear long skirts. They voluntarily, often enthusiastically, place themselves into traditional communities (even if their parents actually abandoned such communities long ago). They welcome, sometimes fanatically, constraints and embrace the place to which they are assigned. They hold the freewheeling streets of Paris and Boston in contempt.

Perhaps this migration signals the dark side of equality and placelessness. Has contemporary society, imbued as it is with the spirit of the creative individual, become a swirling mass of free-floating atoms who belong nowhere and to no one? Aristotle would surely say yes. He would find our condition deplorable. Many people today seem to agree. But who's right?

Aristotle is an elitist who believes that some people just are better, and have better lives, than others. He thinks that the city should be stratified and that it will be well run if people occupy their proper place in the hierarchy. He would find the nursing homes of today, in which degraded lives are indefinitely sustained at great cost, absurd. Without doubt, his view is dangerous and easily abused. What prevents Bob from claiming to be an Aristotelian and then simply (and sincerely) declaring his superiority? He might then try to force other people to do what he says, or identify a group he dislikes as intrinsically inferior. What prevents him from declaring that a woman's place is in the home, and then trying to impose this view on his wife and daughters? Perhaps the dangers of Aristotelian-style elitism, and its conception of human nature and political place, are so great that they should be rejected out of hand.

Resolving the Dispute: Social-Political or Solitary?

Aristotle and Rousseau are at loggerheads on the principal question of this chapter. Are we most ourselves, most "according to nature," in a community and conversing with others, or when we wander alone, far from gossip and gaze? Do we belong in a city, in a place, or can we flourish on our own?

How can this dispute be settled? What counts as evidence or good reasons to prefer one competitor over the other? Perhaps, you might suspect, evolutionary psychology or neuroscience can answer our question. What if the human brain, having developed for so many millennia, is now hard-wired for social interaction? Does that mean we should give the nod to Aristotle? It might, for if this is the case then perhaps we are indeed "by nature" political. On the other hand, even if our species is genetically disposed to live with others it doesn't follow that every individual must or should do so. For, just as Rousseau argues, human beings are capable of fighting against animal instinct. So, for example, like all organisms we are genetically disposed to struggle hard in order to stay alive, and the vast majority of us will do so. But not everyone.

What if a social scientist presents us with data showing that people who are well integrated in communities and feel a strong sense of identification with a group report that they feel happier than those who live in a society that prizes individualism and privacy? What if statistical evidence indicates that the suicide rate climbs as social cohesion plummets? Maybe such findings would lend support to Aristotle as well.[4]

Conversely, perhaps the high level of creativity and economic productivity found in a country like the United States, which values individuality so highly, is to be prized. The streets of Brooklyn are wild with diversity and impulse, the inventiveness of Silicon Valley has changed the world. Perhaps this is evidence that a strong sense of political identification actually weighs people down and impedes genuine human flourishing.

To resolve this dispute a comprehensive account of human nature and of the political community is required, and every available resource should be tapped in order to reach it.[5] Empirical science, both natural and social, needs to be studied, as do the competing philosophical theories that have been developed to defend each of the two sides.

Recall something that was said in Chapter 1 about Socratic questioning. Even if it results in no definitive answer, it nonetheless teaches us what a good answer, a compelling *logos*, would be like. It must articulate and defend both its presuppositions and its consequences, and do so without contradiction. It must be both consistent and comprehensive; that is, a logical whole, a rigorously connected body of well defended propositions.

Needless to say, reaching such a goal requires massive effort. Do either Aristotle's *Politics* or Rousseau's *Discourse on the Origin of Inequality*, supplemented by their many other writings, fit the bill? Obviously, a great deal of reading is required before reaching a verdict.

Prior to that, however, you can still take an important step on your own. Hold a mirror to yourself and try to figure out where you stand, however provisionally, in this debate between Aristotle's vision of a political self and Rousseau's solitary one. Doing this will obviously not settle the dispute. Still, it is a valuable exercise, even a necessary one, for only by performing it will the debate be transformed from a merely academic one to one in which you have some skin in the game. So, ask yourself the following sorts of questions.

If you were presented with an attractive job offer that would require you to live apart from your family, would you accept it? Or does your family mean more to you than economic advancement? Do your friends? What if the job were in another country? Would you be content to live as an expatriate and communicate with those back home only by Skype?

How do you react when you are reminded that over two thousand American soldiers, two thousand fellow citizens, have died in Afghanistan during our long war there? Does a stab of pain rip through you, or is this just another bit of uneventful information on a screen chock-full of them?

Do you vote? If so, do you study the candidates' positions or do you rely on TV advertisements? Do you pay attention to what your government is actually doing by reading serious publications? Or do you feel that your life is just too busy for that?

Do you go to a church or a synagogue or a mosque? Does the sense of common purpose and solidarity that can be found there warm you, or vaguely repulse you?

When you were younger did you have school spirit? Do you enjoy going to stadiums in order to root passionately for the home team? Do you love the feeling of being part of a crowd as it explodes in communal joy when the game is won in the last second? Or does this sort of mass hysteria strike you as a pitiful escape from the responsibility of being an individual? Do you prefer team sports or games like golf?

How do you react when, on the streets of your city, you bump into strange people from all over the world, many of whom are not speaking English? Do you celebrate the fact that the global population is now a motley crew of free agents no longer restricted to national borders? Or do you lament the disappearance of a common language? Do you yearn for the good old days when everyone around you looked pretty much the same and shared many of the same values?

Do you think that talking – about your hopes, problems, passions, political inclinations, ideas, questions – makes your life better? Or are you suspicious of people who gab so much? Perhaps you think that the best thing to do is simply hunker down on your own and take care of business.

Do you check your phone constantly and always stay connected to your network of screens? Or do you occasionally unplug and indulge in those sessions of sweet silent thought in which there are no interruptions? Do you enjoy walking alone in the woods?

When you have compiled your answers, see if they are consistent with one another. If they are not, try to identify and explain the discrepancies. Why, for example, do you love rooting for your local football team, but hate going to church? Why do you vote, but remain ignorant about the current situation in Iraq? Why do you think it is valuable to talk about politics, but not about personal relationships? Why do you spend hours on Facebook when you actually feel better, and more yourself, when you are disconnected?

Most important, if after engaging in this sort of self-inventory you find yourself inclining to one side of the debate or the other, toward either Aristotle or Rousseau, challenge yourself by rereading your opponent as sympathetically as you possibly can. For only this will force you to think hard about our question. Finally, then, this chapter has been no more than an invitation for you to do that.

Notes

1   Many philosophers have developed state of nature theories. The one most directly opposed to Rousseau's is that of Thomas Hobbes. In his great work *The Leviathan* (originally published in 1668), especially in chapter 13 of Part I, titled "Of the Natural Condition of Mankind, As Concerning their Felicity, and Misery," Hobbes argues that by nature human beings are competitive, aggressive, and deeply concerned with what others think of them.

2   Gary Shteyngart, in his superbly satirical novel, *Super Sad True Love Story* (New York: Random House, 2011), splendidly captures Rousseau's critique of socialized man. Set in the near future, his characters are propelled by *amour propre* gone haywire. Their super-smartphones, to which he gives the name "äppärät," can scan a room and instantly rank people in terms of wealth, sexual attractiveness, health, and intelligence. No one in this world sees anyone else, or himself, except through the lens of comparison. Shteyngart's satire works so well because it is close to present reality.

3   An excellent updating of Aristotle's conception of biology, which provides a powerful counterpoint to Richard Dawkins, is Leon Cass's book, *The Hungry*

Soul (Chicago: The University of Chicago Press, 1999). You can also consult a recent book by Armand Leroi titled *The Lagoon: How Aristotle Invented Science* (New York: Viking, 2014).

4   My mention of suicide here is inspired by remarks made by Emile Durkheim in his classic work, originally written in 1897, *On Suicide: A Study in Sociology*, translated by John Spaulding and George Simpson (New York: Free Press, 1979). Here Durkheim argues that suicide, which seems "to be a phenomenon relating to the individual is actually explicable etiologically with reference to the social structure" (13). In other words, even the most personal of decisions, such as taking one's own life, is a "social fact" (37–38) that can best be understood through rigorous scientific and statistical analysis. To oversimplify his conclusion, people who live in isolation from community are more likely to commit suicide. In other words, he thinks, with Aristotle, that human beings are by nature social.

5   The contemporary version of this debate is between those thinkers today called "liberals" and "communitarians." The former would, broadly speaking, line up more with Rousseau's individualism, and the latter with Aristotle's dictum that human beings are political by nature. A good introduction to this controversy can be found in the essays edited by Michael Sandel in his *Liberalism and Its Critics* (New York: New York University Press, 1984). Here you will find important essays by, among others, Isaiah Berlin and John Rawls (two liberals), and Alasdair MacIntyre and Sandel himself (two communitarians).

3
What Should We Do?

The Question

Do you agree with Rousseau that in the final analysis you're at your best when alone? Do you distance yourself from those groups or communities that have invited you to join? Do you believe that you're entitled, perhaps even obligated, to disregard the desires of your fellow human beings? Even if you hold such radically antisocial views, you nonetheless have taken a stance about how to comport yourself toward others. In other words, you have adopted a *moral* position on how you ***should*** act, on what you should do.

It happens frequently, at least to most of us. Before actually doing something, you pause and ask, "should I?" You're sitting on a bus and the guy next to you, slumped against the window, is fast asleep. He's well dressed, but you can smell the alcohol and you know he won't be awakening soon. His wallet is sticking out of his jacket pocket and you can see that it's filled with cash. You're broke. Why not reach in and just grab a few bills, and then quickly get off the bus? He wouldn't notice. When he wakes up he won't remember much anyway. You pause and wonder: should I?

You're pregnant. And you're very young and don't yet have a job or your own apartment. You know that there is little chance the relationship you are currently in will last for much longer. Your irresponsible partner has given no indication that he intends to make a home with you. Having a baby now, while you still live with your parents, haven't finished college, and don't have a job, would destroy your dreams of a better future. You live in a city where there is a Planned Parenthood clinic, and so it would be possible for you to get an abortion. Should you?

Thinking Philosophically: An Introduction to the Great Debates, First Edition. David Roochnik.
© 2016 John Wiley & Sons, Inc. Published 2016 by John Wiley & Sons, Inc.

You've been invited to a party, one that promises to be exciting. And then your roommate, who is unattractive and socially awkward, asks what you're doing tonight. It's obvious he wants to join you. You like him well enough. After all, he's smart, kind, and sometimes funny. But you know he'll need your assistance at this party, and that's something you're not eager to provide. There's action to be had and you want a piece of it. You wonder: should you tell him that you're going to the library? Should you lie?

The dinner party is lovely, but the main course is steak. You're a devout vegetarian and believe that killing animals in order to feed ourselves is needlessly cruel and even unjust. When you see your friends at the table cheerfully gorging themselves with meat you wonder whether you should speak up and explain to them that what they're doing is wrong. Such a tirade would likely be taken as boorish and disruptive at such a refined gathering. But perhaps you should tell your friends what's on your mind anyway.

These questions all include the word "should." They put us into the driver's seat of our lives. For by answering them we make choices that will shape our futures. We don't have to steal money from sleeping strangers, get abortions, lie, or eat meat. The question, then, is whether we should or not. But how do we go about figuring that out?

Mill's Answer

 John Stuart Mill, *Utilitarianism*

John Stuart Mill proposes a straightforward and apparently commonsensical answer to the question. When you're debating whether to steal, have an abortion, lie, or eat meat, ask yourself this: will my action generate more or less happiness in the world? Will it affect more people, and perhaps other animals, on the positive or the negative side of the ledger? As Mill puts it, *"actions are right in proportion as they tend to promote happiness; wrong as they produce the reverse of happiness"* (7). This principle is the foundation of his moral theory, which he calls *Utilitarianism*, the title of his 1863 book.

Think of the guy on the bus whose money you have stolen. Yes, he will be unhappy when he wakes up and finds out it is gone, but he may well have spent that money on more booze. Plus, his fine clothes suggest that its disappearance likely won't harm him too much. You, by contrast, are strapped and can put the money to good use. You'll now be able to afford the textbooks for a course you're taking. As a result, you'll pass the exam, graduate from college, and thereby be both happier and a more productive citizen. The world will be a better place if you take the money. Or perhaps the guy on the bus will be so distraught when he discovers what has happened that he'll go on a violent rampage. Or perhaps his loss will help him see the error of his ways. He'll give up drinking and return to the straight and narrow.

It's possible that your having an abortion will eventually generate more happiness for more people. You're too young to raise a child well. By not having a baby you will be able to pursue your education and then your career, and so you will be both happier and better equipped to contribute to society. Your parents will surely be glad that you are doing so. And, you reason, so too will the children you hope eventually to have be happier, for they will have a parent ready and eager to raise them properly. But there are arguments again this position. The fetus will be deprived of all future or potential happiness by being aborted. Or, to cite a more general worry, the ready access to abortion, which in some cities is as easy to arrange as a trip to the dentist, has (arguably) diminished our appreciation of human life. On this view, the availability and convenience of abortion have transformed the most vulnerable among us, the unborn, into easy victims of those who have the power to pursue their own well-being at the expense of others. Such a culture cannot, on this view, be counted as one that is truly happy.

Should you lie to your roommate so that he won't trail you at the party and thereby slow you down? In fact, you tell yourself, not only will you be happier if he stays at home, but he will too. For at the party he's sure to be shunned. Lying to him is really just a way of protecting him from the inevitable dejection he would have felt. But what if he finds out you lied to him? Your friendship will be ruined. For once trust has been broken it can't easily be repaired.

Should you raise your voice in protest at your host's decision to serve grilled meat? You don't want to spoil your friends' evening, but you honestly believe that eating animals only because they taste good is a genuinely bad thing to do. You want to explain to your friends that cows too are capable of experiencing happiness and the wholesale slaughter of them shuts that possibility entirely down. Perhaps, you reason, the sermon you plan to deliver will make them so uncomfortable that they will reconsider their eating habits. It might, therefore, be your duty to intrude on their pleasant chatter. After all, the well-being of animals is a far more important topic than real estate or the hot new restaurant downtown.

The conversations imagined above take Mill's utilitarian principle as their point of departure. On his view, we should decide what to do by staying focused on the *consequences* of our actions.[1]

Mill is an excellent thinker and in one decisive respect we should emulate him. He understands that in order to develop the strongest possible position he must anticipate challenges to his own theory, and then try to rebut them. He must, in other words, engage in a kind of internalized competition. Following him as he engages in this process will allow us to think through his position, which is just what he wants us to do.

What Is Happiness?

The first challenge Mill issues to himself is to clarify the foundational principle of utilitarianism: actions are right insofar as they promote happiness. But what in the world is happiness? He responds: "*by happiness is intended pleasure and the absence of pain; by unhappiness, pain and the privation of pleasure.*" Or as he also puts it, "*pleasure and freedom from pain are the only things desirable as ends*" (7).

Why believe this is true? Because, Mill argues, it is a "psychological fact" (36):

> The only proof capable of being given that an object is visible is that people actually see it. The only proof that a sound is audible is that people hear it ... In like manner, I apprehend the sole evidence it is possible to produce that anything is desirable is that people do actually desire it ... *No reason can be given why the general happiness is desirable, except that each person, so far as he believes it to be attainable, desires his own happiness.* (35)

Mill argues against his imaginary opponent by citing what he takes to be strong empirical evidence. Even casual observation or introspection, he thinks, discloses that people pursue their own happiness. He uses the same strategy in defending his equation of happiness and pleasure:

> And now to decide ... whether mankind do desire nothing for itself but that which is a pleasure to them, or of which the absence is a pain, we have evidently arrived at *a question of fact and experience*, dependent, like all similar questions, upon evidence. It can only be determined by practiced self-consciousness and self-observation, assisted by observation of others. (39)

Like all good philosophers, Mill demands that his readers be honest with themselves. What makes you tick? What is it you pursue and why do you do so? Isn't it, he asks, because you want to attain happiness, conceived as pleasure, and avoid pain?

Utilitarianism Is Crude

An opponent might object: even if Mill's "psychological fact" is true, and happiness-as-pleasure is what we all seek, it can't possibly function as the "directive rule of human conduct" (11). After all, pleasure seems to be a mighty low standard by which to measure the goodness of human action. People can get pleasure from all sorts of nasty stuff; from rolling in the mud to having sex in airplane bathrooms. How, then, can a "moral" theory, a lofty word whose very sound smacks of dignity, possibly take its bearings from happiness-as-pleasure? Utilitarianism seems to be a low-life theory that would be just as applicable to swine as to human beings.

Mill responds: pleasure is indeed what all human beings desire, but it is not a singular phenomenon. Instead, there are different kinds. Some pleasures, like rolling in the mud, we may share with pigs. But there are others. "*Human beings have faculties more elevated than the animal appetites*" (8). We have minds and an ability to delight in literature, the theatre, music, friendship, movies, mathematics, and social activism. And these pleasures, which are "of the intellect, of the feelings and imagination, and of the moral sentiments," are "*higher*" than those associated with the body. Thus they "*are more desirable and more valuable than others*" (8). As such, he continues, they will invariably be preferred and chosen by anyone who has experienced both kinds of pleasure.

> Of two pleasures, if there be one to which all or almost all who have experience of both give a decided preference, irrespective of any feeling of moral obligation to prefer it, that is the more desirable pleasure. If one of the two is, by those who are *competently* acquainted with both, placed so far above the other that they prefer it, even though knowing it to be attended with a greater amount of discontent ... we are justified in ascribing to the preferred enjoyment as superior in quality. (9)

This is, yet again, an empirical argument whose conclusion, that some pleasures are higher than others, is grounded on observation. If someone has experienced both high and low pleasures, Mill contends, she will opt for the higher one even if it is "attended with a greater amount of discontent."

A simple example: at the moment I am neither drunk nor intoxicated. I could be either if I wanted to since it would be easy for me to buy a bottle or purchase some drugs. But I don't want to and for one simple reason. However difficult and frustrating it can be, I like what I'm doing now, which is trying to read, write, and think. I prefer working soberly in my office to the warm pleasure of intoxication. This is not to say that being intoxicated is bad, for it surely is not. After all, it's pleasurable. In fact, when I return home this evening I may well enjoy a glass of wine and I look forward to the "highly pleasurable excitement" (13) of the party I'm going to on Saturday night.

Mill's point is that intellectual activity, even if it is a struggle often attended with discontent, is ultimately more enjoyable than, and therefore preferable to, brute physical stimulation. Anyone who has experienced both and who therefore is in a position *competently* to judge the relative merits of the two pleasures, will (predicts Mill) invariably choose the higher over the lower. As he puts it,

> *Now it is an unquestionable fact that those who are equally acquainted and equally capable of appreciating and enjoying both [high and low pleasures] do give a most marked preference to the manner of existence which employs their higher faculties.* (9)

Imagine you were presented with these two options. First: you inherit a huge fortune and so you never have to work again. You live in a giant McMansion in a gated community, with a swimming pool, a hot tub, and a well-stocked refrigerator and bar. You can have sexual partners of your choosing who will appear and then comply upon request. You have both a masseuse and pharmacist on 24-hour call. The only problem is that you are not allowed to have any other visitors, your sexual partners are not allowed to talk and you have no books, TV, or computer. Your physical pleasures are nearly endless. You just don't have any mental stimulation.

Second: you have to keep your demanding job and continue living in a modest apartment in the city, where you have access to theatres, concerts, bookstores, friends, restaurants, and conversation. You have a cable package with access to all the premium channels, which means that you don't have to watch commercials.

Which would you pick? The second option will bring with it hard work and frustration. The books you read aren't always easy. Television series like *The Wire* and *Breaking Bad* are emotionally wrenching, even grueling.[2] Reading the bad news in the newspaper is demoralizing, arguing with your friends about politics usually seems to go nowhere, and you often become baffled when trying to translate Thucydides.

Now, if you've never watched the *Wire* or seen a play or heard live music or engaged in a debate about the war in Afghanistan then you won't recognize the appeal of the second option and you might well pick the first. But if you have experienced both, Mill is confident that you'll pick the second, the higher form of pleasure.

Is he right? Perhaps his is an overly optimistic conception of the human condition. You may insist that if pleasures, however low, are strong enough they will invariably be preferred. Mill takes the point. He realizes that drinking and drugs can trump better options. By his lights, however, this occurs only when there's a breakdown. At times, when the going gets rough, it can surely feel like ignorance is bliss. When the struggle becomes consuming it is tempting to drown sorrows in drink. As he puts it, those with intellectually ambitious and therefore readily thwarted aspirations are "capable probably of more acute suffering" (9) than the simpleton. The chances of going downhill fast are considerable since the "*capacity for nobler feelings is in most natures a very tender plant, easily killed.*" Anyone anywhere can all too easily succumb to drugs and even the best among us may "addict themselves to inferior pleasures" (10). Once that happens the game is over.

Nonetheless Mill is adamant. He sums up his conviction in these memorable words: "*Better to be a human dissatisfied than a pig satisfied; better to be Socrates dissatisfied than a fool satisfied*" (10).

Imagine what Mill might say about the scourge of drug abuse in America. Our policy has long been to tell young people that drugs are bad. Our motto, popularized by the late Nancy Reagan, is "Just say no," and the American strategy has been to declare a war on drugs and to criminalize both their sale and use. This policy has failed. Drug use remains high, prices are low, and entire countries, especially in Latin America, have been victimized by narco-terrorism.

Mill's remedy would begin with the proposition that drugs, because they produce pleasure, are good. That's why people choose them. It is therefore senseless to demonize and then attempt to eliminate them through the threat of punishment. Instead, the goal of public policy should be to show young people that superior pleasures are available. Remember, Mill argues that having been exposed both to high and low pleasures people will opt for the former. The best way to combat drug abuse, then, is to fight pleasure with pleasure; that is, to make the higher pleasures more accessible and familiar to more people. And this, above all else, requires a greater commitment to *education*. This doesn't mean that more information should be dispensed about the harm of drug abuse. No, what Mill has in mind is education that enhances the capacity to experience the higher pleasures.

When I was in college a friend recommended that I take a class in the history of Western music, a subject about which I was totally ignorant. Before he suggested this, it had never occurred to me to do so. But I admired him and so I followed his lead. During the two semesters of the course I was exposed to everything from Gregorian chants to Stravinsky. Even though I was no great shakes in the classroom, my capacity to enjoy music grew enormously. Having been educated, even if only a little, I now have more avenues of pleasure available to me. For 40 years I have gone to concerts and listened to music at home. These days, rather than drink a lot when I travel on airplanes, I take a good set of headphones with me, turn the volume up, and lose myself in my playlist.

Education, broadly understood as the acquired capacity to enjoy the higher pleasures, is the best antidote against boredom; that insufferable feeling of dull repetition when life seems to be going nowhere. In turn, boredom is often the catalyst for stupid and destructive behavior. For bored people will resort to almost anything, even the lowest of pleasures, to spice things up. Unemployed young men, for example, often engage in random acts of violence just to get their juices flowing. And people of all sorts and ages will drink heavily – anything to ward off the weary tedium in which they feel mired. But an educated person has a set of tools with which to stimulate herself. When there's nothing else to do and I'm feeling restless, I can take pleasure in reading a novel or going to the museum. Because I am knowledgeable about baseball I can visit the web site of the Boston Red Sox and review boxscores.

Genuine education is far more than the mastery of technical skills or the absorption of information. It is the development of intellectual capacities whose exercise can become a life-long source of pleasure, and it is essential for human happiness. For this reason, Mill is remarkably optimistic about the prospects of improving the human condition. He believes that it is possible to create the conditions for making more people happy. As he puts it, "*the present wretched education and wretched social arrangements are the only real hindrance to [happiness] being attainable by almost all*" (13). He is a progressive who honestly believes life can be made better for people through reform. There is no reason, he thinks, that vast numbers of human beings must suffer a life of deprivation. "Poverty, in any sense implying suffering, may be *completely extinguished* by the wisdom of society" (15), he claims. Illness and premature death "may be indefinitely reduced by good physical and moral education" (15). In fact, "*all the grand sources ... of human suffering are in a great degree, many of them almost entirely, conquerable by human care and effort*" (15). (Compare this to Rousseau's dictum that "most of our ills are of our own making.")

We are, thinks Mill, morally obligated to try to make life better for as many people as possible. Extending the reach of education causes better pleasures, and thus more happiness, to be available to more people. Even if you ultimately disagree with utilitarianism, it is surely not a swinish or crude doctrine.

Utilitarianism Is Selfish

Because it is a moral theory that makes happiness paramount, utilitarianism may initially seem selfish. As the previous section should have already made clear, however, this is not the case. Mill states this point forcefully:

the *"standard is not the agent's own happiness, but the greatest amount of happiness altogether"* (11). When debating what to do, the question should not be, will my proposed action benefit me? Instead: will it benefit the most people possible?

Built into this notion is another one. Since utilitarianism prohibits me from privileging myself, it implies that my happiness is no more important than yours or anyone else's. Human beings are, in other words, morally equal. "As between his own happiness and that of others, utilitarianism requires [the agent] to be as *strictly impartial as a disinterested and benevolent spectator"* (17).

Because of its *egalitarian* foundation and consequent concern for the well-being of others, Mill claims that his moral theory is fully compatible with the teachings of Christianity:

> In the golden rule of Jesus of Nazareth, we read the complete spirit of the ethics of utility. "To do as you would be done by" and "to love your neighbor as yourself" constitute the ideal perfection of utilitarian morality. (17)

It is useful here to summon a contrast (and thereby trigger a debate). Recall Aristotle's defense of natural slavery. He argues that by nature some human beings simply are better, because they are smarter, than others. Such a view is, by Mill's lights, anathema to the Christian ideal whereby every person is a child of God and therefore deserving of the same level of moral respect.

Aristotle might respond that, despite his claim to being an empiricist, Mill is peddling idealistic claptrap. A quick glance at the real world reveals that most people are concerned only with their own well-being, not that of others. Mill has a rejoinder and by now it will be familiar. While it may be true that most people are at present selfish, there is no reason that this predicament cannot change. What is required is moral education:

> Education and opinion, which have so vast a power over human character, should so use that power as to establish in the mind of every individual an indissoluble association between his own happiness and the good of the whole (17).

Reformulated: education can expand the capacity of human beings to identify themselves, and their interests, with others. Literature is especially good at teaching this sort of lesson; in other words, in teaching us how to empathize. Reading stories exercises the imagination. It enhances the ability to feel with others, and to recognize that characters who initially seem alien to us are not in fact all that different. However unlike we may seem to be, we are finally all in the same boat. This is a basic idea for Mill and so we'll return to it shortly.

Utilitarianism Becomes Moral Fanaticism

If Mill is right that "all the grand sources ... of human suffering are ... conquerable by human care and effort" (15), then are we morally obligated to work 24 hours a day for the betterment of our fellow human beings? If every "should" question must be viewed through the lens of the greatest happiness principle, then must every decision be made with an eye toward maximizing the happiness of other people? Is Mill thereby demanding that we become full-time social activists? Or, even more extreme, moral saints?

If I decide to make a cup of coffee in my office instead of buying a double-skim cappuccino at ten times the cost, I could use the saved money to help others. Am I morally obligated to do so? I have several pairs of expensive leather shoes even though cheap canvass ones could probably substitute. Does Mill's moral theory require me to abandon all trappings of bourgeois consumerism and dedicate myself to "promoting the general interests of society" (18)? If so, then does it exceed the capabilities of normal human beings? If Mill is right then shouldn't most of us feel guilty most of the time for falling so short?

Mill anticipates this objection. He explains that even though the job of his theory is to spell out our moral obligations, we are not obligated to be moral all the time:

> No system of ethics requires that the sole motive of all we do will be a feeling of duty; on the contrary, *ninety-nine hundreths of all our actions are done from other motives*, and rightly so done if the rule of duty does not condemn them. (18)

This is hard to figure out (at least for me). By Mill's lights, most of the time it is permissible for my actions to be motivated by non-moral considerations. Perhaps it's okay, then, for me to drink expensive coffee and wear leather shoes. But what about eating meat, driving a fancy sports car, and wearing a stylish jacket? Where do I draw the line? Is there a special corridor of life that is officially "moral," and only while present there must I invoke the greatest happiness principle? Mill insists that "there is nothing in the utilitarian theory inconsistent with the fact that there are other things which interest us in persons besides the rightness and wrongness of their actions" (20). But how can we distinguish between what in our lives is morally relevant and what not?[3]

Utilitarians Are Frigid

Similar to the arguments of the previous section, one might challenge Mill by claiming that his theory transforms human beings into moral-calculation machines. If the ultimate standard invoked by utilitarianism is "the greatest amount of happiness," then determining whether you should do something or not seems to require adding up units of anticipated happiness that will be generated by the action. As usual, Mill anticipates the challenge by himself raising the possibility that *"the dry and hard consideration of the consequences of actions"* (20) will turn the utilitarian into an ice-cube. Once again, however, he responds to the objection. "Utilitarians," he says, "are quite aware that there are other desirable possessions and qualities besides virtue" (20). At the same time, he is also aware that his moral theory runs the risk of turning its practitioners extremist and cold. He believes, however, that this is a risk worth taking. The severity of moral calculation is better than fuzzy sentimentalism. As he puts it, "if there is to be any error, it is better that it should be on that side" (20). Maybe the spasm of guilt that accompanies the double-skim cappuccino isn't the worst feeling in the world.

Utilitarianism Is Expedient

Mill acknowledges that because it is a moral theory that takes its bearings from the consequences of actions, utilitarianism might be accused of dealing in *expediency*. To explain what he means, consider lying. On some occasions, it seems to be the obviously right thing to do. If, for instance, I hear a knock on the door and upon opening it meet a man who begs me to hide him from a deranged killer, I may well let him hide in my basement. When the bad guy comes to the door and asks if I've seen his intended victim, shouldn't I say "no"? After all, if I tell the truth then the killer likely will find him. Or if a child who is extremely sick asks me whether she will soon get better, and I know that, barring a miracle, this will not occur, shouldn't I say, "of course you will"? Mill would say yes. Although he holds truth telling to be a "sacred" rule, he allows it to be violated under just these kinds of circumstances. As he puts it, lying is morally permissible,

> if the withholding of some fact (as of information from a malefactor or of bad news from a person dangerously ill) would save an individual (especially an individual other than oneself) from great and unmerited evil. (23)

To his credit, Mill understands that this sort of consequentialist defense of lying is risky. Return to the example of the socially awkward roommate who wants to accompany you to a fast-paced party. The easiest way to get rid of him is to tell him you're going to the library. Perhaps, you say, you'll give him a call if you decide to grab a beer later in the evening, even though you know this won't happen. You tell yourself that you are lying in order to protect your roommate's feelings – that is, to make him happier – but it is more likely that you're protecting yourself. It would be painful and time consuming to explain the situation honestly to him. Regardless of how it is rationalized, in this sort of case a lie is told for self-ish purposes; that is, for the sake of expediency.

The dilemma is this: utilitarianism counts some lies – those that benefit others – as morally permissible. But once consequences are allowed to justify lying, is the door opened to a vast number of possible justifications, not all of which are genuinely altruistic? Mill says no. In other words, he thinks that utilitarianism has the conceptual resources to reject lying on almost all occasions. Specifically, it is disallowed when it is "for the pur-pose of getting over some momentary embarrassment, or attaining some object immediately useful to ourselves or others" (22); that is, when it is merely expedient to do so.

There are, Mill thinks, good utilitarian reasons to tell the truth (almost all of the time). For while lying may *seem* to be beneficial, even the white lie will likely have bad consequences. First and foremost, lying (if discovered) undermines trust, which is crucial in developing lasting relationships, which in turn are crucial in promoting long-term happi-ness. If your roommate discovers that you actually went to the party instead of the library, your friendship will be, if not destroyed, at least made insecure. How will he know you're not lying the next time you tell him you're going to the library? Such a loss will ultimately be more painful than the party was pleasurable.

Second and perhaps even worse, lying can become a habit. If your ruse succeeds and your roommate never finds out what you really did, your dishonesty has been reinforced and you may well become convinced that lying, justified in terms of benefiting others even when it is no more than self-protection, is an effective social strategy. You run the risk of become a habitual liar. And this is a disaster. As Mill explains, "*a sensitive feeling on the subject of veracity [honesty] is one of the most useful*" attributes a human being can have. For it is the foundation on which reliable and enduring relationships are built, which are the source of so much happi-ness. Simply put, we need to be confident that those close to us are telling the truth. Honesty, then, is not only the "principal support of all present social well-being" but also the basis of "everything on which human happi-ness on the large scale depends" (23). For this reason, even if lying achieves a short-term gain, in the long run it is ultimately harmful. It undermines trust and thereby destroys the possibility of being confident in others. To his detriment, and to yours, your roommate may never confide in you again. Furthermore, habitual liars will eventually become incapable of distinguishing truth from falsehood. At that point, they will not only be unreliable and useless or even dangerous to others, but also lost to themselves. They will no longer know what they really mean or what they really want.

Think of the great cyclist Lance Armstrong. For years he stood before TV cameras and adamantly insisted that taking drugs had nothing to do with his spectacular victories in the Tour de France. We now know that he was lying. But how was he able to maintain the façade of a fierce truth teller for so long? I for one was taken in. I simply couldn't imagine that this man's reality was at such odds with his steadfast appearance. How did he pull it off? Perhaps it was by telling himself that deep down he wasn't really cheating. All elite cyclists of that period were probably engaged in doping. Armstrong may have convinced himself that he was simply putting himself on a level playing field, and so in fact he beat his opponents fair and square. How else could he have developed that tremendous sense of conviction in his own superiority? Perhaps Armstrong had told these lies for so long that he believed that their falsehood paled in comparison to what he believed was a deeper truth.

Lance Armstrong is a fractured human being. Not only will he never be trusted again by other people, it is likely that he no longer can be honest with himself. He is the supreme example of what Rousseau sees as the socialized man for whom "being something and appearing to be something became two completely different things."

In sum, the disposition to be honest can, Mill thinks, be fully supported on utilitarian grounds. It makes abiding relationships not only with others possible, but also with oneself. Still, he does allow that there can be good (moral) reasons for not telling the truth. For *"even this rule [one ought to tell the truth], sacred as it is, admits of possible exceptions"* (23). There will be occasions, such as the killer-at-the-door scenario conjured above, where on balance the negatives of lying are trumped by the positive consequences that will ensue. But can we really determine what those occasions are? And if lying is allowed on these few special occasions, might it not be so as well for less admirable ones? Ones that are baroquely rationalized in terms of benefiting others but are ultimately selfish? Perhaps it would be morally safer, then, to disallow lying in every possible situation. As we will soon see, our next philosopher (Kant) certainly thinks along such a line. Before turning to that, however, let's linger with Mill for just a little while longer.

Utilitarianism Is Unjust

There are 20 people in the room. I propose to the group: let's make Bob our slave. He can take on all the menial jobs that we hate to do, and the rest of us will be happier as a result. Bob will be miserable, but 19 people will be better off as a result of his sacrifice. Doesn't that add up?

The general question at issue here is this: does utilitarianism fail as a moral theory because, with its singular focus on the greatest happiness for the greatest number, it offers no protection of individual human rights? Does it become a ruthless form of calculation? If a few individuals have to go down the tubes for the greater good, so be it.

Mill anticipates this objection and he responds in much the same way as he did to the charge that utilitarianism leads to expediency. Yes, it may seem that enslaving poor Bob will benefit and make happier the other 19 people in the room. But it won't. For in the long run, violating Bob's rights (which is also known as injustice) will cause the other 19 people in the room to feel insecure. After all, if Bob can be enslaved, how do I know I won't be next? In Mill's words, the utilitarian has a great "interest" in protecting the rights of individuals – that is, in being just – in order to foster a feeling of security, which in turn is "the most vital of all interests" – in fact, *"security no human being can possibly do without"* (54). For without it, the future looms only as a debilitating threat. In times of great insecurity planning ceases, hopes dwindle, and paralysis ensues. Therefore, enslaving Bob, which would render everyone else in the group insecure, is the wrong thing to do.

But is this utilitarian defense of rights strong enough? What if we figured out a way to enslave Bob while keeping the other 19 people in the room ignorant that we had done so? What if we told them that Bob was no longer with us, when in reality he was buried deep in a mine shoveling coal (which will bring our heating bills down)? Perhaps they would continue to feel secure. If so, what utilitarian-moral reason could then be summoned to make this the wrong thing to do?[4]

Or think of this: a terrorist has been captured and his interrogators are convinced that he has knowledge of where a bomb, soon to explode, has been planted. Should they torture him in order to extract this information? Doing so will violate his basic human rights, but as Jack Bauer on the TV series *24* regularly (if misleadingly) informed us, torture is an effective means of getting bad guys to talk, and thereby saving the lives of innocent people.[5] Is it thus morally right? If it is not, can the utilitarian explain why not?

Utilitarianism Is Fantasy

Recall that a possible objection to utilitarianism is that, because it makes happiness the ultimate goal of human striving and of morality, it is a *selfish* doctrine. If something makes me happy, then why shouldn't I go for it regardless of whether my actions have a negative impact on others? Mill's response: the standard invoked by his moral theory is "not the agent's own happiness, but the greatest amount of happiness altogether." A critic might object, however, by saying that this is folly. People simply don't care about other human beings.

Mill disagrees. He believes that a "*feeling of unity with our fellow creatures*" (27), which he calls "*sympathy*" (28), and we would call "empathy," is present in all of us (unless we are sociopaths). It pains me to see you in pain. Therefore, I will do what I can to alleviate your suffering.

Mill's "sympathy" is similar to what Rousseau calls "pity," the natural repugnance we feel at seeing another human (or any sentient) being suffer, and he thinks that empirical observation confirms that such feelings lie deep in the human heart (or DNA). In fact, he invokes just such observation to justify the greatest happiness principle:

> The ultimate sanction, therefore, of all morality (external motives apart) being a *subjective feeling in our own minds*, I seen nothing embarrassing to those whose standard is utility in the question, What is the sanction of that particular standard? We may answer: the same as of all other moral standards – *the conscientious feelings* of mankind. (29)

Mill doesn't care where sympathy (or empathy) originates; that is, whether it "is innate or implanted" (30), natural or the result of socialization. What matters is only that it exists and can be empirically observed. As he says, "the social feeling of mankind … is a powerful principle in human nature" (32).

The critic retorts: say what? Just look around. Far from being animated by feeling for others people are selfish dogs who do not hesitate to victimize those weaker than themselves. Perhaps you can now predict Mill's response: sure, this is the way people often behave, but if they do it is because their moral or social education has been inadequate. Fortunately, however, that failure can be remedied. As he puts it, "the smallest *germs* of the feeling are laid hold of and *nourished by the contagion of sympathy* and the influences of education" (33).

Note the metaphor. Germs of sympathy can be found in even the most stunted and selfish of souls – the violent criminal cares about his mother – and they can be nourished and then grow. Sympathy is contagious. It can become viral and spread. This it will do so if people are properly educated. Again, this does not refer to the transmission of information or technical skills. Instead, Mill is thinking of the process whereby our imaginations are strengthened and our capacity to put ourselves in someone's else shoes is enhanced. We learn that those who seem other than ourselves are actually similar.

One of the more striking TV shows in recent years is *Transparent.*[6] It features a 60 something man who has three adult children and is divorced from his wife. He has decided finally to act on an impulse he has harbored since childhood: to become a woman. As the show progresses, we see him become her, and it is not a comfortable sight. She is tall and has a deep voice. She looks and sounds peculiar. But as we get to know her better we realize that she is no different from any of us. All she wants is to feel comfortable in her own skin. She is struggling to support and understand her children. She longs to be understood. In short, she's no different from the rest of us.

Or think of the 2002 film *Secretary.*[7] It begins with a young woman being released from a psychiatric ward and returning home to her mother. She's a "cutter," a masochist, who inflicts damage on her own body. She takes a job as a secretary only to discover that her boss is a sadist who gets pleasure from inflicting pain on others. These are two of the more peculiarly perverted people I have seen on screen. But it turns out that they complement each other perfectly. In a strangely effective twist they end up getting married and living happily ever after, even though their relationship is based upon his inflicting and her absorbing pain.

Secretary was troubling. In fact, my wife, who detests the appearance of male violence against women, walked out of the theatre. I stayed and think I was rewarded by doing so. For by the end of the movie I cared about these two characters and wanted the best for them. This movie was a success because I learned that however strange and even objectionable these people seemed to be, they were no more than two needy souls longing to connect. Just like me, they were pathetic creatures trying to stay afloat.

These examples illustrate what Mill has in mind when he says that the germs of sympathy (or empathy) can be nourished by education. If this is true, then we are morally obligated to build an educational system in which young people are "taught" to care about others. Such "teaching" requires repeated exposure to a wide variety of characters and stories, which function like calisthenics for the sympathetic imagination. Mill is confident that however distant his own society may be from achieving the goal of mutual moral concern, it is nonetheless both feasible and defensible. It is possible for people to feel that the well-being of others actually matters to themselves. Such, at least, is the hallmark of a healthy society, one in which we should all aspire to live.

It should now be clear that Mill's reasoning above implies another basic feature of his moral theory, one that was implicit in the general happiness principle from the beginning: *egalitarianism*, the view that human beings are morally equal:

> Now society between human beings, except in the relation of master and slave, is manifestly impossible on any other footing than that the interests of all are to be consulted. Society between *equals* can only exist on the understanding that the interests of all are to be regarded *equally*. (32)

Aristotle would disagree.

Whatever your reaction may be to Mill's moral theory, you must give him credit for possessing intellectual grit. He forces himself to challenge his own position, to compete against himself. This is the only way, he thinks, to determine whether his theory is strong enough to stand on its own. He believes it is. Whether he is right or not, he provides a model of intellectual rigor that we should all emulate. Next, however, we will test Mill by presenting him with a critic other than himself: Immanuel Kant.

Kant's Answer

 Immanuel Kant, *Grounding for the Metaphysics of Morals*

Mill's moral theory is optimistic, humane, socially responsible, and seems to provide concrete guidance for those who wish to figure out what they should do. Another philosopher, however, thinks it is terribly inadequate. This is Immanuel Kant. He denies that we can determine whether an action is right or wrong by calculating its consequences. He rejects happiness as the ultimate standard of moral judgment and doesn't think the capacity for human sympathy, while both empirically observable and encouraging, is conceptually strong enough to mandate that individual human rights be protected. We will follow his argument by tracking the first moves he makes in his book, which has the forbidding title, *Grounding for the Metaphysics of Morals* (1785).

The Good Will

Kant opens the First Section of his book with the following words:

> *There is no possibility of thinking of anything at all in the world, or even out of it, which can be regarded as good without qualification, except a good will.* (7)

Many things seem to be good. Some, like intelligence, a sense of humor, a capacity for self-discipline, or a powerful memory, are qualities that belong to, or are somehow in, us. Others, like inherited wealth, come to us from the outside. And others, like being physically coordinated or having a robust constitution, are a result of good (genetic) luck. All, however, suffer from the same limitation. They can be misused or deployed for bad purposes. It's possible for a violent criminal to be handsome, strong, rich, and smart. All of these putative goods, then, are saddled with a qualification: they have to be used well in order to become truly good. So, for example, if you just won the lottery, you can spend your newfound riches on fancy clothes that you don't need, or give a sizable chunk of it away to those who are poor. When you decide what to do with your money it will then be your *will* that directs your action. It is, therefore, the will that transforms a qualified or potential good such as wealth into a really good one. As such, only the good will has "*intrinsic unconditional worth*" (7). Kant elaborates and explains.

Consequences and Morality

A good will is good not because of what it effects or accomplishes, nor because of its fitness to attain some proposed end; it is good only through its willing; i.e., it is good in itself. (7)

Imagine that Bob is thoroughly enjoying a superb dinner with a lively group of attractive people. His phone rings. It's Sue, a close friend. She's very sick and has run out of her medicine. She asks Bob to pick it up for her at the pharmacy since she can't get out of bed. And she badly needs it now. Because the party is magnetic Bob doesn't want to go. But because he believes that friends should help each other, he thinks that he should, and so he wills himself away from the table. He gets into the car, drives to the pharmacy, and buys the medicine. On his way to Sue's house, through no fault of his own, he is blindsided by a drunk driver. His car is wrecked and his phone destroyed. Fortunately he suffered no serious injury, but he did get a bump to the head and is dizzy, and he has to remain at the accident scene for hours. As a result, he fails to deliver Sue her medicine.

This wasn't Bob's fault. He did what he, as a friend, was morally obligated to do. He fulfilled his duty even if his mission failed. It's possible, of course, that at first Sue was angry with him when he didn't show up. But her anger dissipated when she learned the reasons why (and finally got her medicine); when she realized that her friend had the best of intentions, which were thwarted only by terribly bad luck.

The lesson here is that consequences are not the true measure of the moral worth of an action. If they were, then Bob's leaving the dinner party to get Sue her medicine would be morally deficient, when in reality it was admirable. From a moral perspective, then, what matters is not what happens but what Bob intended to happen, what his will directed him to do. As Kant puts it,

> If with the greatest effort it should yet achieve nothing, and only *the good will* should remain (not, to be sure, as a mere wish but as the summoning of all the means in our power), yet would it, *like a jewel*, still shine by its own light as something which has its full value in itself. (8)

In more technical language he also says this:

> An action done for duty has its *moral worth*, not in the purpose that is to be attained by it, but *in the maxim according to which the action is determined*. The moral worth depends, therefore, not on the realization of the object of the action, but merely on *the principle of volition* according to which, without regard to any objects of the faculty of desire, the action has been done. (12)

A maxim is a "subjective principle of volition" (13). Think of it as a "should" statement or imperative that we utter to ourselves. Bob told himself that he should help friends in need, and so even though he was sorely tempted to stay at the party, he forced himself to abide by what he said to himself. His maxim directed his action, and it rather than the consequences of the action caused by it determines moral worth.

Duty

The lesson learned above can be reformulated: "*the concept of duty*" (9) is the crux of the moral enterprise. Bob did what morality demanded of him; that is, his duty. And from a moral perspective this is what matters, not the fact that he never actually delivered the medicine to Sue.

The concept of duty allows Kant to categorize our actions from a moral point of view. He suggests that there are four different ways in which an act can relate to duty. He illustrates by means of examples (which I modify).

Acting contrary to duty Let's assume that we are in fact morally obligated to help friends in need. Next, imagine that when Sue called Bob he couldn't bear to leave the splendid party and so he said to her, "Sorry, no can do. My car is in the shop. You'll have to ask someone else."

This case is easy to understand. Bob is a liar and a bum who has acted "*contrary to duty*" (9). His action is immoral.

Acting in accord with duty but not really wanting to   Let's change the scene. This time, Bob is so bored at the dinner party that his legs are twitching. When Sue calls he's delighted at the prospect of being able to leave. Now, Bob's not a particularly generous person so, as he would himself admit, had the party been a blast he would have lied to Sue and stayed at the table. He doesn't really want to help his friend. But because the party is a drag he welcomes the excuse and is glad to leave.

Bob did the right thing but for the wrong – that is, for a selfish – reason. He's using Sue's request to benefit himself, which is all he cares about. Let's imagine that in this scenario Bob succeeds in delivering the medicine to Sue, who thanks him profusely when he arrives. From Mill's point of view, which prioritizes the consequence of an action, Bob's action is positive. As he puts it, "*the motive has nothing to do with the morality of the action*" (18). Kant disagrees and this case is meant to show why. For simply performing the action doesn't make Bob morally admirable. Instead, it was almost by accident that he happened to do the right thing. For him to be morally admirable he must not only do the right thing but also act for the right reason. Even though his action was "*really in accordance with duty*" (9), it wasn't genuinely moral because he had "no immediate inclination" (10) to do it.

Acting according to duty and really wanting to   You own and run a bakery. A kid comes in with a few bills and asks for a loaf of bread. It would be easy for you to charge her more than the listed price or give her the wrong change. But you don't. Because we have the duty to be honest this is the right thing to do. You have acted according to your moral duty. Still, even though you really want to do the right thing, you are still being pushed by a selfish reason. For you understand that if it were discovered that you were cheating little kids your reputation and business would be damaged. In this case, your "own advantage required [you] to do it" (10).

I think of this example often when I go to a local restaurant. The waitstaff treats me very well. They greet me warmly, laugh at my jokes, and let me taste new dishes. Clearly their motive is double-edged. On the one hand, they may be genuinely hospitable people who believe in treating others well. On the other, it is also in their interest to do so. After all, one reason I keep returning to the restaurant, and spending a good bit of money there, is because of how well I'm treated. Like the imaginary owner of the bakery, the staff not only do the right thing – they act in accord with duty – but they also want to do the right thing. It is possible, though, that their wanting to is infected by a more selfish purpose than that of morality.

Acting according to and from duty   You have a chronic illness that keeps you in constant pain. Entirely dependent on your caregivers, you no longer enjoy any aspect of your life. Furthermore, you are imposing significant financial and emotional burdens on your family. Enough of this, you think. Better to end it all now. In other words, you are mightily tempted to commit suicide. Now, assume that (as Kant thinks) suicide is morally wrong, and that you have always aspired to be a moral person. So even though every fiber of your being longs for life to end you resist the impulse. And you do so only *because* you think suicide is wrong. As with the characters mentioned in the prior two examples, you have acted *in accord with duty*. Far more important, however, and unlike the other two, you have acted *from duty*. For it is only *because* you believe that you are morally obligated to resist the temptation of suicide that you are alive today.

Kant describes such a person:

> If adversity and hopeless sorrow have completely taken away the taste for life, if an unfortunate man, strong in soul and more indignant at his fate than despondent or dejected, wishes for death, and yet preserves his life without loving it – not from inclination or fear but *from duty* – then *his maxim indeed has a moral content.* (10)

If you're reading this book you are, I am pleased to say, alive. This means that you too did not commit suicide this morning. As such, you acted in accord with duty. But because you are a healthy and reasonably happy person suicide tempted you not at all. You are immediately inclined to stay alive simply because life is pleasant to you at the moment. There is, of course, absolutely nothing wrong with this. Kant's point, though, is that neither is there anything moral about your not committing suicide this morning. By contrast, the chronically ill person described above has no inclination to stay alive. Indeed, he is attracted to and inclined toward death far more than life. His action of resisting suicide therefore counts as a moral achievement.

To reiterate: Kant does not think that those of us who refrain from suicide simply because we're glad to be here are inferior to the chronically ill person who desperately wants to die but stays alive for moral reasons. The purpose of his examples is only to illustrate four different ways in which an agent can relate to the concept of duty, which lies at heart of morality. To act both according to and from duty, as shown in the fourth case, is an example of a moral will at its most pristine.

Universality

Duty, Kant says, is *"the necessity of an action done out of respect for the law"* (13). The chronically ill person in the example above refuses to yield to the temptation of suicide only because he respects, and so is willing to subordinate his own inclinations to, the moral principle that disallows it under any circumstances. Of course, the next question we want to ask is, what are these principles, what is this moral law? Kant doesn't tell us yet, but he does disclose an essential feature of morality. A moral imperative, he thinks, must be *universal*. It must apply to everyone.

This is a notion that most us can readily grasp. For example, one often hears a child complain that her treatment hasn't been "fair." Her older sister was allowed to stay up late playing on the computer, why can't she? What her complaint implies, even given the child's limited understanding, is that people should all be treated in the same way. To favor one person over another seems unfair. Even the child, then, has an inchoate sense of equality and morality.

Or think of the familiar question people often ask themselves before they act: what if everybody did it? Should I steal the guy's money? What if everyone were a thief? Should I cut in line even though I came late? If everyone were to do so chaos would ensue. Even without knowing what this question exactly means, or why it is reasonable to ask it, it nonetheless represents an impulse that Kant thinks lies at the heart of morality. We are capable of stepping outside of our particular selves, even just a little, in order to scrutinize an action from a perspective that tries to encompass everyone.

Here's a slightly more circuitous way to think about this point. Most of us are comfortable breaking rules when we are convinced that doing so will not harm anyone else. This regularly goes on behind the wheel of a car. You see a stop sign a few feet ahead of you. But you can also see that no one is behind you and the intersection is clear in every direction. You're driving slowly and so you don't fully stop. In other words, you break the law even though you believe that, in general, drivers should obey the law. In this case you make an *exception of yourself* because you predict that going through the stop sign will cause no harm. Or remember the room-mate who asks if you're going to a party. You believe that both you and he will end up unhappier if you tell him the truth. So you lie. But notice the thought process you undergo before doing this. You are simultaneously acknowledging the force of the general rule even while you are breaking it. This is why you feel impelled to rationalize your action. You tell yourself, yes, it's wrong to lie, but in this case, when my roommate's feelings are at stake, it's okay not to tell him the truth ... for his own good. When people tell their white lies they typically are not embracing a life of deception. Instead, as Kant states clearly, *"when you tell a lie, you merely take exception to the general rule that says everyone should always tell the truth"* (15).

The next time you tell what seems to be an inconsequential or white lie, pay close attention to the thought process that accompanies it. Even as you violate the general rule against lying, you explain to yourself why you are justified in doing so; why you are an exception. This is evidence, Kant thinks, that even in disobeying the rule you tacitly acknowledge its existence; that is, you acknowledge that morality asserts itself in the form of universal demands.

Kant encapsulates this line of reasoning by presenting what he calls the *"categorical imperative"*: *"I should never act except in such a way that I can also will that my maxim should become a universal law"* (14). To illustrate, he uses an example, which I'll modify. I'm broke and badly in need of some cash. I borrow 20 bucks from you and promise to pay you back, knowing full well that I will not be able to do so. Remember that for Kant consequences are not the true measure of an action's moral worth. So even though I will now be able to buy some food with your 20 bucks, and fend off my family's starvation for another day, this does not justify the act. Instead, to determine whether the action is moral or not I must,

> *ask myself whether I would really be content if my maxim (of extricating myself from difficulty by means of a false promise) were to hold as a universal law for myself as well as for others.* (15)

Following this procedure, Kant thinks, will lead to an unambiguous "no" to the question, should I make a false promise? For if I universalize the maxim that led me to lie in order to get some money from you, the result will be unsustainable. As he puts it, I cannot will a "universal law to lie" because "by such a law there would really be no promises at all ... Therefore, *my maxim would necessarily destroy itself just as soon as it was made a universal law*" (15). If there were a universal law that allowed us to break promises whenever it was convenient to do so, then the very concept of promise making would evaporate. Upon universalization all lies would be justified, lying would become the norm, and so *"there really would be no promises at all*" (15). Or as Kant later puts it, upon being universalized, the maxim that one should make false promises reveals itself to be "*self-contradictory*" (31). In other words, in order for promises to make any sense at all, there must be a presumption that one ought to tell the truth. Again, if the maxim *It's okay to break promises when it is convenient to do so* were universalized, the notion of keeping a promise would become incoherent. Kant believes that the categorical imperative does no more than formalize what is latent in what he calls the "*ordinary knowledge of morality*." Even though most people would never dream of explaining their actions and deliberations in terms of the universalizability of maxims, "the ordinary reason of mankind in its practical judgments agrees completely with this" (14). The fact that we use the word "fair" as often as we do, and that in telling and then rationalizing white lies we actually pay heed to a general rule to which we make exceptions of ourselves, is evidence that our gut-level sense of morality requires universality.

Still, Kant's moral theory may seem easy to reject. Remember the story of the murderer who knocks on your door. You are sheltering his potential victim in your basement. When the bad guy asks you, "Is he in the basement?" almost all of us would likely say "no." It seems obvious that most of us (and John Stuart Mill) would gladly violate the general prohibition against lying in order to save a life, and that to do otherwise would be a moral rigidity bordering on insanity. But Kant invites you to think about this situation further in the following way. What if you lie to the murderer but, without your knowing that he had done so, the potential victim had just escaped from your basement and was running away? When the murderer leaves your doorstep and arrives at the sidewalk in front of the house, he bumps into his victim and kills him on the spot. Conversely, what if you had told him the truth? Perhaps the murderer, who went down to your basement only to find it empty, would then have failed to commit his dastardly deed.[8]

In the first prong of this little story, the guy in the basement gets killed because you lied to protect him. Would you be responsible for his death? No, you'd say, it was an accident. Your intentions were all good. By contrast, in the second prong, where you told the truth to the killer, you actually saved the victim's life. However happy a result that might be, it too would have been an accident. Kant's point here is that consequences are always liable to precisely such accidental twists. Therefore, he reasons, if we take our bearings from them we are throwing the fate of our moral lives into the winds of chance. Morality, however, requires us to take responsibility for our actions, and what is in our control is only our will, our ability to try to do the right thing. We can choose to act such that the maxim of our action can be successfully universalized, and avoid those actions whose maxims lead to self-contradiction. Regardless of what beneficial consequences may be predicted to occur, the fact remains that it is simply wrong to lie. The maxim cannot be universalized. Lying, therefore, is wrong. Full stop. Kant believes that a decent person knows this.

(Also: note that there's nothing in Kant's moral theory that forbids you from punching the murderer in the nose or pulling out your 9 mm pistol and detaining him until the police arrive.)

The man in unrelenting pain that the doctors say will never end while he is alive (and conscious) wishes to commit suicide. Were he to do so, the maxim of his action would be "from self-love I make as my principle to shorten my life when its continued duration threatens more evil than it promises satisfaction" (30). Perhaps surprisingly, suicide, which seems to be driven by self-hate, is actually driven by self-love. Its purpose, in this example at least, is to end the torment and spare oneself future suffering. For this reason Kant believes that a maxim promoting suicide cannot be universalized. His reasoning is this:

> One sees at once *a contradiction* in a system of nature whose law would destroy life by means of the very same feeling that acts so as to stimulate the furtherance of life. (31)

Suicide does not make moral sense because upon universalization it becomes incoherent. It pits the impulse to life – namely, a desire to avoid pain – against itself. Thus, regardless of the positive consequences it might seem to generate, it is wrong. Full stop.

Egalitarianism

If morality is essentially bound to duty and universality, as Kant thinks it so plainly is, then it is also egalitarian at its core. For if the moral law applies to everyone, then everyone must be equally subject to it. On his view all human beings deserve the same moral treatment and respect.

Now, recall that Mill also agrees people should be treated equally (fairly), but for reasons very different from Kant's. For him, treating people unfairly (unjustly), favoring some at the expense of others, has bad social consequences, the worst of which is the insecurity it produces. If Bob can be singled out and harmed in some way, even if the stated reason is for the common good, then perhaps such treatment will someday be meted out to you or me as well. Because a widespread sense of security is needed for a society to flourish, it is morally imperative to promote it.

If treating even a few people unfairly works against that objective, then it is wrong. There are thus, Mill thinks, good consequentialist reasons to protect individual rights.

For Kant, however, the utilitarian defense of individual rights is just not strong enough. For while it may be true that in most circumstances treating people fairly is beneficial to the whole society, it is conceivable that in some cases this principle may not apply. If oppression of a few can be cloaked in secrecy, then perhaps it would not weaken the sense of security felt by the many, and so society would not be harmed by it. In short, the utilitarian attempt to justify an action through its consequences is forced to rely upon the unpredictability of actual events in the world. Therefore, Kant reasons, there must be grounds stronger than social consequences to support the inviolability of moral imperatives and the essential egalitarianism of the moral law. And these, he thinks, can only be found in what he calls "practical reason."

Consider the question of whether slavery is morally justified. For Kant this requires an examination of the maxim that would affirm it. Can it be successfully universalized? No. Why it cannot becomes especially clear when Kant offers another version of the categorical imperative:

> *Act in such a way that you treat humanity, whether in your own person or in the person of another, always at the same time as an end and never simply as a means.* (36)

My computer is a thing that I own. I can do what I want with it, and I surely can use it as a means to further my own ends. When it ceases to serve my needs, or even if I just get tired of it, I can sell or otherwise get rid of it. Kant's reformulated version of the moral imperative is that I should never treat another person like a thing, which of course is precisely what is done to a slave. Treating someone as if he were "simply a means" to gratify my desires – which is what I do with my computer – would rob him of the dignity that is his simply because he is human. I am morally required to treat every person as an "end"; in other words, to respect them. Slavery is thus morally wrong.

This does not imply that we are absolutely (morally) prohibited from treating others as a means. Of course we benefit from many of our relationships. The administrative assistant of my department has, for example, been very useful to me over the years. We're not friends and professionally we're not equals. But there's nothing wrong with that. What would be wrong, what would be immoral, is if I conceived of him as merely a tool whose purpose was to further my ends. While it is perfectly okay for me to use him as a means, and in turn for him to do the same with me, it is not acceptable for either of us to treat the other "*simply* as a means." The "simply" is the key. To conceive of someone else exclusively as a means to an end is to transform him into a thing and thereby to violate his humanity.

This form of reasoning would apply even to a convicted terrorist. However grotesque his crimes, he too is a human being. Therefore, he should not be tortured just to provide information. Doing so would reduce him to a something like a computer. He would become an information machine rather than a person.

Perhaps this sort of moral rigidity seems counterintuitive. It may seem obvious to you that a terrorist suspected of knowing when and where the next bomb is going off should be subject to any form of enhanced inter-rogation that would make him talk. After all, innocent lives are at stake. But remember Kant's story of the murderer who knocks at the door. Consequences are unpredictable and so anticipated benefits should never get in the way of moral analysis. Torture is wrong because it transforms people into tools. It is wrong because it diminishes their humanity, even if the person in question is a bad guy. Full stop.[9]

Two of Kant's examples discussed above, making a false promise and committing suicide, can also be illuminated through this version of the categorical imperative. The old man who wants to end his life in order to save both himself and his family from suffering is in effect treating himself as a means to the attainment of a goal: the cessation of pain. It's as if he wants to transform himself into a narcotic or analgesic rather than main-tain his status as a dignified human being who has intrinsic value (who is an end). And if in asking you for 20 bucks I tell you that I will pay you back, knowing full well I won't be able to do so, then I've transformed you into an ATM machine. This I simply should not do.

Ordinary Moral Intuitions

At this point, Kant's moral theory may seem forbidding. But it is impor-tant to remember that he claims to be doing no more than articulating the grounds of "ordinary moral knowledge." Although his prose can be dif-ficult and his thinking abstract, he is actually trying to justify what he takes to be the basic moral intuitions that, by his lights, most people already share. It is wrong to lie. It is wrong to treat people as if they were things. These ideas are not complicated and so, as he puts it, "*neither science nor philosophy is needed in order to know what one must do to be honest and good, and even wise and virtuous*" (16). You don't need a complicated theory to be decent. You only need to be decent.

This side of Kant's moral theory, its simplicity, will come into sharper focus if we contrast it again with Mill's. Recall his consequentialist position on lying. On the one hand, Mill certainly believes that honesty is the best policy. He knows that deception undermines trust, and that this has bad consequences for all future relationships and thus for society itself. But he's equally clear that on some occasions it is morally permissible to lie. To repeat what he says, "even this rule [that one ought to be truthful], sacred as it is, admits of possible exceptions." If other people will actually be benefited by telling lies, then the prohibition is lifted.

I've been smoking a few cigarettes a day since graduate school. When my daughters were young I almost never smoked at home and I regularly echoed the message they were getting at school: smoking is bad for your health. I certainly didn't want them to smoke and so while I didn't blatantly lie to them I tried to give them the impression that neither of their parents were puffers. Not surprisingly, they finally caught me. I tried to talk my way out of the jam by explaining to them that I smoke very little and do so only because it helps me stay at my desk. It's difficult for me to sit for hours and try to concentrate. Nicotine relaxes the muscles and stimulates the brain. Like coffee, it's what I need to work. Naturally my children were upset. Had I been lying to them? Did I lose their confidence? Or had I succeeded in communicating the right message, at least for a while? Smoking is bad. As far as I know, neither of my daughters has ever smoked. (Of course, they could be hiding it from me as I did from them.) This is good. But did I do the wrong thing at the beginning? I'm honestly not sure.

Utilitarians invariably enter into these kinds of difficult, even excruciating, deliberations. They must calculate benefits and measure them against potential harm. As Mill puts it,

> If the principle of utility is good for anything, it must be good for *weighing* these conflicting utilities against one another and marking out the region within which one or the other preponderates. (23)

Deceiving my children about my smoking was a negative. But if it kept them away from cigarettes perhaps it was also a positive. The point of my example is this: the moral life of the utilitarian invariably gets complicated with justifications, calculations, and rationalizations. Kant's view is different: just stick with the basics. Be honest. Don't treat people as things. Never enslave anyone. Don't commit suicide. This may all sound terribly superficial to a sophisticated mind. But its force, if it actually has any, can perhaps be better appreciated by comparing Kant here with Rousseau.

Rousseau thinks in the state of nature we were animated by pity, by the instinctive repugnance we felt simply at seeing other sentient beings (not just humans) suffer. But everything changed when we entered society and the world of language, comparison, and moral reasoning. There our lives were ruined. As he so powerfully puts it, in society "the most decent people *learned* to consider it one of their duties to kill their fellow men." From the father who spanks his child because he (sincerely) believes it will make the kid better, to the pilot who drops a bomb knowing full well it will kill not only enemy combatants but also civilians, we are all capable of reasoning ourselves into doing things that, simply left to our own natural impulses, we would otherwise not do. For no human, argues Rousseau, would harm another in the state of nature unless his immediate survival depended on doing so.

In a similar vein, Kant thinks that our moral lives are actually quite simple:

> I need no far-reaching acuteness to discern what I have to do in order that my will may be morally good. Inexperienced in the course of the world and incapable of being prepared for all its contingencies, I only ask myself whether I can also will that my maxim should become a universal law (15).

To repeat, however abstract it becomes, Kant's theory is meant to buttress the simplest of moral imperatives. Keep your promises. Don't commit suicide. This is nice, but does it offer any guidance whatsoever when it comes to a complicated case? Consider this one. In 2014 Israel invaded the Gaza Strip. By the end of this war, over 2000 Palestinians and some 70 Israelis had been killed. Notable among the Palestinian dead were hundreds of children. The question is whether Israel was morally justified in using its vastly superior military force to attack the Palestinians, knowing full well that their bombardment would kill civilians. Did the Israelis try their very best to limit civilian casualties? If so, does that alter the moral equation? Did Hamas use civilians as shields by concealing its weaponry in hospitals and schools? If so, are they ultimately to blame for the innocent blood that was shed? Did they cause the war by firing rockets into Israel? If so, did that give Israel good reason to invade? If in the long run this invasion somehow leads to fewer deaths, then perhaps it did. But what if the war of 2014 only causes the next battle to be fought?

Does the categorical imperative give us a tool to navigate such treacherous moral terrain? It is arguable that both the Israelis and Hamas used civilians in Gaza simply as a means to further their ends. Should both sides, then, be damned?

The Dear Self

Kant might seem to be a cold-blooded rationalist who requires us to analyze situations in order to determine what our duties are. His version of
morality, encapsulated by the categorical imperative, refuses to allow projected benefits to play a role, and so steers clear of the messiness of flesh
and blood reality. He has at least one good reason for holding such a view.
To explain, consider the following scenario.

You are walking on the street and a poorly dressed woman asks you for
some money. She tells you that she has children who need food. She does
not seem like a schizophrenic or a drug addict, and so you give her $20.
Why did you do it? Because you believe in the moral obligation to be
charitable? Did you act from duty? Or did you have a selfish purpose
steaming inside you as well? Perhaps giving her the money made you feel
better about yourself or allowed you to look impressive in the eyes of others. Perhaps having just been to the ATM your wallet was too full of $20
bills and you wanted to lighten your load.

The point here is that, regardless of how resolutely we examine ourselves, it is impossible for any of us ever to be certain about our actual
motivations. As Kant puts it, correctly I think, "*we can never, even by the
strictest examination, completely plumb the depths of the secret incentives
of our actions*" (19). The reason for this is that "if we look more closely at
our planning and striving, we everywhere come upon *the dear self*, which
is always turning up" (20). In other words, no matter how confident we
may be that we are doing something for the sake of others it is always possible that in fact we are doing it to benefit ourselves.

I once made a promise to someone. He had heard that a few people in my
department were planning to form a reading group and he wanted to join.
The problem was that I thoroughly disliked this man. He was a big, self-
indulgent talker, and his raspy voice made me cringe. I truly did not want
him ruining our reading group. But I had promised him that once the group
decided on its schedule I would inform him. A few days later the plans were
set for our first meeting. I did not want to call this man. But I did, and (it
seemed) only because I had promised to do so. Even in this apparently clear-
cut case, however, I may not have accurately diagnosed myself. For the "dear
self" may well have entered my deliberations without my being aware of its
doing so. Perhaps what really pushed me to call him was the fear of the guilt
that would haunt me had I not done so. Or of the embarrassment that might
ensue if I withheld the information and then he discovered my subterfuge.
At the moment of acting I took myself simply to be abiding by a promise.
But about what ultimately prompted me to act, I will never be certain.

Another example: I enjoy teaching. But why? Why do I come to life in front of students and put so much time into preparing my classes? Is it because I'm eager to assist young people? Or because I'm trying, however minimally, to make the world a better place? Am I some sort of altruist or does the pleasure I get from teaching come from the feeling of power that attends my position as the professor. I dole out grades to my students, and so they have a stake in listening to me. I'm a lot older and know a lot more than they do (at least in the subjects I'm teaching). Perhaps I just like being the top dog in my classroom. After all, it's the only place in which I can make this claim.

I honestly don't know what has pushed me into a life of teaching – or into the writing of this book – and so on this issue at least I agree with Kant. I am incapable of completely plumbing the depths of the "secret incentives" of my own actions. This region of reality – let's call it "the empirical self" – is not fully penetrable. For Kant, this implies that it should play no role in moral reasoning. Instead, we should rely solely on the clear light of practical reason to help us understand our duties. We should, for example, keep our promises. That, for Kant, is demonstrably a moral imperative. But even when we abide by (act according to duty), and so resist the temptation to break a promise, it is impossible to determine whether our action was driven by either moral or selfish reasons. So what? The job of moral reasoning is not to tell us what makes us tick, but only how we should act.

Resolving the Dispute: Consequences or Duty?

Should we make moral choices based upon a calculation of how the world will be made better by what we do in specific situations, or by following strict rules that admit of no exception? On empirical study, or on a rational examination of the subjective principles of volition that we are considering? On projected consequences or on duty? How can this competition, whose great champions are Mill and Kant, possibly be resolved?

Perhaps we should first ask which of these two philosophers has better defended his presuppositions. So, for example, both assume that human beings possess free will. Many thinkers, however, have challenged this view. A theist, for example, might hold that because God is omniscient and omnipotent, He knows the future before it occurs, and so human choice is actually an illusion. A mechanist might maintain that the universe is a giant machine and so, as a result, what we do now is caused by events outside of our control. Perhaps such causes are encoded in our genetic strands. Can either Kant or Mill argue against such opponents?[10] That's a tough question, and so a great deal of study awaits you.

Even at this juncture, however, with only two simplified options on the table, your philosophical inquiry can commence. As usual, start with some introspection. Can you remember an occasion when you did something that was actually a result of a moral deliberation? Have you ever been in any situation that resembles the several scenarios that were offered to you in this chapter? Did you pause before acting and ask yourself, should I do it? If so, then how did your thinking unfold? Did you weigh the conflicting utilities of your options, and then decide on the basis of which would benefit the most people? Did you then act on the basis of your calculation? Or are you someone who has strict principles and so, regardless of predicted outcomes, you stick to your guns at all costs?

Do you admire a character like Jack Bauer and his willingness to torture suspected terrorists in order to extract useful information from them? If so, then how do you respond to Kant's ingenious example of the murderer-at-the-door? Remember, if you lie to this guy in the hope of saving the victim, you may actually be hastening the victim's death. Analogously, the consequences of torture may be far less positive than expected (extracting false information, creating an enemy for life, tarnishing the image of America in the world). Or does torture strike you as something Americans simply should not do, and for one reason only? Because it is wrong.

Where did you stand on the debates triggered by the Israeli invasion of Gaza in 2014? In your mind, was the loss of civilian life justified on the basis of future benefits? Does a country have a right to protect itself against rocket fire by any means necessary? May it legitimately kill children if it deems it necessary to do so? Or is that too simply wrong?

Or think of it this way. Because it takes its bearings from consequences, Mill's moral theory requires us to look toward the future. By contrast, Kant forces us to stand still and scrutinize our maxims. It might thus be useful here for you to ask yourself what relationship you have with the future. Do you have your key out of your pocket before you reach the locked door of your office? Or are you more concentrated in the moment, and attentive to what is standing before your eyes? The former disposition might be more up Mill's alley, for he is, after all, the great progressive. The latter, coupled with an attraction to the logical clarity of principles, could be closer to Kant.

Another possibility looms. Upon honest introspection, you may discover that moral reasoning of either the Kantian or the Millean stripe plays no role in the actual deliberations you make before acting. Upon reflection, you may further conclude that a debate between representatives of these two schools on an issue like abortion or physician-assisted suicide will ultimately become no more than an abstract exercise. Logical wheels will spin and arguments will duel, but they will be without existential punch. Some other form of reasoning, you suspect, is needed in order best to confront the "should" question. If this is your (provisional) line of thought, then the next two chapters should be to your taste.

Notes

1   Utilitarianism is a complex doctrine. For a good overview see the entries titled "Consequentialism" and "Rule Consequentialism" in the *Stanford Encyclopedia of Philosophy*:
    http://plato.stanford.edu. This is, by the way, a good resource for further investigation of many topics discussed in this book. The articles tend to be rather scholarly and sometimes technical, however.

2   *The Wire* is a TV series that appeared on HBO from 2002 to 2008. *Breaking Bad* appeared on AMC from 2008 to 2013.

3   The philosopher Peter Singer has argued to great effect that our relationship to the happiness of non-human animals is morally relevant. Inspired by utilitarianism, he has argued on behalf of vegetarianism. See his *Animal Liberation* (New York: Harper Collins, 2009), which was originally published in 1975.

4   The most well known expositor of the view that utilitarianism lacks the conceptual resources to provide an adequate defense of individual human rights is John Rawls. His magnum opus is *A Theory of Justice* (Cambridge, MA: Harvard University Press, 1971), a book that has influenced political theorizing for nearly 50 years.

5   Jack Bauer is the hero of the TV series *24 Hours*, which appeared on Fox from 2001 to 2010.

6   *Transparent* is a 2014 TV series that was produced and broadcast on Amazon.

7   *Secretary* is a 2002 film directed by Steven Shainberg.

8   Kant's example about the person who by lying inadvertently aids, rather than hinders, a murderer is found in his essay "On a Supposed Rule to Lie Because of Philanthropic Concerns." It can be found in the same volume as the *Grounding for the Metaphysics of Morals*.

9   A good book that discusses the morality of torture, and whose title expresses a Kantian conviction, is *Because It Is Wrong: Torture, Privacy and Presidential Power in the Age of Terror*, by Charles Fried and Gregory Fried (New York: Norton, 2010). They authors can be seen discussing it in this video: https://www.youtube.com/watch?v=WiWweN9s3zA.

10 The question of free will is discussed very widely in contemporary philosophy. For a thorough overview of the debate, which includes a selection from Kant, see *Free Will*, edited by Derk Pereboom (Indianapolis: Hackett, 1997).

4

Whom Should We Emulate? (1)

The Question

The "should question" is integral to human life. Without it we would be unable to recognize ourselves. (Without it we would not be free.) This does not mean, however, that Kant and Mill have exclusive dibs on it. For it is possible to ask the "should question" without moralizing it. The two thinkers we examine in this chapter, Aristotle (again) and Nietzsche, will illustrate what this means. Neither will be primarily concerned with establishing rules or principles that tell us what we should do. Nor will their books tackle dilemmas such as the moral legitimacy of torture and suicide that cropped up in the previous chapter. Instead, their question will be, to what finally should we aspire? What is the fullest expression of a life well lived? What is human excellence, and who among us best supplies a model or paradigm to emulate? While such questions are obviously similar to that asked by the moralists, they also transform it. By greatly expanding the purview of the "should," they invite us to examine life as a whole.

Aristotle's Answer

 Aristotle, *Nicomachean Ethics*

Happiness and Excellence

From an Aristotelian perspective, the dispute between Mill and Kant is wrongheaded from the start. Asking, what's the right thing to do?, and then trying to work out the answer, is too narrow a lens through which to

Thinking Philosophically: An Introduction to the Great Debates, First Edition. David Roochnik.
© 2016 John Wiley & Sons, Inc. Published 2016 by John Wiley & Sons, Inc.

examine the "should" aspect of our lives. Unlike many contemporary philosophers, and despite the fact that he invented "ethics," Aristotle is not preoccupied with a set of moral problems, such as those concerning abortion or lying. Instead, he has his eyes fixed on a different prize: understanding the best life available to human beings. His focus is on human "excellence," or what the Greeks called *aretê* (also translated as "virtue"). He wants a full-blown picture of what it means to be a human being on top of his game. This, he thinks, will give us the best guidance as we try to navigate through the turmoil of our days.

We begin with the first few paragraphs of the *Nicomachean Ethics*.

(1) Human beings, Aristotle says, seem to do everything for the sake of some "good" (1094a1). These goods can also be called "ends" or "goals." To use a word that appeared in Chapter 2, during our discussion of the *Politics*, human action is "teleological."

You're reading this book for a reason. Perhaps you have a passion for philosophy and you thought it might be interesting. Or perhaps it was assigned by a teacher and you want to get a good grade. Whatever your answer, the point is this: you're not a machine and so you acted with a goal in mind, something you projected as a good, when you picked it up.

(2) Human goods form a hierarchical sequence. They are like steps on an ascending ladder of means and ends. For example, Bob washes dishes in a restaurant (means) because he wants to make some money (end). But he wants the money (means) to buy a car (end). What had been an end, the money, is now a means to a higher end, the car. And he wants the car as a means to reach an even higher goal: getting to the beach.

(3) This sequence of means–end must terminate, Aristotle argues, for the following reason:

> If there exists an end [*telos*] in the realm of action which we desire for its own sake, an end which determines all our desires; if, in other words, we do not make all our choices for the sake of something else – for in this way **the process would go on infinitely so that our desire would be futile and pointless** – then obviously this end will be the good, that is, **the highest good**. (1094a18–22)

Aristotle's argument here is indirect. He begins with a proposition, shows that it leads to untenable (or absurd) consequences, and from this concludes that the proposition has to be rejected. So, if the means–end sequence did *not* terminate, if it were infinite, then no achievement of any goal whatsoever would significantly advance an agent up the ladder. Every end would simply become a means to something else. If the ladder were endless, then no single step upward could count as real progress, and every desire to take such a step would thereby be rendered "pointless." Life would become meaningless and there would be no reason to get out of bed in the morning. But Aristotle is confident that desire is *not* futile and pointless, that life is not meaningless. After all, the vast majority of us do get out of bed in the morning. We work hard to achieve goals we set for ourselves. Deep in our bones, then, we must believe that progress is possible. Aristotle agrees. Therefore, the ladder of means–ends cannot be infinite. It must stop somewhere. And this terminus would be the "*highest good*"; the final end that is not a means to something else; the end we seek simply for itself.[1]

(4) "As far as its [the highest good's] name is concerned, most people would probably agree: for both the common run of people and cultivated men call it *happiness* [*eudaimonia*]" (1095a19). This is because most people would agree that "we always choose happiness *as end in itself and never for the sake of something else*" (1097b1).

If I ask Bob, why do you wash dishes in that miserable restaurant?, his answer would be, to make some money. The content of his answer (money) is different from that of the question (washing dishes). By contrast, if I ask Bob, why do you want to be happy?, he replies, because I want to be happy. The content of his answer reproduces that of the question. Bob wants to be happy not in order to achieve something else, but just because he wants to be happy. There is no other reason, no higher objective. Therefore, Aristotle reasons, happiness must be the highest good. It is what all human beings ultimately want. But the next question is obvious: what is it?

(5) "To call happiness the highest good is perhaps a little trite, and a clearer account of what it is, is still required. Perhaps this is best done by first ascertaining the proper *function* of man" (1097b24–25).

This move should give us pause. Without explanation Aristotle has connected happiness to "function," a concept he has not yet explained. Fortunately, in the next step he does so.

(6) The "function" of human being cannot be "simply living," for we share this "even with plants" (1097b34). Nor, he argues, can it be found in the use of our senses, since all animals, not just us, have senses. From this

we can infer what a "function" is: a natural capacity that is **uniquely characteristic**. It is what allows an individual to be identified as a member of a species.

(7) Next, Aristotle tells us what the specific human "function" is. Because being alive and exercising the senses, because bodily activity in general, is not unique to us, it does not qualify. Therefore, what "remains then is an active life of the rational element [of that which has *logos*]" (1098a4). Only human animals have "language" or "speech," "reason" or "rationality," all of which are possible translations of *logos*. Therefore, rational activity (whatever exactly that means) is our characteristic activity, or "function."

(8) Happiness, which is the highest good, is the best, the fullest actualization of the human function. It is, therefore, the maximal and sustained exercise of the human capacity for rational activity. As Aristotle puts it, it is the "activity of the soul [*psuché*] in conformity with excellence or virtue [*areté*]" (1098a16). (*Psuché* is the root of "psychology" and its meaning here is close to "mind." In other words, it is that which is responsible for rational activity, and it is not the body.)

To clarify and sum up so far: the concepts of "function" and "excellence," *ergon* and *areté*, go hand in hand. If you know the function of X, you can determine whether X is excellent. The job of a clock is to keep and display time. If it does so well, it is an excellent clock. Analogously, Aristotle identifies *logos* or rational activity as the human function. Therefore, doing excellent rational work is the best and highest achievement available to human beings. And this, he thinks, is just what happiness is.

Even though being rational helps us enormously in securing other goods, it has more than **instrumental** value; that is, it is not only a means to the achievement of other ends. Instead, it can be an end in itself. Its value can be **intrinsic**. In turn, this is precisely the feature of rational activity that conforms to Aristotle's requirements for the highest good, which is happiness.

It should now be clear that "happiness" is not quite satisfying as a translation of Aristotle's Greek word, *eudaimonia*. "Flourishing" or "well-being" might do a better job, for what this word names, the excellent actualization of the soul (*psuché*), is something like the health of the body. Consider this parallel. Unless they have a disability, human beings have legs that enable them to walk and run. But if a woman rarely walks and never runs, her legs will become soft and begin to atrophy. By contrast, if she is a dedicated jogger who regularly exercises, her legs will be good and strong. They will flourish as they increasingly actualize their natural capacity. The woman will then take pleasure in walking and running, and so she will gladly do more of both. This positive feedback loop and continually expanding mode of activity is like Aristotelian happiness, which is the sustained exercise of the rational capacity. Just as the runner enjoys working out, so too does the virtuous or happy person enjoy doing his rational work on a daily basis.

The pleasure or gratification the runner feels in jogging is a by-product or an accompaniment of the activity. By itself, however, feeling pleasure is no guarantee that someone is actually happy. After all, Bob feels pretty good when he lies in the sun on the beach. Happiness, then, is not simply a sensation that someone happens to feel. Instead, it is an *objective* condition. Bob may sincerely believe, or be *subjectively* certain, that he is happiest when he is sunning himself, but because he is not fully exercising his rational capacity, not fulfilling his nature as a human being, he is wrong about himself.

Even if you are sympathetic with Aristotle's reasoning so far, you may still have reservations about his definition of happiness, for it may seem to be excessively intellectual. Is it true that we are most ourselves, are happiest, when we are exercising our rational capacity; when, for example, we're solving algebraic equations? There's more to life, you may think, than that. After all, our emotions, bodies, and social life are also part of who we are. Aristotle has a response to this objection, and it emerges when he begins to explain what rationality (or *logos*) is.

Logos, he tells us, has two sides. There is that which "obeys the rule of reason" and that which "possesses and conceives rational rules" (1098a5) on its own. The first may seem especially puzzling. How can someone merely obey and yet be rationally active at the same time? Isn't obedience passive? Perhaps not. Consider this example. I compose a syllabus for all my courses. On it are the reading and writing assignments for each class of the semester. It is rational for students to follow these directives; that is, to "obey" me. I am a veteran teacher who is knowledgeable about the course material, and I have a pretty good idea at what pace students can handle it. They, by contrast, know little about the subject. It thus makes good sense for them to abide by the instructions on the syllabus. This doesn't mean that they should blindly follow every command I or any other professor issue. Some teachers are terrible and so what they say should be ignored most of the time. But if students have grounds to believe the professor knows what he is doing – if, for example, they have heard from reliable friends that he teaches a solid course – then the reasonable default position for them is to follow the rules.

Another scenario: two parents exhort their eight-year-old daughter to clean her room. The girl doesn't want to do it. The parents have discussed this issue thoroughly with each other, and have decided that the child should be forced to perform this task. They want her to become a responsible member of the family, and so they plan to threaten punishment if she balks. When she does, they stick to their guns and sternly issue their threat. Fortunately, the child obeys. Even without understanding why, she may well sense that her parents know better and are acting in her best interest. Or perhaps she fears the punishment that will ensue if she disobeys. In either case it makes sense, and thus represents a rational act, for her to do what her parents tell her.

If the parents are consistent in imposing this discipline – if, say, they require the girl to clean her room every Sunday morning – eventually she may well incorporate their voices into her own head and begin to do the cleaning without having to be told. She can't yet grasp or articulate the reasons why she has to do this every Sunday instead of playing outside, but she has done it so often and with such regularity that it has become a *habit*.

This last word is critical in Aristotle's conception of the good life. In fact, the Greek word for "habit," *ethos*, is at the root of "ethics" itself. But what is it? As usual, begin with some introspection.

I start almost every weekday morning by taking a shower. After getting dressed, I pick up the newspaper at the front door. Then I make coffee and breakfast, which I eat while reading the sports page. After putting the dishes in the sink, I then walk to work, always following the same route. I barely think about what I am doing. My morning routine, which I have repeated for decades, feels almost automatic.

A habit, then, is a relatively fixed pattern of behavior. The result of much repetition, it operates with little or no conscious intention. Instead, it becomes a part of who we are. Frequently, as in the example of the parents who force their daughter to clean her room, habits initially take root through external pressure. Many of us regularly brush our teeth before going to bed, and likely because we were forced to do so when we were children. In these cases, a habit has been inculcated through discipline or training.

Habits take place in a sort of cognitive gray zone. On the one hand, they don't require much if any deliberate thought. My walking to work every morning is thus quite different from my sitting here now at my desk and wondering, should I touch the top of my head? I weigh the pros and cons, and then decide, yes. I touch my head. The act of doing so is bathed in the light of consciousness. On the other hand, habitual action is not like the mindless beating of my heart. It is not automatic, even if it sometimes feels that way. I can and occasionally do skip my morning shower or read world news instead of sports. Even though deviating from a routine can sometimes be slightly disorienting, it's not particularly difficult to modify these behaviors. Habit, then, operates somewhere in between the beating of the heart, which occurs in cognitive darkness, and the bright light of explicit self-consciousness. In Aristotelian terms, it is the actualization of the "obedient" side of our rational capacity. While not as fully active or rational as, say, studying mathematics, it is not passive. Furthermore – and this is Aristotle's response to the worry that his conception of happiness is excessively intellectual – habituation involves the entirety of a person. The child who cleans her room may well be motivated by fear of punishment or a desire for praise. The students who obey the directives on the course syllabus may be motivated by a passion for success. Such emotions are harnessed in the process of habituation. They are shaped by the force imposed by the rational agent (the parents, the professor) who issues the commands. When the inculcation process is successful, the child and the students can then impose that force upon themselves. The child cleans her room without being told to do so. In fact, at some point in her development failing to do so will actually cause her some pain. The students in my class, at least the conscientious ones, regularly refer to the syllabus and complete the assignments without needing a reminder.

It is no accident that both of these examples involve a younger person (the child and the student) and an older one (the parents and the teacher). Obedience and inculcated habits represent the level of rationality appropriate for the former. Children are incapable of comprehending and then abiding by a logical explanation of why they should clean their rooms. College students need to develop, and professors should attempt to instill in them, the habit of studying every week rather than just cramming for an exam at the end of the semester.

More generally, what we call "socialization" is really a kind of habituation. Parents, teachers, coaches, elders (should) monitor children carefully, and try to redirect their behavior when it deviates from the norm. They repeatedly tell them, for example, to be polite, and reprimand them when they are not. They exhort them to share and be fair. They force them to tidy themselves up before going to school. Sometimes such socializing practices take the form of traditions or rituals. Little league baseball players are required to line up and shake hands with their opponents at the end of every game in order to instill in them a regard for sportsmanship. Christmas gift giving reinforces the idea that generosity is good. Some families say grace before a meal, others make sure that no one picks up a fork until a parent says "*Buon appetito,*" in order to make sure that children show some respect, if not gratitude, for the trouble an adult took to put food on the table. Other families, instead of going to church, devote Sunday mornings to cleaning the house. Such repeated and regularized practices inculcate good habits. Eventually, if they take root, they become forms of excellence. They become virtues.

More specifically, they become what Aristotle calls "ethical" virtues – remember that *ethos* means "habit" – or what some scholars call "virtues of character." (The Greek word for "character," *êthos*, is also closely related to *ethos*.) When we say about someone, she is honest, we ascribe a trait to her. Consistently being honest is a quality that makes her who she is: someone who finds lying so distasteful that she can be counted upon to tell the truth. She does so not because she is thinking about Mill's greatest happiness principle or reasoning through Kant's categorical imperative, but because she would not recognize herself if she told a lie. It would be out of character, and so would be painful. Likely her parents were honest people too.

A large portion of the *Nicomachean Ethics* is devoted to explicating these ethical virtues, which arise through habituation and represent the actualization of the obedient side of our rational capacity. But remember, rationality has a second side: that which can think things through on its own. This is actualized in what Aristotle calls "the intellectual virtues." These require teaching. So, for example, the biologist who does excellent work in her field had to go to graduate school first. The level of her rational activity, and thus her virtue and happiness, is higher than that of the well-disciplined person who has been habituated to tell the truth or be generous.

One of the intellectual virtues is "practical wisdom." This is particularly important because it spans the ethical and the intellectual. To explain, return again to the parents who deliberated and then decided to threaten their daughter with punishment if she did not clean her room. Let us assume that in this particular case their decision proved to be a good one. The child responded well and now cleans her room without needing to be told. When it comes to their younger daughter, however, the situation is different. This child has an instinctive aversion to commands of any sort, and so typically refuses to obey them. The parents realize that in her case a threat of punishment would likely be counter-productive, and so they adjust their strategy. Instead of raising their voices when she disobeys, they ignore her and with their older daughter go about the task of cleaning the house on Sunday. Their hope is that the little girl will feel ashamed of herself and turn her behavior around.

The point here is that just as excellent rational activity is found in the study of biology or mathematics, so too can it be found in the realm of practical deliberation. If the parents are smart about how to influence the behavior of their daughters, if they accurately diagnose the differences between these two children, and prescribe the appropriate regimen for each of them, then they will succeed in getting them to clean their rooms on their own; that is, they will shape them as responsible members of the family. The parents actualize their rational capacity, but unlike the biologist they do so in the human or practical sphere.

Recall a point made in Chapter 2. Aristotle is an elitist who believes that some people are better, and have better and happier lives, than others. Children are not yet ready to actualize their potential as rational beings, and in this sense are inferior to adults. Furthermore, there are adults who are much like children. They are incapable of regulating their own lives, of disciplining themselves (likely because they were raised badly), and so still require the forceful guidance of others in order to stay in line. The best they can aspire to, and it's not so bad, are the ethical or habituated virtues. Furthermore, there are gradations even within the intellectual virtues. While practical wisdom is a fine thing, it pales in comparison to the fullest expression of human rationality: philosophy.

This is but a bare outline of what Aristotle means by the interrelated concepts of rational activity (*logos*), excellence or virtue (*aretê*), and happiness (*eudaimonia*). Suffice it to say that the purpose of the *Nicomachean Ethics* is precisely to fill in the details. It is a monumental work whose purview is almost every dimension of human activity, both practical and intellectual. By its last chapter, the book has painted a comprehensive picture of a life well lived.

Let's summarize by highlighting the ways in which Aristotle's ethical thinking differs from that of Kant or Mill. For the latter two, morality is essentially oriented to others. They are egalitarians whose basic principle is that selfishness is immoral. (They are Christians, after all.) Mill expresses this in his general happiness principle. In assessing the moral content of any action the criterion is how much pleasure or utility can be generated for the greatest number of people. For Kant it is found in the categorical imperative, which tests the morality of a maxim by examining whether it can be universalized. By contrast, Aristotle takes the best life to be one in which the agent himself is happy and flourishes. *Eudaimonia* is the highest good and so, by his lights, people should act with an eye toward maximizing their capacities and fulfilling their natures. Some people will succeed, others will fall short.

This sounds both self-centered and elitist, and from the moralists' perspective it is. But do recall the following point that was critical in Chapter 2: for

Aristotle "human being is by nature political." This means that in order to fully actualize one's humanity and thereby be happy, one must have positive relationships with, as he puts it, "parents, children, a wife, and friends and fellow citizens generally" (1097b8). Maximizing one's own well-being requires living and acting well with others. This is why, for example, he counts justice as a virtue or form of excellence.

Compared with the general utility principle or the categorical imperative, both of which are meant to guide us in determining the right thing to do, Aristotelian *eudaimonia* is such a broad notion that it does not readily translate into concrete guidance in specific situations. It does not offer an algorithmic approach to ethical decision making. As the next section will show, Aristotle is fully cognizant of this limitation. And he doesn't apologize for it.

Precision in Ethics

Early in the *Nicomachean Ethics,* Aristotle offers a warning about the work on which he is about to embark. "Our discussion," he says, "will be adequate if it achieves clarity within the limits of the subject matter. For **precision** cannot be expected in the treatment of all subjects alike" (1094b10–14). So, for example, when it comes to mathematics, whose subject matter is abstract and formal, the highest level of precision and clarity is possible to attain and therefore is expected. It is unacceptable for a geometer to state that, more often than not, the sum of the interior angles of a triangle is equal to the sum of two right angles. Instead, a proof is required to demonstrate that this is a necessary truth, an invariable fact about all triangles. Its steps follow logically one from the other and its conclusion admits of no exceptions. Such a proof is the paradigm of precision.

By contrast, it would be, Aristotle thinks, a terrible mistake to expect such mathematical rigor in all other disciplines. When it comes to ethics, whose subject matter is human happiness – the dimension of human life concerned with and guided by a conception of what is good – there is obviously great dispute, and there always will be. In China, for example, free speech is not accorded much value, whereas in the United States it is. In Saudi Arabia women are not allowed to have a driver's license; in Sweden this is considered absurd. Because there are a vast number of divergent answers to the question, how should we live?, it is tempting to think that values, or conceptions of the good life and happiness, exist only "*by convention*" (1094b17), that they have no deeper root in reality other than the fact that people agree about them.

That Americans greet each other with a handshake, while Japanese do so with a bow, is clearly no more than a minor cultural difference. But does such conventionalism apply to the question, what is the best life? Many people, let's call them *relativists*, believe this is the case. For them, there is no right answer to a practical question, except the one that a culture or a community has put into place.

Aristotle disagrees. He thinks happiness, activity according to virtue or excellence, objectively grounded as it is in the human function, is a matter of *nature* (1094b17), *not convention*. This means that in principle there are objectively correct answers to ethical questions that are not determined by cultural practices. It is arguable, for example, that the suppression of free speech in China, however widely it is approved there, is just plain wrong. At the same time, however, Aristotle acknowledges that this region of reality, the practical or ethical, is not amenable to mathematical proof. The best he hopes for, then, is "a rough and general sketch" (1094a20), an "outline" (1104a2) rather than a technical treatise or systematic exposition of the good life. For the practical realm is so complicated, contingent, and variable that it simply does not admit of precise solution. In short, the "problems" of ethics are quite different from those in geometry. The latter can be solved with clarity and distinctness. The former cannot. There are no foolproof decision procedures or clear-cut rules to guide people struggling with the messy challenges of the good life. There is no analogue to Mill's greatest happiness principle or Kant's categorical imperative. Nonetheless, Aristotle refuses to hand ethical questions over to the relativists.

You have a friend whose life is going downhill fast. Listless and disengaged, she's drinking a lot, missing work, ignoring her family, and sleeping far too late. You want to help. The question you're struggling with is, should you suggest that she see a therapist, or should you more forcefully intervene by calling her parents? You worry that if you act too hastily she might resent your interference. You might alienate her and, despite your best intentions, make things worse. But you also worry that waiting too long to get help will bring disaster. When would it be best to intervene?

Unfortunately, there is no application on your smartphone that you can consult in order to find an answer. Unlike the question, what is the sum of the interior angles of a triangle?, this one cannot be indisputably resolved. Instead, you must size up what Aristotle calls "*the specific occasion.*" What sort of person is your friend? Is she too proud to accept help, too stubborn to acknowledge faults? Would intervening now push her further into her own disintegrating shell? Perhaps it would be best to let her find her own way and tell her only that you're there if she wants to talk. On the other hand, she might be suicidal. If so, forcefully intruding into her life right now would be the best course of action.

Imagine that in this scenario intervention on Tuesday would be too early while waiting until Saturday would be too late. There is a right time to act, one not too early and not too late. What that is, however, cannot be determined in advance or by means of an abstract calculation. Instead, it emerges from the specific occasion. Only by correctly diagnosing the particulars of the situation, only by being practically intelligent and by caring very much what happens to your friend, will you get the answer right.

Now, even a staunch relativist would agree that there is an appropriate time to intervene at which the friend would be saved from suicide, and that someone with intelligence will figure out what it is. The relativist would deny, however, that this is anything more than instrumental reasoning; that is, figuring out how to achieve a stipulated goal, one that itself is neither good nor bad. For Aristotle the story teaches a different lesson. It illustrates practical wisdom at work. The goal, helping a friend in need, is what a good or virtuous person aims for. Furthermore the means to attain such a goal can in principle be grasped by intelligence. The practically wise person, the pinnacle of ethical virtue, is animated by the right goal and has the smarts to achieve it. In him ethical and intellectual virtue work in tandem.

To elaborate, consider another scenario. Despite having taken precautions, an unmarried young woman who already has one child has become pregnant and is considering an abortion. We should ask, is this a good thing to do or not?

The Catholic Church has a ready reply. In its view, abortion is morally wrong. Full stop. No exceptions. So too can the relativist answer this question, albeit very differently. It depends on the culture or group to which the woman belongs. If she happens to be a member of a strictly Catholic community, then she should not abort. But if she happens to live in an authoritarian country where a one-child policy is strictly enforced by the state, then she should abort. For the relativist, neither this nor the Catholic answer is in itself RIGHT. Instead, there are many right answers and they vary depending on what community upholds them.

Aristotle's own view fits somewhere in between these two. Like the Catholic, he thinks right answers exist independently of convention. He is no relativist. But he also rejects the sort of unyielding position advocated by the Catholic Church. Instead, his reasoning on this issue takes the following shape.

A fetus is a potential person and therefore has enormous value. Indeed, as Aristotle understands as well as any thinker in the Western tradition, life itself (and not just human life) is good. Powerful reasons must therefore be adduced in order for abortion to be counted as good. If the adults making the decision have such reasons, then it is acceptable to abort. The young woman in question might, for example, reasonably determine that her future value to her family and community would be irreparably diminished by having to raise two children as a single parent. It is conceivable that she may be right. The rational concerns raised by adults can, on some occasions, override the very strong claim of the fetus to life. But what are these occasions? Aristotle doesn't specify. He does, however, draw one firm line: "abortion should be induced before perception and life arises" (*Politics* 1335b25). He is referring here to what has traditionally been known as "quickening," the moment when the mother feels fetal movement in the womb. Prior to this, there are occasions when abortion is acceptable.

Aristotle's ethics may seem rather unsatisfying at this point. Is his conception of practical wisdom – the intellectual virtue capable of discerning the right means to achieve virtuous ends – too vague to offer any concrete guidance? After all, his response to a question like, should a woman have an abortion?, seems to be: yes, if the practically wise person determines that this is a good thing to do in the situation. But how can this possibly help the rest of us? It is conceivable, however, that what may appear to be a deficiency in Aristotelian ethics is actually a strength. For even as it acknowledges the messiness of the practical realm and rejects the possibility of clear-cut moral rules or imperatives, it refuses to succumb to the temptation of relativism. It allows for the possibility of good answers to practical questions, but denies that their truth can be proven with certainty. It affirms the possibility of ethical knowledge, but refuses to allow mathematics to be the governing paradigm of all knowledge.

From an Aristotelian perspective, both Kant and Mill's versions of moral reasoning aspire to an excessive level of precision. Mill's moral problems can (in theory) be resolved through weighing conflicting utilities. Kant's moral questions can (in theory) be answered by testing a maxim in order to determine whether it can be universalized. In contrast to both, Aristotelian ethics operates closer to the rough ground of lived experience. We struggle when we wonder how we should best live. We are never completely sure since strict rules to guide our actions are rarely available. But we should never relinquish our inquiries or transfer our decision making to the conventions of the community in which we happen to live. Instead, we should strive to make good decisions, to be astute and caring, to attain practical wisdom. And this, in turn, requires keen sensitivity to the particular circumstances of the "specific occasion" as well as a commitment to the goals that animate an ethically virtuous person.

In sum, Aristotle's path is a middle way. Practical wisdom can attain the truth. It is, however, an imprecise and precarious affair. Guided by only a few general principles (such as, it is always wrong to abort after quickening), the practically wise person is alert to the particularities of the specific occasion, and judges well. But how, you might still be asking, can we determine that any given judgment is actually a good one?

Character

Imagine you're sitting on a jury in a courtroom. The defendant has been charged with aggravated assault. He was riding his bicycle on Commonwealth Avenue, pedaling away in the bike lane, when a large SUV took a quick right turn directly in front of him. The car nicked his front tire and the cyclist fell to the ground. He wasn't hurt, but he exploded in rage nonetheless. The driver of the SUV stopped to see what had happened, and when he opened the window to express his concern the cyclist began screaming at him. Many expletives flew. The driver jumped out of the car and responded in kind. The two were nose to nose when the cyclist punched the driver in the face. Even though blood was pouring, the cyclist did not relent. Instead, he shoved the guy to the ground and kicked him three times in the ribs. It was the driver of the SUV who ended up in the hospital.

In the courtroom, the cyclist seemed genuinely remorseful. He shouldn't have lost his temper, he explains, and knows that he shouldn't have beaten the man so badly. But he had been blinded by his rage at the driver's carelessness, and he just lost it. He apologized profusely and tried to assure the jury that such behavior was out of character, and would never happen again.

Your question is this: does the cyclist mean it? Is he a decent guy whose violent outburst was an aberration triggered by an unusually dangerous event, or is he a menace to society who needs to be punished? He did a bad thing, that's for sure. But is he a bad person? It's hard, likely impossible, to be certain. Nonetheless, as a jury member you must reach a verdict. You must assess the cyclist's character, even while acknowledging that your resources for doing so are limited.

If moral philosophy is required to attain a level of clarity and precision that approximates mathematical proof, then a character-based ethics will fall short. For as this example is meant to suggest, it is impossible to be certain that the cyclist is genuinely remorseful. Perhaps he's just a good liar who is spinning a tale to keep himself out of jail. Because the human psyche can shroud itself with layers of disguise, plumbing its depths is dicey. This does not imply, at least for Aristotle, that we should abandon the task of judging character. Instead, he thinks this is another example of how we must adjust our epistemic expectations when it comes to the practical realm. Some people, those with practical wisdom, are exceptionally good at discerning the characters of others, determining whether they are telling the truth, reading their faces. There is no rulebook, however, for doing so. Practical wisdom is imprecise. Everyday (ethical) life is not amenable to technical reduction. Nonetheless, right answers can be discovered. Truth is possible. The ethical challenges of our lives can be well or virtuously navigated by someone with good judgment.

Again, perhaps you think that Aristotle has relinquished his responsibility as a philosopher. His notion of happiness is amorphous, and practical wisdom seems to be a largely ad hoc affair, and therefore indistinguishable from relativism. You might thus reasonably prefer Mill. By conceiving of happiness as pleasure, he seems to have made it concrete and measurable.

Aristotle on Climate Change

Here is one last example to illustrate the debate between Aristotelian ethics and Kant or Mill's (Christian) morality. Consider this question: in the age of global warming, should each of us burn less fossil fuel?

Let us assume that Aristotle, were he to appear in Boston tomorrow, would agree with what most educated people now believe about climate change. Because of the enormous amount of fossil fuel being burned around the world, and the consequent emission of carbon dioxide and other greenhouse gases, the atmosphere is warming. As a result, it is able to absorb more water vapor, which in turn leads to the atmosphere warming even more. Consequently, average temperature around the globe will continue to climb, there will be increasingly intense storms and fires, sea levels will rise, and disease will spread. Millions of people, most of them poor, will likely suffer the consequences of all these things happening. It seems, therefore, that a reasonable and decent person will wonder what to do in response.

A moralist might argue like this: because (1) emission of greenhouse gases contributes to global warming, and (2) global warming will harm innocent people, and (3) harming innocent people is immoral, (4) individuals should reduce their carbon footprint. On this view, we are morally obligated to turn the lights off when they are not needed and to keep the thermostat low in our homes and offices. As much as possible, we should ride bicycles, walk, and take public transportation instead of driving in private cars. If we don't do these things, we should feel guilty.[2]

Aristotle would likely agree that we should take these actions. His reasons for why, however, are not moralistic. By his lights, at least as I imagine them here, during the winter we should wear warm clothing inside of our homes instead of turning up the heat, not because of our duty to the human race or our obligations to those less fortunate than ourselves, but because it is stupid to squander a valuable resource. We can be quite comfortable in a moderately heated house if we put on a sweater. For this reason, someone who jacks the heat up to 75° and then wears a T-shirt is acting in an unbecoming fashion. Just as there is nothing wasteful in an excellent work of art, so too should there be nothing wasted in an excellent life. Those who needlessly burn oil are therefore leading lives that aren't quite as good or beautiful as they could be.

Why ride a bicycle in Boston instead of driving a car? In Chapter 1, I suggested a few reasons: efficiency in travel, saving money, improving health, participating more viscerally in the street life of the city, having some fun, and so on. None of these are moral reasons. Instead, they are ways in which the quality of *my* life has improved since I took to the bike. Yes, getting rid of my car has the consequence of reducing my carbon footprint and so taking a step, however miniscule, to slowing the pace of climate change. This is not, however, my motivation for riding a bike. I do so because at this stage of my life I don't need to own a car. If my commute to work were very long, or if my children still lived with me and I had to shuffle them around town, then I would certainly buy one. But living as I now do, in a small city that is easy to traverse, and where car sharing is readily available, owning a car is an unnecessary appendage that would make my life more clunky. With my bicycle, walking, public transportation, and occasional rental of a car, my days are more active and compact than they would be were I able to hop into a car every time I had to go somewhere. Now I have to think about how to complete the various tasks required of me and then take responsibility for getting to where I must go. I must drive myself to get through my day, and so I am more engaged and present in its unfolding. Even though my travels are occasionally demanding, they can also be interesting and gratifying, and I am at the center of them. The elements of my life fit together better than they would if I depended upon a car.

While my actions might be described as benefiting other people, my reasons for forgoing the car are selfish rather than altruistic. Aristotelian ethics argues that we should fulfill our natures as human beings and thereby live the most active, fullest, most beautiful and happiest life possible. Strikingly, in this particular case at least, following such a directive leads not only to my life being enhanced, but other lives as well. For by taking to the bike, I pump a little less carbon into the atmosphere.

Nietzsche's Answer

 Friedrich Nietzsche, *On the Genealogy of Morals*

The title of the book to be discussed in this section, *On the Genealogy of Morals* (1887), already provides a clue to Nietzsche's thinking. Morality, it claims, has a "genealogy," a family tree that records a line of descent from ancestors. This implies that it was born and, because it is (or at least is like) a living being, it will die. Morality, on this view, is neither a permanent nor a necessary feature of human existence.

Think about your own family tree. My parents, for example, met on a blind date. At least as he told the story, my father wasn't enthusiastic about this occasion and agreed only in order to please the friend who had invited him. Because he was a devoted handball player, he refused to miss his game on the very afternoon he was supposed to meet my mother. The game ran late and he was tempted to skip the date altogether. But for some reason he went, even though he was dressed in his shorts and still sweaty.

That our parents and grandparents happened to join together to produce offspring was largely a matter of luck. Standing here today and looking back, we may feel that our lineage was inevitable. In reality, however, the branches of our family tree could easily have veered into different directions. Of course, once the process of sexual reproduction is underway the laws of genetics kick in and continuity between one generation and the next can be safely predicted. But my father could just as easily have played another game of handball and I would not be sitting here today. Genealogy, then, bespeaks the role of chance.

In the "First Essay" of his book, Nietzsche sketches what he takes to be the line of descent, or history, of morality as it was operative in nineteenth-century Europe (and still is today). Because he was trained as a philologist (someone who has studied languages, in particular Greek and Latin), he takes his bearings from words. "What light," he asks, "does linguistics, and especially the study of etymology, throw on the history of *the evolution of moral concepts?*" (55).

The ancestor of modern morality can be found, Nietzsche claims, in the archaic distinction between "good" (*gut*) and "bad" (*schlecht*). Even though these two words signify basic values, their original meaning was not moral. Instead, they were used by aristocrats to distinguish themselves from those who were beneath them. The "good" were the "noble, powerful, high-stationed and high-minded," while the "bad" were the "low,

low-minded, common and plebian" (26). A key point he makes about this normative dichotomy is that it had "no inculpatory implication" (28). Those who were "good" or high did not blame those who were "bad" for being low. In much the same way that a gifted athlete will look down upon an inferior who represents no threat or competition, so too did the archaic aristocrats feel largely indifferent toward those who were beneath them. They possessed a "powerful physicality, a flourishing, abundant, even *overflowing health*" (33), but this did not translate into hostility toward those inferior to them. Instead, the aristocrats took the lowly to be inconsequential. If anything, the strong felt some sympathy for the weak. So, for example, Nietzsche claims that the words the archaic Greeks used to describe the "bad,"

> are continuously mingled and sweetened with a kind of pity, consideration, and forebearance, so that finally almost all the words referring to the common man have remained as expressions signifying "unhappy." (27)

Even in my basketball playing prime, had I gone one on one with Michael Jordan there would have been absolutely no doubt, on his part or mine, that he could defeat me. He could surely have held me scoreless if he put his mind to the task. More likely, however, my negligible presence on the court would have bored him. Perhaps he would have taken pity on me and let me get off a few jump shots, and I might even have made a couple. But the outcome of the game would have been sealed from the outset. His confidence would have been total, and I would have been no more than a minor distraction.

The archaic value distinction, which Nietzsche labels the "*knightly-aristocratic*" (33), was something like this. It divided those who knew themselves to be powerful from the weak:

> The protracted and domineering fundamental total feeling on the part of a higher ruling order in relation to a lower order, to a "*below*" – that is the *origin* of the antithesis of "good" and "bad." (26)

Nietzsche may well be thinking here of the heroes of Homer's epic poems, Achilles and Odysseus. They were the best of the best, the warriors par excellence, and it would never have occurred to either of them to doubt their superiority. In their own minds they deserved every bit of praise they received, and glory became the guiding principle of their lives. The lowly many (like Thersites or Lycaon in the *Iliad*) were little nobodies hardly worth a glance. For such was the effect of "*the pathos of*

distance" (26), that feeling of near indifference the truly strong feel
toward the weak:

> **To be incapable of taking one's enemies, one's accidents, even one's misdeeds
> seriously for very long** – that is the sign of strong full natures in whom
> there is an excess of the **power** to form, to mold, to recuperate and to
> forget … Such a man shakes off with a single shrug many vermin that eat
> deep into others. (39)

My roommate in graduate school was the most intelligent person I have
ever met. He was a self-contained but pleasant person who rarely asserted
himself in public. Deep down, however, he knew that he was almost always
the smartest guy in the room. He once told me a remarkable story. After
he had applied to our PhD program he received a letter of rejection.
He was neither angry nor disappointed. Instead, he was confident that
there must have been a clerical mistake. And so there had.

Nietzsche's praise of strength, indeed his language in general, can make
readers uncomfortable. But that's exactly what he wants it to do, for his
thesis is disruptive. The origin of morality was not itself moral, and so
what we take for granted – namely, the fundamental dignity and worth of
all human beings, a notion at the heart of both Mill and Kant's theories –
was not always thought to be, à la Jefferson, self-evident. It would never
have occurred to Achilles to ask himself, can the maxim of my action be
universalized? Such a question would have put him on the same level as
everyone else, and this the Homeric hero surely did not do. Nor would
he have calculated the impact of his actions on the general population.
As Nietzsche puts it, "the viewpoint of utility is inappropriate as it possibly
could be in the face of such a burning eruption of the highest rank-ordering,
ranking defining value judgments" (26).

In contrast to the knightly-aristocratic dichotomy between "good"
and "bad," the moral distinction is between "good" (*gut*) and "*evil*"
(*böse*), and this is a whole new ballgame. It came into being – at least
according to Nietzsche's speculative reconstruction of the history of
Western culture – as a result of "*the slave revolt in morality*" (34). At
some point in the deep past resentment built up among the lowly weak
and was directed against the strong, from whom they eventually wrested
power. In turn, this led to a fundamental inversion of the archaic value
system. The "good" of the knightly-aristocratic distinction, the one full of
himself and instinctively confident in his superiority, became identified as
"evil," while the "good" of the good–evil distinction became those who
formerly had been "bad."

This revolt was led, Nietzsche claims, by the Jews. They mobilized the cumulative resentment of those who were sick of their own powerlessness and,

> with awe inspiring consistency, dared *to invert the aristocratic value equation* (good = noble = powerful = beautiful = happy = beloved of God) and to hang on to this inversion with their teeth, the teeth of the most abysmal hatred (the hatred of impotence), saying *"the wretched alone are the good*; the poor, impotent, lowly alone are the good; the suffering, deprived, sick ugly alone pious, alone are blessed by God, blessedness is for them all – *and you, the powerful and noble, are on the contrary the evil*, the cruel, the lustful, the insatiable, the godless to all eternity; and you will be in all eternity the un-blessed, accursed and damned!" (34)

The slave revolt turned the tables on the aristocrats, and vilified their pride and self-affirmation as the pinnacle of immorality. Characters like Achilles and Odysseus, formerly heroes, became paragons of selfishness; that is, of evil.

Again, Nietzsche's language may seem offensive. It can easily lead to the charge of anti-Semitism. In fact, however, he makes it clear that even if the Jews led the slave revolt – indeed, they "had a world-historic mission" (36) to do so – it was Christianity that institutionalized and ultimately bears the responsibility for it. As he sardonically puts it, *"one knows who inherited this Jewish revaluation"* (34). It was the spread of Christianity that obliterated the distinction between strong and weak, high and low, and demanded that all glory be given to God, not to heroes. It was Christianity, in which all human beings were construed as children of God sharing equally in His love, that ushered in the age of moralism. With its advent "the people have won – or 'the slaves' or 'the mob' or 'the herd' or whatever you like to call them" (36).

Nietzsche's philologically based argument cannot be evaluated here. Fortunately, what matters for us is not the historical accuracy of his claims, but the idea he is trying to convey. By proposing that morality has a genealogy, and so is not written in stone, Nietzsche invites his readers to critically examine it. (In this sense, his account of the slave revolt of morality can be read like Rousseau's about the state of nature and the fall into society; namely, as a philosophically provocative story.) He does so by asking the following question:

> Under what conditions did man devise these value judgments good and evil? *And what value do they themselves possess?* Have they hitherto hindered or furthered human prosperity? Are they a sign of distress, of impoverishment, of the degeneration of life? Or is there revealed in them, on the contrary, the

plenitude, force and will of life, its courage, certainty, future? (17)

An unsettling question: is morality itself good, or is it the "danger of dangers" (20) that, far from representing human progress, is actually a symptom of decay and self-hatred? Is it a symptom of psychological health, or does it require the denial of genuinely human instincts? The great contribution of Nietzsche's book is not its putative reconstruction of the genealogy of morality, but the questions he raises about the well-being of the moralist. His diagnosis is brutal:

> The slave revolt in morality begins when *resentment itself becomes creative and gives birth to values: the resentment of natures that are denied the true reaction, that of deeds, and compensate themselves with an imaginary revenge.* While every noble morality develops from a triumphant affirmation of itself, slave morality from the outset says NO to what is "outside," what is "different," what is "not itself"; and this NO is its creative deed ... in order to exist slave morality always first needs a hostile external world; it needs, physiologically speaking, external stimuli in order to act at all – *its action is fundamentally reaction.* (37)

In order to convince himself that he is "good," the moralist needs to condemn those who are "evil." He is a self-righteous naysayer whose fuel is only ignited when he finds fault with others. As such, his actions are really just reactions. And his targets are those who celebrate or assert themselves, and honestly feel superior to others.

To clarify by contrast, let's return to Kant for a moment. He sketches four possible ways in which a person can relate to moral duty, only one of which has genuine moral worth: that of resisting a selfish inclination in order to act in such a way that the maxim of the action can be universalized. His example is someone in terrible pain who wants to end his life, but refuses to do so because he thinks suicide is morally wrong. By contrast, the actions of someone like the baker who gives a child the right change – that is, someone who acts according to duty but does so for twin purposes (in order to be honest but also to safeguard his reputation among his customers) – has no moral worth. Kantian morality, expressed via the categorical imperative, requires a negation of the agent's special claims for himself. Because it demands that the maxim be universalizable, it requires the agent to put himself on the same level as everyone else. Anyone who fails to do this should be condemned as immoral. It follows from this that moral rules do not allow exceptions. In fact, the essence of immorality is precisely making an exception of oneself to general rules, and then rationalizing the doing so.

By contrast, Nietzsche celebrates the exceptional and accuses the moralist of pathological self-deception. For those who don the mantle of the righteous universal, and profess benevolence, are actually seething with resentment. They need to lord themselves above those whom they castigate as selfish. They claim to be concerned with the well-being of others, but deep down their moralism is an expression of a desperate need for self-assertion and power.

Think of the prominent politician or preacher who enthusiastically denounces homosexuality, but is actually a closeted homosexual himself. He is a twisted soul whose righteous condemnation of others cloaks the very lust that courses through his veins. His crusade against evil is actually expression of his own self-hatred. Unable openly to express his own desires, he lashes out at others in order to maintain his equilibrium.

This extreme example is illuminating because it forces us to consider the dark side of righteous indignation. On Nietzsche's view, although moralism appears to require the abnegation of the agent's power, it is in fact fueled by the impulse to assert that power. Although it identifies self-assertion as evil, it itself is a disguised form of self-assertion. For only by castigating wrong-doers as "evil," and therefore deserving of punishment, does the moralist secure his own status as "good." Despite professing love of humanity, what he really enjoys is meting out punishment. Although he denounces the sin of pride, he does so proudly.

By contrast, the "good" of the "good–bad" distinction, the knightly-aristocrat, was clear through and through, and so he had no need to orient himself toward others in order to maintain a strong sense of himself. He felt the force of his power deep in his bones and was eager to express it. From Nietzsche's point of view, he was more honest and healthier than the moralist:

> the noble mode of valuation: *it acts and grows spontaneously, it seeks its opposite only so as to affirm itself more gratefully and triumphantly* – its negative concept "low," "common," "bad" is only a subsequently invented pale, contrasting image in relation to its positive basic concept – *filled with life and passion through and through* – "we noble ones, we good, beautiful and happy ones!" (37)

Nietzsche's greatest fear about the fate of European culture, shaped as it is by (among other forces) the moralism of Kant and Mill, is that its egalitarianism will so thoroughly level the playing field that true excellence, which is always an exception, will become impossible. For both the categorical imperative and the general happiness principle throw a blanket over the assertiveness of the exceptional few, and thereby over life itself.

> *The diminution and leveling of European man constitutes our greatest danger, for the sight of him makes us weary.* We can see nothing today that wants to grow greater ... Here precisely is what has become a fatality for Europe – together with the fear of man we have also lost our love of him, our reverence for him, our hopes for him ... what is *nihilism* today if it is not that? We are weary of man. (44)

The good–evil distinction of Christian modernity leads to nihilism, the belief in nothing, precisely because it denies the possibility of greatness, of joyful action spontaneously performed by those who love themselves. It is a form of disease.

At this point, you may have serious reservations about Nietzsche. His language is inflammatory and seems to open the door to terrible abuses. In fact, it has been invoked in order to justify many a bogus claim to superiority. His writings were, for example, exploited by the Nazis in the 1930s, and in a famous case from 1924 they inspired two teenagers, Leopold and Loeb, to murder a boy only in order to prove to themselves that they were (what they took to be) Nietzschean heroes. It's arguable that his language is so dangerous that it should be taken off the table. That, however, would be a mistake.

Recall the phrase "pathos of distance." Rather than hate or wish to harm the lowly many who are "bad," the aristocratic few felt them to be inconsequential. They had no urge to single them out for blame or punishment, as the moralists do with the "evil." Instead, according to Nietzsche's linguistic analysis, they felt a mild sympathy for those who were beneath them. In fact, he suggests – and here he daringly inverts a Christian platitude – only in the aristocratic days of the "good–bad" distinction was a "genuine 'love of one's enemies' possible" (39). No such love is possible in the age of moralism. For the "good" are consumed by hate ... a hate of the "evil" disguised as benevolence and moral indignation.

Another conciliatory note that might mitigate the fear that Nietzsche's prose will give birth to violent monsters can be found in the following scenario. A poor man borrows money from a rich one, from an aristocrat, but fails to repay his debt on time. According to the rules of strict justice he deserves to be punished. The aristocrat, however, is so rich, in both wealth and spirit, so imbued with the "pathos of distance," that the poor man's transgression is inconsequential to him. As a result, instead of applying the abstract rules of morality, he exercises *mercy*. The bestowing of mercy violates the principle of fair treatment of all. It exempts some from punishment for no reason other than those who have the power have decided to be merciful. But this apparent lack of fairness (or justice) troubles the aristocrat not at all. He,

> *winks and lets those incapable of discharging their debts go free*. He ends, as does every good thing on earth, by overcoming itself. *This self-overcoming of justice*: one knows the beautiful name it has given itself – *mercy. It goes without saying that mercy remains the privilege of the most powerful man*. (73)

Instead of seething with a resentment disguised as a passion for justice, Nietzsche's aristocratic man "winks" at the ineptitude of the low. He feels no urge to inflict pain on those below him. Wealthy and strong, he can afford to be merciful, even if that means breaking the rule that people should either pay back their debts or be punished for not doing so.

Nietzsche hopes that his genealogy of morality, as disruptive as it may be, will rejuvenate the European spirit. By his lights, contemporary culture had been thoroughly poisoned by the "bad air" (44) exhaled by Christian moralists like Kant and Mill, which righteously suppresses the exceptional few, and calls them "evil," in the name of equality. His scathing critique aims to clear the ground so that a healthier kind of human being can once again roam free, someone who possesses a spirit "strengthened by war and victory, for whom conquest, adventure, danger and even pain have become needs ... it would require, in brief and alas, precisely this *great health*" (96). He expresses this hope in the following, radically non-Christian, prayer:

> But grant me from time to time – if there are divine goddesses in the realm *beyond good and evil* – grant me the sight, but one glance, of something perfect, wholly achieved, happy, mighty, triumphant, something still capable of arousing fear! *Of a man who justifies man*, of a complementary and redeeming lucky hit on the part of man for the sake of which one may still believe in man! (44)

Whether the dangers of Nietzsche's sometimes overwrought prose outweigh its philosophical merits is yours to ponder. Has the spirit of moralism, of egalitarianism, so often identified with the progress of civilization, actually harmed us? Has it impeded the spirit of creativity and obliterated the possibility of "great health?" Or does it reflect an altogether justifiable and humane concern for others less fortunate than ourselves?

When my children were in elementary school, they would occasionally come home with ribbons declaring them to be winners in some sort of athletic competition. This was surprising to me since neither of them liked or was good at sports. What had happened was that every kid in the class had received similar ribbons just for participating. Is this a cautionary tale or an inspiring one that should be admired for its concern that no child's feelings ever get hurt?

Whatever your initial reaction might be to Nietzsche, at least give him credit for this: he is grappling with the question, what is the best, the healthiest, most truly human form of life? And he refuses to accept conventional or comfortable answers. For him, the excellent life is liberated from the debilitating constraints of morality, and thus can celebrate its own exceptional power. He tells a little story, or parable, to encapsulate his view:

> That lambs dislike great birds of prey does not seem strange: only it gives no ground for reproaching these birds of prey for bearing off little lambs. And if the lambs say among themselves: "These birds of prey are evil; and whoever is least like a bird of prey, but rather its opposite, a lamb – would he not be good?" there is no reason to find fault with this institution of an ideal, except perhaps that the birds of prey might view it a little ironically and say: "we don't dislike them at all, these good little lambs; we even love them; nothing is more tasty than a tender lamb." (45)

That his words echo the Christian image of shepherd and flock is hardly an accident. Nietzsche, however, turns it inside out. To demand that the bird of prey show the lamb moral respect and treat it as an equal would negate its essential being. Eating lambs is what the bird does, and to require it to do otherwise would destroy its animating power. Such is Nietzsche's conception of the excellent life. He dreams of a time when the powerful and strong, the creative and spontaneous, will no longer be shackled and afraid to offend the many by declaring their superiority. His ideal is a psychological vitality in which repressed desires no longer do their hidden damage. Again, this may all sound rather frightening. Or, as his comments on mercy and the "pathos of distance" could suggest, it may ring of promise and thrilling hope.

Resolving the Dispute: Virtue or Power?

However divergent their stories may be, Aristotle and Nietzsche stand on some common ground.[3] For they share a question: whom should we emulate? In their answers, both reveal themselves to be elitists. Their ideal is one of maximal activity, flourishing, vitality, great psychological health.

From the moralists' perspective, both come off as terribly self-centered, and in a sense they are. But they also disagree on much, and this arises from the fact that they conceive of the self so differently.

For Nietzsche, the human animal is at bottom willful, creative, and assertive. The completely actualized, and the most honest, life is thus one that unabashedly expresses its power to change the world; in particular, its power to create values. For this is precisely the message of the *Genealogy*: what counts as good changes over time, and the agents of such change ultimately have great power over the rest of us. For Aristotle, the human good is a stable target (or *telos*) at which everyone, knowingly or not, aims. It is happiness, and it is found in virtuous activity, in the sustained and excellent exercise of rationality in all its manifold (and graduated) manifestations. It is human nature fully realized. This implies that it is an objective good, and can be discovered by reason. This is precisely the task of the *Nicomachean Ethics*: to articulate a truthful *logos*, a rational account, of happiness; of, that is, the meaning and purpose of our existence.

Nietzsche, by contrast, is a relativist (of some sort) who opposes teleology in any form. By his lights, what is counted as "good" changes shape depending on whether it is opposed by the "bad" or by the "evil." And there are more options than just those two. Values are up for grabs, and those who are powerful and creative are the ones who do the grabbing. As opposed to Aristotle, truth plays no privileged role in this process. And so Nietzsche allows for the possibility that a "positive spirit," one who imposes his will upon others, may ultimately do no more than "replace the improbable with the more probable, ***possibly one error with another***" (18). What matters is not whether a value system or conception of human nature is objectively true, but only the fact that it has been created and is in play. Aristotle would be appalled. Above all else, he seeks truth, a project which for Nietzsche is at best problematic, at worst laughable.

Can empirical science help us here? Perhaps the neuroscientists can tell us whether the human brain is at bottom creative or rational. Perhaps the anthropologist who has studied foreign cultures has data that suggest that each of them has its own peculiar worldview and attendant set of values; that, in other words, no system of values is etched in stone.[4]

As always, the criteria needed to adjudicate this philosophical competition include the consistency of the account, the clarity and truth of its presuppositions, and the tenability of its consequences. The task for serious readers, then, remains the same: they must study both authors carefully. Before commencing to do so, however, I again recommend a preliminary exercise. You need to figure out where your intuitions lie so that you that you can participate fully in this debate.

First, take a step backward and ask yourself whether you want to partake in this debate at all. Before rereading the *Nicomachean Ethics* and the *Genealogy*, gauge your reaction to the elitism that they seem to share. Perhaps your sympathies have always been with Jefferson, and you believe it is self-evident that all people are created equal and therefore deserve the same set of human rights. Or you may believe that we are all children of God and so equally share in His unbounded love. If so, then both Aristotle and Nietzsche will likely put you on the defensive, or at least on edge. On the other hand, if you are someone who relishes competition in everything you do, who suspects that athletics, with its struggle for victory, and then its winners and losers, offers a useful model of life best lived, then perhaps one of the two thinkers we have just met attracts you. If so, how will you decide between them?

Turn next to a different kind of self-assessment. Gauge your reaction to the kind of language each of these thinkers uses. Aristotle's prose, which rarely sparkles, is bereft of rhetorical flourish. There is little pleasure in reading it out loud. This is hardly surprising, for he is above all else a theoretical thinker who works slowly, patiently, and with a keen eye for detail. By contrast, Nietzsche's writing can sometimes be manic and thrilling. It is almost poetic.

Which do you prefer? This may seem to be an irrelevant question, at least for a philosopher. After all, it seems to ask only about style, not content. On the other hand, perhaps the way these two write tells much about how they think. Aristotle's calm, methodical, sometimes tedious expositions bespeak his conviction that truth is the ultimate prize (which only a few will attain). In his view, because the meaning and purpose of life is stable and intelligible, sustained intellectual work can result in an understanding of human nature. The way he writes implicitly calls upon his readers to join in the theoretical enterprise. By contrast, for Nietzsche creativity and the willful expression of power are integral to the best life, and his explosive prose mirrors this view. Which do you prefer?

As you may have already begun to suspect, Nietzsche's position might be vulnerable to the following sort of attack. He is, you recall, a relativist who denies that there is an objective good or ultimate purpose to human striving. Instead, he believes that values are created and therefore change throughout history. How, then, can he consistently maintain his own version of the excellent life, which he seems to do with such ferocity, as well as his criticisms of conventional morality? If all value systems are in flux, one being created as another is destroyed, then how could one be counted as superior to another?

Philosophers call this "the self-reference argument," and it has long been deployed against relativists. When their claim that "there is no objective truth" is applied to itself, it self-destructs. For if is true, then it is false. If there is no objective truth, then there is no more reason to believe that "there is no objective truth" than there is to believe that "there is objective truth." Now consider the statement "all values are created." If this is true, as Nietzsche asserts, then no value is intrinsically superior to any other. Instead, all value systems are but temporary manifestations of a particular power surge and will be replaced in the future by a competitor. But Nietzsche's own critique of modern Europe is so strident that he surely cannot believe that it is on par with, say, the Homeric Greece he admires so greatly. By privileging one culture over another, as he seems so clearly to do, does he thereby contradict himself? Such, at least, would be the verdict that Aristotle would reach about him.

How would Nietzsche respond? Perhaps by thumbing his nose at the Aristotelian. Who cares, he might say, if I contradict myself! I'm a free spirit, a creative force, and I'm not in the business of making rational arguments, of offering a *logos*, at all. Truth be told, my language is closer to that of the poets. Their job is not to logically defend their propositions. Instead, it is to express, however they can, the crisscrossing currents and powerful impulses that drive the human animal.

These are just suggestions, but I hope they stimulate you to think long and hard about this debate. For the competing positions in play here are fundamental. Indeed, we will confront versions of them in the next chapter as well.

Notes

1 Aristotle's argument on behalf of the existence of a highest good – at least as I have reconstituted it here (as an indirect argument) – is vulnerable to criticism. Try to figure out where.

2 A book that argues that both individuals and governments have a moral obligation to take action to reduce the pace of climate change is *Climate Matters: Ethics in a Warming World*, by John Broome (New York: Norton, 2012). For an impassioned call to political action read *Eaarth: Making a Life on a Tough New Planet*, by Bill McKibben (New York: Times Books, 2010).

3 A good book that will help you continue your study of Aristotle is *Aristotle's Nicomachean Ethics: An Introduction*, by Michael Pakaluk (Cambridge: Cambridge University Press, 2005). Paul Katsafanas's book, *Agency and the Foundations of Ethics: Nietzschean Constitutivism* (Oxford: Oxford University Press, 2013) offers an excellent, albeit rather difficult, defense of Nietzsche.

4 Bronislaw Malinowski, in his seminal anthropological work, *Argonauts of the Western Pacific* (Long Grove, IL: Waveland Press, 1984 [originally published in 1922]), is very interesting on the question of diversity: "In grasping the

essential outlook of others, with the reverence and real understanding due even to savages we cannot but help widening our own. We cannot possibly teach the final Socratic wisdom of knowing ourselves if we never leave the narrow confinement of the customs, beliefs, and prejudices into which every man is born. Nothing can teach us a better lesson in this matter of ultimate importance than the habit of mind which allows us to treat the beliefs and values of another man from his point of view" (518).

5

Whom Should We Emulate? (2)

The Question

Who among us best represents human beings at the pinnacle of achievement?
Who most fully embodies our greatest possibilities? How do they comport
themselves? What do they talk about? What does it feel like to sit next
to them? While the moralists ask a related question – what should we
do? – they don't engage in this sort of inquiry. By contrast, Nietzsche and
Aristotle do. So too do two great thinkers from China, Confucius and
Lao-Tzu. While their books differ considerably in style from those we have
studied so far, the questions they grapple with will be familiar. They too
explore what counts as an excellent life.

Confucius's Answer

 Confucius, *The Analects*

Filial Piety

The seeds of excellence, according to Confucius in his *Analects* (or *Sayings*,
compiled some time in the fifth century BCE), must be planted early.
"A young man's duty," he asserts, "is to behave well to his parents at home"
(I.6).[1] These words describe the virtue known as ***filial piety***. Children
should respect and obey their parents. At first glance, this seems no more
than an especially trivial platitude. For Confucius, however, it goes far
beyond that. So, for example, he thinks that children should not only defer

Thinking Philosophically: An Introduction to the Great Debates, First Edition. David Roochnik.
© 2016 John Wiley & Sons, Inc. Published 2016 by John Wiley & Sons, Inc.

to their parents, but live with them for as long as possible. "While father and mother are alive, a good son does not wander far afield; or if he does so, goes only where he has said he was going" (IV.19). Even more extreme, he insists that the demands of filial piety reach beyond the grave. "If for the whole three years of mourning, a son manages to carry on the house-hold *exactly* as in his father's day, then he is a good son" (IV.20).

This last directive reveals a decisive feature of the Confucian worldview. It is deeply "*conservative*" – a word whose Latin root (*conservare*) means "to keep, preserve, guard" – and "*traditional*" (from *traditio*, a "handing down" or "delivering"). The father passes down a way of life to the son, who is required to maintain it and then pass it to the next generation. Simply put, in a traditional society children take their bearings from their parents. Its goal is to keep things the way they are. Its vision is cyclical, not linear or progressive.

Boring, you might think. But Confucius believes that filial piety is the root of all that is good in our social and political lives:

> Those who in private life behave well towards their parents and elder brothers, in public life seldom show a disposition to resist the authority of their superiors. And as for such men starting a revolution, no instance of it has ever occurred. It is upon the trunk that a gentleman works. When that is firmly set up, the *Way* [*Tao*] *grows*. And surely proper behavior towards parents and elders brothers is the *trunk* of Goodness. (I.2)

Like the deep roots of a flourishing tree, filial piety gives rise to a trunk and many branches. And so a child who behaves well toward his parents will grow into a young man who will defer to both "his parents at home and to his elders abroad" (I.6). He will respect authority, be socially responsi-ble and, most important, never start a "revolution." He will become a true "gentleman" or "superior man" (a *chün-tzu*). Such is the Way, the *Tao*, the natural process of social development that begins in the primordial (biological) relationship between parent and child.

This notion of the Way as an organic development helps to explain why Confucius requires a son to mourn for his father – and to maintain the household exactly as he inherited it – for three years. By his reckoning, this length of time corresponds to the initial stage of child rearing. "Only when a child is three years old does it leave its parents' arms" (XVII.21). The rituals of mourning symbolize, and are meant to inculcate an appre-ciation of, the natural cycles of a good human life. It should end with the elders being cared for by those whom they took care of.

When I was in my fifties I was sandwiched between two sets of respon-sibilities. My father was very old and I had taken charge of his affairs, and my children were still young enough to need a good bit of attention. I was kept busy on both fronts. Somewhat surprisingly, however, I only occasionally felt frustrated about others eating up my precious time. In fact, I count that period as one of the most rewarding of my life. The best explanation that I can come up with is Confucian. At that stage of my life I was well equipped to take care of others. Having reached a level of intellectual, emotional, and professional maturity, I was ready to take my turn. The two generations flanking me both needed assistance, and it felt right and natural to provide it. My father had taken care of me, and then I took care of him. If all goes well, my children will someday do the same. I was and hope to remain part of a cycle rooted in biological change.

Likely a question is already on your mind: what if the father is a bad guy? Are his children still obligated to obey him? Confucius responds: if you think your parents are being wrongheaded, you should respectfully state your objections, but if you fail to dissuade them, obey anyway:

> In serving his father and mother a man may gently remonstrate with them. But if he sees that he fails to change their opinion, he should resume an attitude of deference and not thwart them; may feel discouraged, but not resentful. (IV.18)

This might be unsettling. What if the father is a drug addict or abusive? Should his children obey him anyway? Aren't there occasions on which even children should think for themselves rather than submit to authority? On a political level, what if you found yourself in North Korea? Should you still defer to those in charge? Or is that too feeble a response? Perhaps you should dissent and even consider rebellion. But Confucius seems to reject that possibility unconditionally.

Such questions encapsulate the dilemma of conservatism. The traditionalist values stability and continuity. Anyone who has had the misfortune of living in a broken or chaotic society will know how beneficial these are. But at times the price to be paid for such social goods is simply too great. How, then, can Confucius defend his seemingly inflexible demand for filial piety and all that follows from it? Before confronting this difficult question, let us examine his thinking a bit further.

Ritual

The crucial tool, he thinks, in maintaining an effective social system is the performance of ritual. So, to cite a random example, "when preparing himself for sacrifice he must wear the Bright Robe, and it must be of linen.

He must change his food and also the place where he commonly sits" (XII.7). The details here are unimportant. Instead, what is instructive in this directive is the light it sheds on the nature of ritual itself. First, it has its own well-established rules, and must be performed in the same way time after time. Adherence to such specific practices is what separates ritual from the haphazard flow of daily life. In the one just mentioned, the practitioner must wear a certain kind of clothing. What matters is not that it be linen, but that it's something not worn on other days. Following a methodical sequence, a ritual draws clear boundaries, both spatial and temporal, around itself, and thereby signals a break from the ordinary.

If you are fortunate enough to have one, think of the Thanksgiving meal you share with your family every November. You don't eat cranberries at any other time of the year. You don't typically open the table and seat a dozen people instead of just your nuclear four, or eat so much in the late afternoon. It's a special day when you are called upon to feel some gratitude for food and family, for being safe and warm when it's cold outside. By interrupting the quotidian flow, a ritual creates conditions that encourage the participants to pause and pay attention. On its proper performance, Confucius stakes all. As he puts it, "he who can himself submit to ritual is Good" (XII.1).

But, to reiterate the same worry occasioned by his insistence on filial piety, is Confucius saying that if we mechanically perform a routine year after year we'll be just fine? No, for he insists that going through a ritual without cultivating a corresponding psychological or emotional state is worthless: "ritual performed without reverence, the forms of mourning observed without grief – these are things I cannot bear to see" (III.26).

Of course, in his day and our own, many (perhaps most) people just go through the motions. Did you really give much by way of thanks on Thanksgiving, or were you preoccupied by your annoying relatives? Certainly Confucius recognizes this phenomenon. Nonetheless, he would insist that the yearly performance be strictly maintained. What he has in mind here, not unlike Aristotle, is the value of *habituation*. Even if you suffered through your last Thanksgiving dinner, it is something to which you are accustomed and would miss if November went by without it. If your own parents regularly hosted this yearly feast, it is probable that when you become the head of a household you will want to do the same. Like an Aristotelian habit, which typically results from external pressure being applied to children, Confucian rituals inculcate patterns of proper action. They are not mindless. They are traditional.

As with Aristotle, the Confucian worldview is both developmental and stratified. Some people, perhaps most, follow traditional practices without much by way of understanding, conviction, or thought. They do so because they are expected to, or have been ordered to, or because they have been effectively habituated. Others (presumably like Confucius himself) comprehend the meaning and value of their rituals. Children, of course, typically fit in the former category. The best they can do is follow the lead of their elders. The same is true of many adults who are still like children; they need strict rules imposed upon them from the outside in order to stay in line. Confucius is blunt in rank ordering these groups:

> To men who have risen at all above the middling sort, one may talk of things higher yet. But to men who are at all below the middling sort it is useless to talk of things that are above them. (VI.19)

Confucius insists that someone who only mechanically goes through the motions, even if regularly, isn't really ritualizing at all. "A man who is not good," he says, "what can he have to do with ritual?" (III.3). In a similar vein, he complains bitterly about people who fulfill the requirements of filial piety, but do so only minimally and with no conviction:

> Filial sons nowadays are people who see to it that their parents get enough to eat. But even dogs and horses are cared for to that extent. If there is no feeling of respect, wherein lies the difference? (II.7)

In short, like Aristotle, Confucius is an elitist. "The common people," he says, "can be made to follow it [the Way]; they cannot be made to understand it" (VIII.9). For him, different kinds of human beings should play different roles in society. "Let the prince be a prince, the minister a minister, the father a father, and the son a son" (XII.11). There are those who rule, and those who obey; those who work in the rice paddies, and those who sell the rice. People should know and keep to their place. Such is a conservative's vision of a stable, stratified, harmonious society.

You may recoil. But before writing him off, however, do consider this. Confucius may be an elitist, but he doesn't think that family connections, wealth, or power are what qualify someone to be a "superior man." Virtue is a matter of character:

> Poor, yet delighting in the Way; rich, yet a student of ritual (I.15) .... Do I regard myself as a possessor of wisdom? Far from it. But if even a simple peasant comes in all sincerity and asks me a question, I am ready to thrash the matter out. (IX.7)

In principle, people from all walks of life can become excellent. This is because human beings are "by nature, near together; by practice far apart" (XVII.2). We share a common nature and a corresponding set of intrinsic possibilities, but we differ widely because of the upbringing we happen to receive. As he puts it, "there is a difference in instruction but none in kind" (XV.38). Like Mill, Confucius is a great believer in the power of education. We are all born with a disposition to follow the Way, and it is only inadequate nurturing that causes so many to deviate from it. It follows from this that those of us who are successful are obligated to work toward the improvement of social and educational institutions for all.

Leadership

I once met a man who had just retired as the director of a prestigious academic organization. He told the story of how he had originally gotten the job. The day before his interview, he happened to bump into a colleague who was a scholar of Chinese culture. Never having held an administrative position before, he asked him for tips about what he should say. His colleague recommended that he mention a simple Confucian principle: a good leader leads by example. The master himself puts it this way: "he who rules is by moral force is like the pole-star [the north star], which remains in its place while all the lesser stars do homage to it" (II.1).

The pole star, distant but distinctly visible, remains fixed in the northern sky, and so navigators can count on it to find their way. So too does the excellent ruler keep his distance, but he shines so brightly in the performance of his duties and the rituals associated with them that he provides guidance. The striking implication of this simile is that the best ruler does not rule with a heavy hand. Most important, he does not threaten punishment in order to inspire good behavior in them. "If the ruler himself is upright, all will go well, *even though he does not give orders*" (XIII.6):

> Govern the people by regulations, keep order among them by chastisements, and they will flee from you, and lose all self-respect. *Govern them by moral force, keep order among them by ritual*, and they will keep their self respect and come to you of their own accord. (II.3)

On this view, leading by example exerts an almost magnetic attraction to those who follow. It activates their natural goodness. By contrast, issuing edicts and then threatening punishment for non-compliance stunts the development of the subjects. Heavy-handed rule operates through fear, and so inhibits the growth of those who obey. Just as water will flow on its own to the sea, so too will people, unless they are impeded, naturally follow the Way if it is illuminated for them by the brilliant shine of the virtuous. As he puts it,

> He who is courteous is not scorned, he who is broad wins the multitude, he who is of good faith is trusted by the people, he who is diligent succeeds in all he undertakes, he who is clement can get service from the people. (XVII.6)

This approach may seem wildly optimistic. Aristotle would certainly think so. By his lights, the majority of people need more than examples to keep them in line. For they are dominated by passion rather than reason, and "passion seems to yield not to reason or speech [*logos*] but to force" (*Nicomachean Ethics* 1179b29). Hence, a well-ordered community requires strict laws (formulated by those who have practical wisdom) that inculcate good habits through the threat of punishment. Confucius disagrees. It is ritual, not law, that best molds the many.

You don't need to be a ruler to weigh in on this line of thought. Perhaps you have already wondered about how best to raise a child, coach a team, or teach a class. How, for example, should a professor get his students not to check Facebook during a lecture? By prohibiting laptops and phones – and penalizing those who violate the rule – or by making the lecture (and the rituals that attend it) sufficiently compelling so that students will actually want to listen rather than check their screens? It is obvious which method Confucius would prefer. Threatening punishment might yield short-term benefits, but ultimately will be counter-productive. The professor's goal is to help his students become mature, thoughtful, self-reliant adults who will act properly of their own accord. Not frightened children who fear the lash.

Teleology

A good story, at least of the traditional sort, is a well-organized whole with a beginning, middle, and end. Confucius tells a little one about himself:

> The Master said, At fifteen I set my heart upon learning. At thirty, I had planted my feet firm upon the ground. At forty, I no longer suffered from perplexities. At fifty, I knew what were the biddings of Heaven. At sixty, I heard them with docile ear. At seventy, I could follow my own heart. (II.3)

In this idealized version of his journey, Confucius tells us that when he reached the age of 15 he began to think for himself. He does not elaborate, and so we have to speculate.

Like most children, when he was very young Confucius had merely followed the orders of his parents and elders. But when he turned 15 he began to wonder what was going on. Perhaps he became curious about the rituals his parents practiced, and so did some research on their origins. Perhaps he became skeptical about his family's traditions and even offered some resistance to participating in them. Whatever he did it was all, at least in his retrospective account, in the service of learning. He had begun the long quest to become an adult who understands what's going on for himself.

Somewhere around 30 he planted his "feet firm upon the ground." Translated into contemporary lingo, he had a steady job, started his own family, bought a house, and became a full-fledged member of a community. The sometimes chaos of youth had subsided. This is not to say that all confusion and doubt had disappeared, for during the next decade he still felt "perplexities." Like many of today's 30-something parents with young children and a mortgage, he occasionally saw the future as bondage without end, and so felt the urge to run away from his responsibilities. But he resisted that impulse and by the age of 40 it had largely passed. Still, he had further to go.

Somewhere around 50, the previous 35 years of learning paid big dividends. He attained knowledge of "the biddings of Heaven" – of, that is, the proper Way of life. He not only performed the rituals but did so with conviction and an understanding of their value. But even then complete psychological harmony, the coordination of external behavior with internal feelings, eluded him. Occasionally there were still stabs of doubt, and he had to look outside of himself, perhaps to his own father or some other elder for guidance. Only at 60, when likely his own father had already died, did the last vestige of resistance disappear. He became "docile." His performance of duty had become self-reinforcing. The unfolding of every year, punctuated as it was by rituals, became a rhythm he felt within himself. Finally, when he reached 70, the "biddings of Heaven" became so thoroughly internalized that he needed only to look within himself in order to determine the best course of action. He could rely on his own judgment. He had come both to trust himself and to deserve to be trusted by others.

This simple story recounts a skeletal version of the Way, of a natural progression each stage of which organically gives rise to the next. It is thoroughly *teleological*; that is, it has a goal, end, or culmination to which all previous steps lead: becoming the superior man, the responsible elder who by following his own heart guides others. Like Aristotelian happiness, the most excellent of Confucian lives is not available to the young. Indeed, on this view the best thing about being young is that it is a prelude to becoming old. Such, at least, is the conviction of traditional societies where elders are venerated. It couldn't be more distant from that found in contemporary culture, so much of which is devoted precisely to forestalling the advent of aging, and to putting people into institutions, and therefore out of sight, when they get really old.

What if the Father Is a Bad Guy?

To return to an earlier question: does the Confucian demand for filial piety, the root of all his conservative beliefs, require a child to obey a father who is a drug addict or abusive? On the political level, what about subjects of a vicious and oppressive dictator? In short, does traditionalism require us to affirm the status quo, regardless of how awful it might be?

On the one hand, there may be good Confucian reasons to say no. Confucius is adamant that rulers should lead by "moral force." Like everyone else, they too should respect their elders, including those who are elderly among their subjects. Like everyone else, they should follow his version of the golden rule: "Do not do to others what you would not like yourself" (XII.2). The Confucian system is anchored in demands for goodness, and so he could not possibly be positive about abusive parents or murderous tyrants. On the other hand, his conservative mentality places such a high premium on stability and propriety that it is difficult to see how a good Confucian could legitimately resist authority.

This is a real conundrum. It is similar to the one we faced in thinking about Aristotle, who in his *Politics* also approves of a differentiated and hierarchical community in which everyone knows, and keeps to, their place. Many of us instinctively recoil from such a notion and denounce it as a denial of human freedom. Others are attracted to the prospect of a more traditional system, perhaps because they lack it and feel rootless, aimless, and alone as a result.

One last thought on behalf of Confucius. The notion of a traditional society implies that there is a way of life that *can* be delivered from one generation to another. But only if the society has functioned successfully for a sustained period of time is this even possible. So, for example, in broken places like contemporary Syria or Somalia the government and the social system have largely collapsed, and so there are no longer any traditions to pass down. Perhaps one could then argue, on Confucian grounds, that people who find themselves in the midst of such misery are no longer bound to obey those in power. On the familial level, it is likely that a father who is a drug addict has no coherent way of life to pass on to his children.

Typically this sort of man is a wreck and thoroughly at odds with himself. Perhaps in such cases, where the father is completely divorced from his duties, and has nothing to contribute or show as a parent, Confucius would allow a child to be released from the demands of filial piety.

Or consider the regime of Kim Jong-un, the supreme leader of North Korea. He surely is no "pole star." Instead of leading by example, he controls his subjects with a very heavy hand. During the decades that he and his family have been in power all aspects of social life have been subordinated to the maintenance of his authority. So, while North Korea does have its own set of state-sponsored rituals, they are imposed from the top down, and their only purpose is to valorize the power of the regime and to keep the people from rebelling. There is nothing organic in the North Korean regime. Instead, order is maintained artificially through surveillance and the threat of punishment. Kim Jong-un treats his subjects not as human beings who are on the Way, but as raw material to be molded according to his desires and whims. He is thus in violation of every Confucian precept. Does this give his subjects legitimate grounds for dissent, escape, or even rebellion? The question, in other words, is this: must a good Confucian obey the edicts of a thoroughly non-Confucian regime? I suspect, or at least hope, not.

Lao-Tzu's Answer

 Lao-Tzu, *Tao Te Ching*

Anti-Teleology

One saying reveals the utterly non-Confucian, and thus non-teleological, character of Lao-Tzu's version of the "TAO" – the "way," "path," or "road" – a word the two thinkers share:[2] "*Be filled with virtue (TE), / Like a baby*" (55). Instead of a venerable 70-year-old, a superior man who incarnates the goal or *telos* of human striving, the *Tao Te Ching* (probably written in the fourth century BCE) locates the sweet spot in our development at its outset. For him, it is the child who shows us who we are at our best. "Sages," Lao-Tzu writes, "become the world's children" (49).[3] But how could a "sage" possibly be like a child? After all, children have not yet reached the age of reason. They are rarely moved by rational argument, and at least until they are seven or so cannot even be held accountable for their actions. This, however, is precisely what captivates Lao-Tzu, and why he elevates them to the pedestal they occupy in his thinking. It is why when he says "I have the mind of a fool" (20), he is not engaged in self-depreciation.

Unless constrained by adult force, children act *spontaneously.* Ignorant of tradition and ritual, oblivious to propriety and expectation, unburdened by anxiety or guilt, they plunge into a world fresh and new, which they experience without filters. When it hurts they cry. When it's funny, they laugh. They play. That's all. Since they have but a minimal share in *logos*, in rational speech and thought, they do not analyze or think tactically. They do not judge, but only engage. If they have any goals at all, they are anything but long term or calculated. Such is the innocent air Lao-Tzu invites us to breathe.

Still, the Taoist message is puzzling. What does Lao-Tzu mean when he says "*banish learning, discard knowledge / People will gain a hundred-fold*" (19)? Or this:

> Pursue knowledge, gain daily.
> Pursue TAO, lose daily.
> Lose and again lose,
> Arrive at non-doing [*wu wei*].
>
> Non-doing – and nothing not done.
> Take the entire world as nothing.
> Make the least effort,
> And the world escapes you. (48)

On the Taoist model the world itself is not a rational structure amenable to *logos*. In fact, it resists articulation altogether. "*TAO called TAO is not TAO*" (1). In other words (ha!), when names are given, that which is named is obscured. Rationality, even talking itself, is thus a weak and ineffectual tool. Not only is it unable to offer truthful access to the world, it distorts it. And so Lao-Tzu tells us that "*those who know don't talk / Those who talk don't know*" (56).

Again, this is a lesson best taught by children. They do not spend much time discussing what they want to do: they just do it. They are not anxious about the future, and so they rarely deliberate or articulate their plans. They don't study reality, predict consequences, or test for logical validity. They are playful, not serious, as they skip, jump, make things, run wild. They laugh.

> The great scholar hearing the TAO
>   Tries to practice it.
> The middling scholar, hearing the TAO,
>   Sometimes has it, sometimes not.
> The lesser scholar hearing the TAO,
>   Has a good laugh.

> Without that laughter,
>   It wouldn't be TAO ...
> TAO hides, no name. (41)

The child, not having yet reached the age of either anxiety or reason, exemplifies a stance toward life – irresponsible, fun-loving, captivated by what is front of his eyes. Somehow the sage achieves (returns to) such simplicity. He is like "plain silk ... uncarved wood" (19). Is he, then, someone who aspires to become a simpleton?

Water

"*Best to be like water*" (8), Lao-Tzu recommends:

> Nothing in the world is soft and weak as water.
> But when attacking the hard and strong
> Nothing can conquer so easily.
>
> Weak overcomes strong,
> Soft overcomes hard.
>
> Everyone knows this,
> No one attains it. (78)

Water is the most expressive symbol of the Taoist worldview because it has no shape of its own. Instead, it assumes the shape of the vessel containing it. It follows the path of least resistance, for it flows only in the direction gravity (or wind) sends it. It submits to the terrain and so, in this sense, is passive. And yet it is also the most powerful of forces. It cuts deep grooves into the surface of the earth and thereby shapes the topography. It is thus both weak and strong, effortless and yet irresistible, formless and yet capable of assuming any form. It is fluid and so, at least in most of our encounters with it (especially in rivers), it continually flows.

Such, Lao-Tzu thinks, is the world. Nothing in it abides or has a permanent structure. Instead, everything flows. This implies that "reversal is TAO's movement" (40) as each thing becomes its opposite. Boston is now cold but soon will be not-cold (hot). Then it will be cold (not-hot) again. In the course of a year Boston is and isn't hot and cold. Or, as Lao-Tzu puts it, "*Is and Isn't produce each other*" (2). To think otherwise, to try to pin the TAO down or grasp it conceptually, is to betray its very nature. The job of the Taoist is to go with the flow, not try to master it through reason or technology.

Paradox

If the world is in fact formless, fluid ,and impossible to grasp, it is resistant to rational analysis and stable description. "Names can name no lasting name. / Nameless: the origin of heaven and earth" (1). Trying to say what the TAO is – or worse, trying to explain it – obscures it. *Logos*, the pride of the mature and responsible adult, serves us poorly, while the child at play, exuberant, fully alive, hopping from this to that, gives us a better model or paradigm to emulate.

There is, however, a big problem lurking in the *Tao Te Ching*. If reality cannot be named and *logos* distorts rather than discloses, then why did Lao-Tzu write anything at all? After all, his book is a *logos*. If he really believes that "those who know don't talk," then why did he say anything? Either he doesn't know what he is talking about, and so there's no reason for us to read his work, or he does know something, in which case he should have kept it silently to himself.

This line of questioning is a version of the "self-reference" argument mentioned in our discussion of Nietzsche (Chapter 4). Recall that statements such as "there is no truth" or "all truths are relative," when applied to themselves, self-destruct. For both make blanket – that is, non-relative – truth claims even as they deny that this is possible.

Lao-Tzu, I imagine, understands this logical dynamic well. Even more so, he embraces it:

> My words are very easy to understand,
> Very easy to practice.
> No one under heaven can understand them,
> No one can practice them. (70)

Lao-Tzu embraces **paradox** even if, or maybe just because, it is offensive to the sensible, logical mind. For him, "true words resemble their opposites" (78). What is cold is hot. What is beautiful is ugly. What is dead is alive.

Consider this remarkable statement: "I am a liar." If it's true, it is false, and if it's false, it is true. The statement continually reverses itself, turns itself inside out. Like an active child at play, or a river, it is never still. It oscillates. Lao-Tzu's writing is something like that. It keeps readers on edge at it tries to wean them away from their dependence on *logos*. His is a language that works against language. Even as his text invites us to read it, it demands that we look elsewhere. After all, its author has confessed that "I have the mind of a fool."

*Non-Action (*Wu Wei*)*

Lao-Tzu pays special heed to one paradox in particular (which was mentioned above). "The sage," he says, "is devoted to non-action [*wu wei*]" (2). To elaborate, he again invokes the symbolism of water:

> Best to be like water,
> Which benefits the ten thousand things
> And does not contend ...
>
> **Only do not contend,**
> And you will not go wrong. (8)
>
> I alone am passive, giving no sign
> Like an infant who has not yet smiled ...
>
> I have the mind of a fool ...
>
> I alone am dull, dull,
> Drifting on the ocean
> Blown about endlessly. (20)

Do not contend. Do not act intentionally and with a plan in mind. Instead, go with the flow – a time-honored phrase that seems to embrace passivity. But that is only half of the story, for from such apparent passivity emerges true activity:

> **Act without acting [wei wu wei]**
> Serve without serving
> Taste without tasting ...
>
> The Sage
> never attempts great things
> and *so accomplishes them*. (63)

Here is an idea we can sink our teeth into, even investigate scientifically, for it opens the door to a fascinating feature of human agency. We are often at our best when we are trying the least. A good illustration comes from sports.

The pitcher on the mound who repeats to himself, "I have to throw a strike, I have to throw a strike," is doomed. Once he becomes self-conscious and deliberately aims the ball, he is over-thinking and this will destroy the fluidity of his motion, and likely cause him to miss the plate. The player who is determined to achieve an objective instead of just playing the game will invariably muck things up.

Every athlete, and many a musician, will recognize the dynamic here. They understand that they are at their very best when in high gear, "in the zone," when their bodies are moving fluidly, almost without effort or thought. When they are trying the least (and so most like a child at play), they most fully tap into their talents. Anyone who has had such an experience knows what this feels like. Even some neuroscientists have weighed in to confirm the Taoist insight. Using functional magnetic resonance imaging techniques, they show that when a subject (like an athlete or a musician improvising) is acting at a very high level, the lateral prefrontal cortex, that part of the brain responsible for deliberate acting, is turned off. I have no idea whether such research holds any experimental water. But precisely because I remember having had such moments (particularly on the basketball court), I'm guessing it does.[4]

The graduate students of my department also illustrate, by sad contrast, this point. They typically choose to pursue a PhD because they loved studying philosophy when they were undergraduates. Soon after they arrive in Boston, however, they become infected by the relentless pressure that university culture imposes upon them to professionalize. They are repeatedly told how hard it is to get a position as a professor, and that it is never too soon to start preparing for the job market. Instead of just enjoying their work – reading, writing, talking about philosophy – they are trained to think tactically. How can I get a paper published or accepted at a conference? What courses will look good on my transcript? Which of the professors in my department is most prestigious? How can I expand my network? Students read the blogs, continually get notices of new publications in their field, check the online rankings to see where their department stands on the national scale. They are consumed by comparison. When their competitors look more successful than they, they feel inadequate and become anxious.

These dejected young people are smart and have, or at least used to have, a lively spark. But as PhD students they no longer take up their studies as an end in itself – as a celebration of questioning – but only as a means to carry them upward to the next rung on the professional ladder.

My advice to such students is a version of Lao-Tzu's "***do not contend***." Do not worry, I say, about getting published or going to conferences. Instead, concentrate on what brought you here in the first place: the love of philosophy. Read widely, and be open to a variety of intellectual options. You will gradually discover what sort of work you find most compelling and enjoyable, and this almost certainly will be what you are best at. Then plunge into it with all you've got. You will need to become very good at what you do in order to succeed professionally. This will happen only if very hard and well. In turn, this you will only do if you identify with your work and find it so engaging that you wake up in the nger to return to your desk. Only if energized by love will you be able to bring words to life and put in the long hours required to accomplish something worthwhile. Only by making your work truly your own will you be able to speak about it with confidence and authentic enthusiasm. And this is precisely what will make you an attractive candidate for a job, if one happens to arise in your area. In short, only by not attempting to reach a goal – a position at a prestigious university, a book that receives critical acclaim – might you reach that goal.

You may not believe it, but I'm offering you practical advice. Plotting the short-term future will fracture your concentration and dilute your work. This isn't to say you should be naïve about the profession. Yes, of course you should publish. But you shouldn't think about publishing now, even though many of your professors are urging you to do so. Instead, just write papers for your seminars, and remember that these are exercises performed in the service of the real goal: gaining knowledge, honing your craft, deepening your convictions. Try to translate the forbidding prose of an Aristotle or a Kant into language that actually means something to you. If you do this, and work very hard, and you have a bit of talent – and some good luck – you will get published. By not trying to succeed professionally you will have a chance of succeeding professionally. *Wei Wu Wei.*

Even as I'm sermonizing, I realize that, given the constant buzz of online culture and the intensely competitive and corporate character of university life, my words likely will have little effect. Still, I hold fast to the Taoist line, and so I repeat these words:

> Pursue knowledge, gain daily.
> Pursue TAO, lose daily.
> Lose and again lose,
> Arrive at non-doing [*wu wei*]
>
> ***Non-doing – and nothing not done***
>
> Take the entire world as nothing.
> Make the least effort,
> And the world escapes you. (48)

Lao-Tzu extends his "action non-action" principle quite far: "Family relations forgotten / Filial piety and affection arise … Banish benevolence, discard righteousness / People will return to duty and compassion" (18–19). The thought here seems to be similar to Rousseau's line on the state of nature. Unburdened by rational analysis, moral obligation, or social pressure, people will – naturally, spontaneously, on their own – not harm others. They will go with the flow, and the flow does no harm. And they will instinctively feel what he calls "pity," the capacity to empathize with the suffering of another human being. By contrast (according to Rousseau), in society we are continually fractured by the demand to justify our actions rationally. And so we all too often convince ourselves that harming others is in fact the right thing to do.

Perhaps something like this is what Lao-Tzu has in mind. If we "discard righteousness" – if we dismiss the Confucian demand for moral rightness and ritual – then we can return to a more natural state: "compassion." Intentional action, carefully deliberated, only distances us from our true selves.

Resolving the Dispute: Superior Man or Child?

The debate of this chapter can be conceived as a competition between two paradigms. On the one side, championed by Confucius, there is the "gentleman" or "superior man." Fully developed, rational, dutiful, devoted to ritual, and old, he is the *telos* of humanity to whom the young should defer. On the Taoist side there is the child. Playful, not driven by goals, oblivious to expectation, fun loving, he acts spontaneously and does not "contend." How can this dispute be resolved?

There's going to be a problem. A rational debate of the sort envisioned here is like a game. It has rules (such as, one must speak clearly and contradictions are illegal), as well as a clear objective: to win by marshaling evidence and good reasons in support of the thesis. As such, demanding that the Taoist engage in such a competition with the Confucian totally stacks the deck against him. After all, like a child he eschews rational argument and does not contend. Therefore, were he to enter the debate he would automatically lose for he would be playing by, and therefore implicitly agreeing with, Confucian rules. To stick to his guns, perhaps the Taoist should jokingly remind his opponent that those who know don't talk, and then walk away chuckling.

What, then, should we who have embarked on the journey that is this book do? Can we adopt an impartial stance and attempt to adjudicate this competition? Perhaps not, for it is the lover-of-*logos* who advocates impartiality and sober-minded rational judgment. In other words, if you have been taking this book seriously and participating in the exercises it has recommended, then you have already declared your allegiance. And it isn't to Lao-Tzu. Or is that too harsh a judgment? You may have great sympathy for Lao-Tzu at this point. But will you be able to defend your position?

This chapter's competition has precedents in material studied so far. Similarities between Confucius and Aristotle have already been noted several times, and we have also detected an affinity between Rousseau's "savage" and Lao-Tzu's "fool." When we reach Chapter 7, and once again confront the thought of Friedrich Nietzsche, you will again be reminded of certain Taoist themes, and so you will be able to revisit the questions raised here. Before that, however, we will examine an entirely different question, one that will take us in quite a new direction.

Notes

1   Many sayings in the *Analects* actually begin with the words, "the master said." I sometimes leave them out.

2   The name "Lao-Tzu" really just means "old master." Very little is known about the author of the *Tao Te Ching*, and the problems of translation are enormous.

3   Legge's translation of #49 is quite different from the one I cited: "The sage has in the world an appearance of indecision, and keeps his mind in a state of indifference to all. The people all keep their eyes and ears directed to him, and he deals with them all as his children." Not knowing Chinese, I am in no position to adjudicate. I cite the translation I did because it harmonizes best with my own, admittedly amateurish, understanding of Lao-Tzu.

4   A book that attempts both to explain and validate the Taoist principle of "non-action" by referring to contemporary neuroscientific research is *Trying not to Try*, by Edward Slingerland (New York: Crown, 2014). Especially see pages 45–50.

6

What Do You Know?

The Question

Do you know what time it is? Yes, I know who won the ballgame last night. No, I don't know what to do. Do you?

You think you know what time it is by looking at your phone. But do you have any idea how its digital clock actually works? If not, why should you trust it? Do you really know what time it is, or are you just relying on the person who programmed the phone in the first place? You read the headline in the sports page of the newspaper. But maybe the printer made a mistake and inaccurate information is on the page. Surely you believe that the nice woman who took care of you for all those years is your mother, and that's why you called her on Mother's Day. But how do you know she isn't an impostor? Has she ever taken a DNA test to demonstrate that she actually gave birth to you? Even if she did, why should you trust the results? What is a DNA test anyway?

"I know what I like." Do you? Or have your desires been irrevocably shaped by social expectations, and so never fully belong to you as an individual? Did you really want to work that hard in high school so that you could be admitted to a fancy private college, or did you do so only because it would make you look good in the eyes of others?

Aristotle claims to know something about human nature. We are, he says, the animal with *logos* and therefore essentially political beings who, in order to be fully ourselves, must enter into cooperative interaction and conversation with others. But how does he know that? Maybe we're most fully ourselves when we are alone and quiet.

Thinking Philosophically: An Introduction to the Great Debates, First Edition. David Roochnik.
© 2016 John Wiley & Sons, Inc. Published 2016 by John Wiley & Sons, Inc.

As suggested in Chapter 1, philosophy aspires to self-knowledge. But is this possible? Or is self-deception inevitable? Can one know oneself in the same way we know that the sum of the interior angles of a triangle is equal to the sum of two right angles? How, by the way, do we know that?

In sum, a question presses hard: what is it to know?

Descartes's Answer

 René Descartes, *Discourse on Method*

Descartes's Education

René Descartes's book, *Discourse on Method* (1637), is autobiographical. But even if he frequently writes in the first person, his is hardly the sort of memoir with which we are familiar today. Instead, it is an account of how he grappled with the question of knowledge. Descartes begins by describing his education:

> I had been nourished on letters since my childhood, and because I was convinced that by means of them one could acquire a *clear and assured knowledge* of everything that is *useful* in life, I had a tremendous desire to master them. But as soon as I had completed this entire course of study, at the end of which one is ordinarily received into the ranks of the learned, I completely changed my mind. For I found myself confounded by so many *doubts and errors* that it seemed to me that I had not gained any profit from my attempt to teach myself, except that more and more I had discovered my ignorance. (3)

To transport this paragraph into the present, imagine that Descartes is describing his experience of attending a liberal-arts college. He had gone to a traditional "high school," one whose curriculum focused on classical texts of literature, philosophy, theology, rhetoric, and mathematics. He anticipated continuing in this vein in college, and hoped that by doing so he would gain "*clear* and *assured* knowledge of everything *useful* in life."

Notice the three adjectives he deploys here. Not surprisingly, Descartes wanted the knowledge he would gain to be "useful." Especially today, when most students enter university in order to receive the training and credentials needed for a job, this is an impulse easy to understand. Unlike most students, though, Descartes's youthful ambition was titanic. He wanted knowledge of "everything useful in life." Everything?

Descartes expected that his professors would teach him material that was "clear." Again, who wouldn't want that? But what exactly is clarity?

That "7 + 5 = 12" is a sentence whose meaning (and truth) is clear, while a line from Joyce's *Finnegans Wake* is not, seems obvious. For just as a clear day is bright and free from cloud or fog, so too can we "see" that 7 + 5 is 12. Nothing obscures its unmistakable truth. By contrast, when Joyce writes, "And that was the first peace of illiteratise porthery in all the flamend floody flatuous world," we don't know what he means. Clarity, then, seems to entail qualities such as simplicity, visibility, and accessibility. For Descartes such attributes belong to genuine knowledge.

The third of Descartes's adjectives is "assured." He expected his teachers to convey to him knowledge that was secure, solid, sure to be true. Unfortunately, they let him down. For what they taught him was, at least in his mind, riddled by "doubts and errors." This phrase tells much. If the epistemic demand is for maximum clarity and assuredness, then even an inkling of doubt or slightest bit of murk becomes intolerable. (Recall that "epistemic" is derived from the Greek word *epistémé*, "knowledge.")

Descartes recounts the subjects that disappointed him in school. First on his list are "languages [Greek and Latin] and ... the reading of classical texts" (4), which were the cornerstones of European education in his day. He explains why they left him cold. Studying books from the distant past, he says, is like traveling to foreign countries. It affords access to unfamiliar ideas and customs, and this seems to be a positive. But it is also risky. For just as someone who travels too much may become "a stranger in his own country," so too may students of antiquity become disengaged from, and therefore useless to, their contemporaries. Next comes literature, or what he calls "fables." These can overly stimulate the imagination and thereby cause readers to think that "many events are possible which are not so at all" (4). Again, the risk seems to be losing touch with reality. Finally, there is philosophy. Even though it (especially the works of Aristotle) had been central in the university curriculum for centuries, "*there still is nothing in it about which there is not some dispute*, and consequently nothing that is not doubtful" (5). For Descartes, this reveals its bankruptcy.

In sum, Descartes became convinced that most of his education, his initiation into the putative "ranks of the learned," was a waste of time. For it distracted him from his real ambition: to find clear and assured knowledge of "everything that is useful in life."

There was, however, one subject he loved:

> I delighted most of all in **mathematics** because of the **certainty** and the evidence of its reasonings. But I did not yet notice its true **use** and, thinking it was of service only to the mechanical arts, I was astonished that no one built anything more noble upon its **foundations** given that they were so **solid and firm**. (4–5)

Only mathematics quenched Descartes's intellectual thirst by providing him with the clarity and certainty he craved. In particular, geometry, with its rigorous proofs, each step of which unmistakably follows from the preceding, delighted him. Its "reasonings" issue in conclusions that ineluctably follow from axioms and definitions. But the crushing disappointment of Descartes's college education was his discovery of how little mathematics was actually appreciated by his teachers. It was treated as one subject among many when in reality it should have provided the "*foundations*" of the other disciplines.

With this one word, Descartes unleashes a metaphor that will resonate throughout the *Discourse on Method*: the design of a structurally sound building. First and foremost, a strong building, one that will last a long time and hold tight through all sorts of weather – one that is "assured" – requires a firm and solid foundation. Without this, even the most elegant architectural masterpiece will crumble. In the *Discourse on Method* Descartes proposes that mathematics can supply the requisite solidity, the clarity and distinctness, needed for a reliable epistemic edifice to rise. He is on the verge, along with Galileo and many others at the time, of inventing mathematical physics, a science of nature that, unlike Aristotle's teleology, utilizes rigorous demonstration. He intuits that, unlike the gibberish of the ancients, the application of such knowledge to the real world will pay powerful dividends. In other words, he foresees that the new physics will lead to powerful technologies that will be "useful" in human life. About this he was surely right.

Descartes makes his agenda crystal clear by swearing allegiance to the following maxim: "*I deemed everything that was merely probable to be well-nigh false*" (5). In other words, if any belief, claim, or assertion is tainted by the slightest bit of doubt, then it must be counted as false. It must be junked. Descartes is no moderate.

Back to his story (updated again): Descartes was so appalled by the sop his professors had been peddling that he dropped out of college as soon as he could. Then he did what the restless young have so often done: he quit school and hit the road. He began to travel. But he soon became disenchanted with the vagabond life, and for the following reason:

> As long as I merely considered the customs of other men, I found hardly anything there about which to be confident, and that I noticed *there was as much diversity as I had previously found among the opinions of the philosophers*. (6)

Descartes's travels reminded him of studying philosophy. Both open the door to "diversity." In Germany people drink beer and in Italy they prefer wine. In France there are Catholics and in England Protestants. The world, he discovered, was replete with competing religions, customs, and conceptions of life. To his dismay, just as in his college classroom nothing firm or assured could be found on the road.

Good fortune then struck. He was in Germany when he got caught in a winter storm. For a full day he was stuck in "a stove-heated room." There was no one to talk to, nothing to distract him, and so "I was completely free to converse with myself" (7). What to others might seem to be a misfortune was for Descartes a boon. Alone with his thoughts, free from the tumult of conversation, confused ideas, and boring professors, he could think for himself. To express his first thought, he reverts to the metaphor of building:

> There is often not so much perfection in works composed of many pieces and made by the hands of various master craftsmen as there is in those works on which but a single individual has worked. Thus one sees that buildings undertaken and completed by a single architect are usually more attractive and better ordered than those which many architects have tried to patch up by using old walls that had been built for other purposes. Thus those ancient cities that were once mere villages and in the course of time have become large towns are usually so poorly laid out, compared to those well-ordered places that an engineer traces out on a vacant plain as it suits his fancy. (7)

The work of a single, domineering architect, who takes complete control of every aspect of the project – a Frank Lloyd Wright, for instance – will be far better, he thinks, than an old house that has repeatedly been renovated by its various owners. Only by being built from scratch will the structure have sufficient unity and integrity to stand strong.

The same principle, he argues, holds when it comes to city planning. Compare Boston to Manhattan. Over the centuries the former gradually developed from a small harbor town into a large city. Marsh and wetland were transformed into solid ground by depositing vast amounts of landfill. The result, even today, is a web of small, crooked streets that follow no predetermined plan, and which is difficult for outsiders to navigate. Essentially Boston is a city of cow paths.

Manhattan also began as an outpost on a harbor and was originally populated mostly on its southern tip. But its growth was planned. Even before people moved northward on the island, a geometrical grid was laid out, with its roads perpendicular to each other. The further north a street was located, or the further west an avenue, the higher a number it received. As a result, it's now easy for anyone to find their way around Manhattan. Go south on 5th Avenue until you get to 18th street, and then take a right. No such directions can be given in Boston. Descartes clearly would prefer Manhattan. He doesn't like being lost.

Descartes deploys this metaphor to explain what he thinks is needed in order to attain real knowledge: a method, a systematic procedure whose purpose is to acquire certain and reliable, as opposed to merely probabilistic, claims to the truth. He develops a set of rules that, if followed, will lead to epistemic success. The first (and the only one we'll consider) is this:

> never to accept anything as true that I did not plainly know to be such; that is to say, carefully to avoid hasty judgment and prejudice; and to include nothing more in my judgments than what presented itself to my mind so *clearly and distinctly that I had no occasion to call it in doubt*. (11)

This passage begins with a platitude: we should think carefully and avoid hasty judgment and prejudice. Okay, no problem with that. But the last clause, the first rule of Descartes's method, is extraordinary and raises the stakes of his game immensely. Only a judgment that *cannot* be doubted, whose truth is so clear and distinct that it is *indubitable*, should be counted as a genuine piece of knowledge. But what sort of judgment could this possibly be?

The Cogito

To answer this question, to arrive at his foundational truth, Descartes (alone in his stove-heated room) follows another rule. He will "*reject as absolutely false everything in which I could imagine the least doubt*" (18). In effect, he establishes a test that can be applied to any proposition. To illustrate by example: I am looking out my window. "It's now raining outside," I say. Is that statement true? There certainly seem to be good reasons for thinking so. I look to the sky and it is dark. Water appears to be falling to the ground. When I stand up from my chair, walk to the window and look down, I see puddles whose surfaces are being punctuated by drops.

But do I really know for sure, with 100 percent certainty, that it is actually raining? After all, I've been wrong about judgments like this in the past. Perhaps what's falling from the sky is not rain but hail. Or radioactive fallout. Or perhaps my windows are so filthy that what looks to be happening outside isn't going on at all. Or what if I unwittingly have an eye infection that has distorted my vision? Or, to make this line of conjecture even more fanciful, what if Bob has spiked my coffee with a hallucinogenic drug that is causing me to think I see stuff that isn't there?

The point is this: my assertion, "It's now raining outside," is based on evidence gleaned from my senses. And these are fallible. As Descartes puts it, "*our senses sometimes deceive us*" (18). About this he is surely right.

And if they sometimes deceive us, how can we be absolutely sure that they are not deceiving us now? Regardless of how confident we are that what we see is real, every sense-based or empirical judgment is in principle dubitable. Therefore, if we are required to reject every assertion about which the least bit of doubt can be entertained, no assertion based on sensible evidence can be counted as true. I may be 99.9% sure that it is raining outside now. I can't, however, bump this up to 100 – because my senses have deceived me before.

Descartes asks himself another question: how can I be absolutely sure that my apprehension of rain outside my window is not a dream? After all, dreams are immensely vivid, sometimes far more so than waking consciousness (fractured as it is by continual stimuli). How, then, is it possible to prove that the vivid experience I now have of seeing rain isn't occurring during sleep? In fact, he says, it is conceivable *"that all the things that had ever entered my mind were no more true than the illusions of my dreams"* (18).

Descartes is fully aware that the skeptical doubts he is marshaling in order to challenge the veracity of sense-based judgments are wildly exaggerated. In fact, I am so confident that it is raining outside that when I leave my office I will bring my umbrella and prepare to get wet, and it makes obvious sense to do so. Descartes's approach here is deliberately hyperbolic because his scheme – cooked up in solitude in a stove-heated room – is designed to discover an extraordinary, a completely indubitable, truth. He tests his judgments so ruthlessly because he is searching for one that can withstand even the most intensely skeptical scrutiny.

To this end, he raises another disquieting doubt about our ordinary conception of knowledge. Consider the following problem in arithmetic: add 59432 and 79392, multiply it by 193 and then divide the result by 3. You know how to perform this calculation. If you were doing it with paper and pencil it might take a while, but eventually you'd get it. After all, you know arithmetic. Nonetheless, you must acknowledge the possibility of making a careless mistake in performing such a lengthy calculation. Even if you were tackling this problem on a calculator, error is possible. Your fingers might strike the wrong keys. Descartes generalizes, and again we know he's right: "there are men who make mistakes in reasoning, even in the simplest matters in geometry" (18). The lesson he extracts here is that because careless error is always possible, no judgment that results from a sequence of steps can ever be counted as completely indubitable. Every such judgment is vulnerable to error and therefore is subject to methodical or hyperbolic doubt. As a result, if there is to be an indubitable truth it must be one so clear – so bright, transparent, and visible – that it can be apprehended immediately; that is, without any prior steps leading to it. What truth this might be we will soon see.

The most epistemically destructive weapon in Descartes's skeptical arsenal is one he wields in another book (*Meditations on First Philosophy*), where he asks his readers to engage in a thought experiment. Imagine, he says, that there is a being every bit as powerful as the God we meet in the Bible. But rather than being supremely good and the source of truth, this one is *"an evil genius"* (62) who has devoted all his diabolical energy to deceiving us. In this wild scenario everything we see with our eyes or hear with our ears – indeed, everything we take to be external to ourselves – is no more than an illusion implanted in us by this titanic deceiver.

My office window allows me to see across the Charles River to the campus of the Massachusetts Institute of Technology. What if some super-geek over there has devised a computer so powerful that it has injected a virtual reality into my consciousness? While I believe I have a body, and it certainly feels like I do, in reality I don't, for my sensations are just the result of the program he is running. I think I see rain puddles on the ground below, but they're nothing but cyber blips so convincing that I take them to be real. Again, this sounds absurd – although it was the premise of the popular and much-commented-upon movie, *The Matrix* – and Descartes will eventually acknowledge that of course there is no such evil genius. But if there were, and if some truth could nonetheless survive in the face of such powerful (even if imaginary) opposition, if it could survive the ultimate epistemic test, then it would qualify as absolutely indubitable. Sure enough, Descartes believes he has discovered one such truth:

> But I noticed that, while I wanted thus to think that everything was false, it necessarily had to be the case that I, who was thinking this, was something. And noticing that this truth – *I think, therefore I am* – was so *firm* and so *assured that all the most extravagant suppositions of the skeptics were incapable of shaking it,* I judged that I could accept it without scruple as *the first principle* of the philosophy I was seeking. (18)

Called by scholars "the *cogito,*" which in Latin means "I think," this one judgment – *I think, therefore I am* – cannot be doubted for its truth is immediately self-certifying.[1] Maybe there is an evil genius who has infiltrated my brain and programmed me to think there is an external world, when in reality my body is actually lying motionless in an incubator. It doesn't matter. As long as I am thinking – in fact, as long as I am doubting that anything is true or that there is an external world – I can be certain that I exist.

Even if your imagination is so vivid that you can actually (sincerely) doubt the existence of your own body, you still can't doubt the proposition "I am thinking." And because "I" am thinking, then "I" must exist. Which means, according to Descartes, that you have just certified, beyond even the most preposterous doubt, that "I" exist. Hence, the *cogito* becomes the "first principle," the rock-solid foundation, of Descartes's epistemic edifice.

To reformulate: I cannot doubt that I am thinking because doubting is a kind of thinking. I cannot doubt that I am doubting.

Years ago, I gave a lecture on Descartes and his *cogito* to a group of senior citizens in a retirement community. During the question period, a man, not terribly old but sitting in a wheelchair, raised his wobbly right arm. He was suffering from what I took to be Parkinson's disease. His body was atrophied from top to bottom, and he could only speak haltingly. What he said, though, made a strong impression on me. He wanted to express his gratitude. For Descartes had taught him that "I" exist simply because "I" think. For this man, whose body was progressively failing, the *cogito* affirmed his very being.

The Existence of God

Even if you are on board with Descartes's train of thought so far, you must be careful. For the "I" whose existence has just been proven is probably not the "I" you typically take yourself to be. The *cogito* only proves that I am *a thinking thing*, or what we might call a *mind*, a "substance the whole essence or nature of which is simply to think" (19). As of yet, you know nothing about the external world, including your own body; not even whether it exists. Like Descartes in his stove-heated room, the result of his argument is completely isolated. I only know that I, as a thinking thing, exist.

Despite having arrived at the "first principle" of his philosophy and (what he takes to be) an indisputable bit of knowledge, Descartes's project is anything but complete. After all, his ambition is to discover "everything that is useful in life," and however clear and certain the *cogito* may be, because it is entirely divorced from the world we experience through our senses, it is useless. To apply the metaphor of building once again: however essential it is, constructing a solid foundation is only the beginning of the project. An edifice must rise upon it in order for it to become functional. Descartes's next task, then, is to bring back the external world; that is, to demonstrate that it too is epistemically accessible. He must show that our minds can grasp empirical reality and that our senses can provide us with reliable information. He must reconnect the mind and the body.[2] Having first raised skeptical doubts in order to demolish our confidence in our ability to know the world, he must next restore it. To do this, he must overcome the very skepticism he introduced at the outset of his reflections. In turn, this requires him to demonstrate that there is no possibility of an evil genius, which was the most powerful of his methodical doubts. If he can defuse the epistemic threat it poses, he will restore the trust we normally have in our ability to know what's going on in the world. And to do this, he must prove the existence of God.

Be careful. Yes, Descartes will offer an argument for the existence of God. His purpose in doing so, however, is strictly epistemic, not theological or religious. This sounds a bit weird, but be patient.

The rudiments of Descartes's proof of the existence of God are few, and can be expressed in the form of a dialogue. Imagine that you are an atheist and I am a theist. We've both read the Good Book and so we share a conception, however vague, of the God it describes. We disagree, however, on whether He exists.

I begin by asking you what it is whose existence you are denying.

"God," you say.

"Okay," I reply. "By your lights, God does not exist. But tell me, what's this God, the one whose existence you deny, all about? What's He like?"

"You know, the God who appears in the silly stories found in Genesis. The one they say created the world, is absolute, all-powerful, all-knowing and good. The one who smote the Egyptians."

"All right. How about this for a definition of God? The ultimate and best thing there is. The most perfect of all beings. The being that lacks nothing and greater than which there is nothing. Does that conform to what you've read in the Bible?"

"Pretty well."

"So, your position is this: there is no most perfect being. It does not exist."

"Right. The Bible peddles nonsense."

"Okay. So God is simply an idea that people entertain, but the idea has no correlate in reality. God is just a fantasy inside of people's heads."

"That's it exactly."

"Let's make sure we're clear here. In declaring your atheism, you invoke the idea of God, or the most perfect being, even as you assert that He does not exist. Is that fair?"

"Yes. I do have an idea of God. I also have an idea of a flying elephant. Neither exists."

"Got it. But you do concede, don't you, that there is at least one point of agreement between us. We both are thinking or using or entertaining the idea of God, the most perfect being, greater than which there is no other. Right?"

"Yes. But you believe it exists and I don't."

"Got it. Let's do this next. Let's get super clear on this idea. Let's analyze it; that is, break it into its component parts."

"What do you mean?"

"Well, here's an example. Take the idea of a triangle. By analyzing this idea, which is what we do when studying geometry, I discover that it is composed of three angles the sum of which is equal to the sum of two right angles. This is something I can prove and I don't need to measure the angles of every triangle in the universe in order to do so. Conceptual analysis by itself does the job. As Descartes put it, 'the equality of its three angles to two right angles is contained in the idea of a triangle' (20–21). The key word is *contained*. Packed inside the idea of a triangle is another idea: that of three interior angles. And then another: the sum of these three angles equals 180 degrees. So when I analyze the idea of a triangle carefully this is what I discover."

"All right, but I don't see what this has to do with anything we're talking about."

"Well, let's perform the same procedure with the idea of God. What ideas does it contain? In fact – and you're not going to like what I'm about to say – we're going to discover that the idea of existence is contained in the idea of God in the same way that 180 degrees is contained in the idea of a triangle. So, just as I say 'a triangle must have 180 degrees,' and know that this is necessarily true, so too will I say that 'God must exist.'"

"No way."

"Just wait. What you'll find is that you, who have the idea of God in your head but deny that it exists outside of your head, are contradicting yourself. Just as the idea of a triangle whose interior angles add up to 360 degrees does not make sense, neither does the idea of the most perfect being not existing. Therefore, it only makes sense to say that God exists."

"You're losing me."

"Think of it this way: if the most perfect being did not exist it would lack something and as a result it would not be most perfect."

"Sorry?"

"The idea of God – and an idea is all we're talking about here – is that of a being greater than which there is nothing. It is most perfect. If such a being did not exist, it would lack something, and this violates the idea itself. Therefore, the most perfect being must exist."

"This is nonsense. First of all, you're assuming that something that exists is more perfect than something that does not exist. But that's crazy. I think the grizzly bear that wants to eat me is better as a fantasy than as a reality. What's up with that?"

"Well, the man-eating bear is not a good, and surely not a perfect, thing. Instead, think of something you take to be good. Let's say a $20 bill. That's good, isn't it?"

"Yes."

"Which would you prefer? A real $20 bill, one that you can use to buy drinks in a bar, or an imaginary $20 bill? You choose."

"Dumb question."

"Maybe. But just listen to yourself here. When something is good, it's better if it exists than if it doesn't exist. This shows that existence is a positive. If God didn't exist, then God would lack that positive and therefore not be most perfect. And this contradicts the very idea of God as an absolutely good being. Therefore, God must exist."

"Nonsense. Think of the most perfectly bad thing. Say the Devil. Doesn't that have to exist too?"

"Not at all. There is nothing in the idea of the Devil that demands its existence. After all, by definition the devil is bad and so a fictitious Devil would be better than a real one."

"But the Devil is supremely powerful. It's just like God but entirely nasty. So it must exist."

"Nope. The Devil is a figment of your imagination. You took a conception of God that you got from the Bible and then pasted onto it the notion of evil, and came up with the Devil. But this is a very confused idea. You're kidding yourself if you believe that you understand the idea of the Devil. For it contains a monumental contradiction within it. God has been defined as the most perfect being. He can't be evil. So the idea of the Devil, understood as God plus evil, doesn't make sense and so can't exist."

"What about the most perfect flying elephant? By your lights, that should exist too. And it doesn't."

"The idea of a flying elephant, which you conjured by merging an idea of bird with an elephant, can make no claim for existence. It's just an idea. Nothing in it guarantees its existence."

"What about a perfect circle?"

"Same deal. I can tell you that all the points on the ideal circle, the one we study in geometry, are exactly the same distance from the center. But that doesn't mean I will find a perfect circle in reality. Only the idea of the most perfect being implies its own existence."

"This is getting weird."

"The idea of the most perfect being is weird indeed. It's an idea that catapults itself into existence through itself alone. In other words, simply by analyzing the idea of God we discover that, just as the idea of a triangle contains the idea of 180 degrees, it contains the idea of existence. You cannot think God without thinking that God exists."

"Then how come I do precisely that? I'm a professional atheist, for crying out loud. I say God doesn't exist for a living."

"That just means you're confused. You haven't analyzed the idea carefully enough and so you don't really know what you think. People who don't remember what they learned in school might say, and might really believe, that the interior angles of a triangle sum to 360 degrees. But they're wrong and if they carefully analyze triangularity – that is, if they study geometry – they'll see where and why they made their mistake. People believe stuff that isn't true when they're confused. And that's what's going on with you. God exists, my friend. Read it and weep."

Traditionally called the "ontological proof of the existence of God," the strength of this argument has been disputed for centuries.[3] For now, concentrate not on whether it is successful or not – although that is a task you should pursue in your free time – but on why Descartes is bothering with it at all. Remember, he needs to build a bridge between the "I" – the mind, the existence of which he has certified through the *cogito* – and everything else in the world. If he can't, then he is left with a useless foundation on top of which nothing will stand. He must, therefore, prove that something exists outside of his mind. And this, he thinks, he has done.

The idea of God, Descartes argues, cannot be a product of my imagination. For if the idea of God were only were a fantasy in my head, then it would depend on me. Now, I know I am not perfect. After all, my thinking is riddled with doubts and I regularly make mistakes. Therefore, if the idea of God originated in and thereby was dependent on me, it would be less than absolutely perfect. But this is a contradiction. By definition, the idea of God is of a being more perfect than which there is nothing. Therefore, God must exist independently of my mind that thinks Him. Descartes puts the point this way:

reflecting upon the fact that I doubted and that, as a consequence, my being was not utterly perfect (for I saw clearly that it is a greater perfection to know than to doubt), I decided to search for *the source from which I had learned to think of something more perfect than I was*, and I plainly knew that this had to be from some nature that in fact was more perfect. (19)

By carefully examining the idea of God, I learn that He exists independently of my mind. By itself, this is a significant achievement. It sets an epistemic precedent, for it demonstrates that something does exist outside my mind. And this is critical in Descartes's quest. God is a kind of bridge that connects my subjective consciousness to external reality. "I" am not alone.

There is another epistemic benefit to proving the existence of God, and it is enormous: the evil genius is vanquished. Recall that the wild fantasy of a being "supremely powerful and clever" – that is, as powerful as God – who is entirely intent on deceiving us, was the capstone of Descartes's methodical doubting. As such, and even if it is only a thought experiment, the evil genius represents the strongest possible objection to any claim to knowledge. But now that God has been proven to exist, the very concept of the evil genius is revealed to be a self-contradiction. God is absolutely perfect and so cannot be either evil or deceptive (both of which are imperfections). Therefore, no being can be the equivalent of God and also be either evil or deceptive. The proof of His existence negates the potency of methodical doubt and thereby restores our epistemic confidence. Most important, knowing that God exists, and the evil genius does not, restores our trust in the veracity of what Descartes calls "clear and distinct ideas." We can trust them to be true because God, in all His perfection, makes it reasonable to do so. He is no deceiver.

A simple example. You and I are sitting in a room. You say "it's cold" and I say "it's "warm." There's no point in debating who's right. "Cold" and "warm" are hardly clear and distinct ideas. So we agree to look at a thermometer. It reads 64 degrees Fahrenheit. We check this result against two other thermometers, and all read the same. You and I can now agree that this is the temperature of the room. We can throw out obscure words like "warm" and "cold" and replace them with a number, and then be more careful with how we talk about the temperature. Instead of saying "it's cold," you will say "I feel cold." That's okay as long as you don't confuse it with an objective judgment about the temperature of the room. If you want to comment on the actual condition of the world you must use statements like "it's 64 degrees in this room right now," for that expresses a clear and distinct idea. Because the existence of God has been proven, and we now know for sure that there is no evil genius, we can trust that such ideas are true. It really is 64 degrees in this room right now.

Descartes summarizes this line of thought:

> For first of all, even what I have already taken for a rule, namely that the things we very clearly and distinctly conceive are all true, is assured *only* for the reason that God is or exists, and that he is a perfect being. (21)

The foundation of Descartes's epistemic edifice is now ready to be built upon. Guided by the reliability of clear and distinct ideas, he can get on with the business of gaining knowledge of the world – that is, with the business of natural science – and discovering "everything that is useful in life"; that is, with developing technologies that apply the findings of natural science.

Two points before going forward. First, perhaps you've detected a potential problem in Descartes's argument. His method for attaining knowledge of the external world requires him to trust clear and distinct ideas. However, he needs to prove the existence of God before he can do so with a good epistemic conscience. As he puts it, "*if I am ignorant of this [the existence of God], it appears that I am never capable of being completely certain about anything else*" (71). But doesn't his proof of the existence of God itself rely upon ideas (such as that of perfection and existence) that he takes to be clear and distinct? And doesn't he trust these? In other words, when Descartes begins to examine the idea of God does he assume what he is trying to prove; namely, that clear and distinct ideas are trustworthy? In my business, this is called "begging the question," and it's a big time no-no. Is Descartes guilty of committing that crime?

Second, Descartes's arguments concerning the *cogito* and his attempt to prove that God exists show him to be a thoroughgoing **rationalist.** In its academic usage, "rationalism" refers to a theory concerning knowledge acquisition. Broadly speaking, it holds that reason on its own is capable of securing access to truth about the world. Traditionally it is contrasted with **empiricism,** the view that experience – specifically, sense experience – is the source of our knowledge of the world. Descartes is clearly in the former camp. Simply by inspecting his ideas of the "I" and of God he has discovered truths about reality. Since he doesn't need to use his eyes or ears to discover that both "I" and God exist, he could have performed these exercises in a completely dark and soundproof closet.

Masters and Possessors of Nature

However problematic his arguments may ultimately prove to be, Descartes believes that having proven the existence of the "I" and of "God," with the latter guaranteeing the veracity of our clear and distinct ideas, we are pre-pared to study the world; that is, to engage in scientific research. It becomes clear in Part 6 of the *Discourse on Method* that here his greatest passion lies. Once again, the architectural metaphor is apt. Yes, a strong foundation is crucial for the long-term stability of the building. But no one lives in the foundation. Instead, we inhabit the upper floors and, unless there is a problem, pay no attention to the basement. Similarly, once the *cogito* and God are in place, we can forget about them and get on with the business of daily life. And daily life for Descartes is the attempt to scientifically grasp (with clear and distinct ideas) the external world, and then apply such knowledge in the form of technology. Don't forget that at the outset of his autobiography he declared that his youthful ambition was to attain "clear and assured knowledge of everything that is useful in life." He explains:

> These notions made me see that it is possible to arrive at knowledge that would be very useful in life and that, in place of that speculative philosophy taught in the schools, it is possible to find a practical philosophy, by means of which, knowing the force and the actions of fire, water, air, the stars, the heavens, and all the other bodies that surround us … we might be able to use them for all the purposes for which they are appropriate and thus render ourselves, as it were, *masters and possessors of nature*. (35)

Physicists study the internal structure of the atom, and then engineers design the machine to unleash its energy. The properties of petroleum are comprehended, the geologists learn how to locate it underground, and the internal combustion engine gets its fuel. Geneticists discover the structure of the human genome, and then pharmaceutical companies manufacture drugs that alter the workings of our bodies. The results of the natural sciences, formulated in the language of mathematics, are applied to the world in order to achieve predictable, and useful, results. They allow us to master and possess nature; to make it bend to our will.

Despite his understanding of the natural world being miniscule compared to our own, Descartes was prophetic. He had a profound intuition of what the scientific revolution, of which he was a charter member, would unleash. Most perspicaciously, he grasped the vast potential latent in the science of medicine. He foresaw that as knowledge of the human body advances, bio-technology will become of towering importance. Not only will it allow us to maintain our health, which he describes as "unquestionably the first good and the foundation of all other goods," but it will enable us to rid ourselves "of an *infinity of maladies, as much of the body as of the mind*." As the last word just quoted shows, he glimpsed that the brain controls the mind. As a result, were he to be transported to Boston today, he would be fascinated by neuroscience and delighted by the way chemicals are being used today in order to treat depression and enhance cognitive abilities.[4]

Most optimistically of all, Descartes envisioned the possibility of forestalling "*the frailty of old age*" (35). He saw a future in which medical science, having comprehended the causes of disease, would generate bio-technical weapons to conquer death. When he was writing four hundred years ago this was no more than a pipe dream. Today, it is inching closer to reality as armies of researchers investigate what causes cells to age and then die. The hope is that if this can be discovered, then the process can be reversed.

We live today in Descartes's world. As every year passes the prospect of being able to master nature, master ourselves, through advanced technology becomes ever more imaginable.

Hume's Answer

 David Hume, *An Enquiry Concerning Human Understanding*

Ideas from Impressions

David Hume is every bit as consumed by the question of knowledge as Descartes. His approach, however, is totally different, for he is the *empiricist* par excellence. That this is so quickly becomes clear in Section II of his *An Enquiry Concerning Human Understanding* (1748), which is titled "Of the Origin of Ideas" (9). Like rationalism, empiricism is a theory that tries to explain how human beings acquire knowledge. For Hume, the answer is straightforward: from experience; more specifically, from sensory impressions, which are the *origin* of all our ideas.

Hume begins this section by asking his reader to perform a little experiment (which I tweak). Light a match. Then put your finger (briefly) into the flame. It's hot and it hurts. Now blow out the match and wait a few minutes. The pain has subsided. You can remember it but it doesn't really hurt anymore.

Or this: you have plans for tomorrow night, which include a fine dinner and a bottle of wine. Imagine sitting at the table and smelling the wine in your glass. Even if you feel the scene vividly, which may be nice, it's not the real thing.

Hume's point, one it's easy to agree with, is this: "*the most lively thought is still inferior to the dullest sensation*" (10). No memory, idea, or expectation – no thought – can match an actual sensation's vivid presence. "Ideas," Hume's term to cover all the cognitive entities just mentioned, are "*less forcible and lively*" (10) than sensory impressions. With such comments he begins to zero in on his empiricism.

The next step he takes is again to ask us to reflect on our own mental lives. It's not too difficult "to form monsters" (11) in our heads. We can think of a flying elephant, for example. Indeed, we can entertain the idea of just about anything we wish. Nonetheless, Hume thinks, our imaginations are actually quite limited:

> But though our thought seems to possess this unbounded liberty, we will find, upon a nearer examination, that it is really confined within very narrow limits, and that *all this creative power of the mind amounts to no more than the faculty of compounding, transposing, augmenting, or diminishing the materials afforded us by the senses and experience*. When we think of a golden mountain, we only conjoin two consistent ideas, *gold* and *mountain*, with which we were formerly acquainted. (11)

Yes, I have an idea of a golden mountain, even though no such mountain (as far as I know) exists on earth and so cannot be experienced. It's easy, though, to determine the source of my idea. I have seen a mountain in New Hampshire as well as the wedding ring on my left hand. To arrive at the idea of a golden mountain I combined the two. This, for Hume, is the constraint upon all ideas: they originate in sense impressions. He expresses the basic tenet of his empiricism when he says, "*all our ideas or more feeble perceptions are copies of our impressions or more lively ones*" (11).

This blanket identification of their origin suggests to Hume a general method for examining ideas. If you come into my office one day and tell me, with great enthusiasm, that you plan to visit a golden mountain located in New Jersey, I will calm you down by asking you to join me in analyzing this thought. You have no hope, I explain, of reaching your destination because the golden mountain is no more than a compound of two mundane ideas – that of a mountain and of gold – and doesn't actually exist in the world. Such a methodical clarification, or reduction, of complex ideas into their simpler elements, all of which are derived from sense experience, can be performed, Hume thinks, on any idea whatsoever. Most important, such a procedure is particularly useful when it comes to the abstract notions regularly utilized by philosophers. Much like Descartes, for whom traditional philosophy is filled with confusion, doubt, and dispute, and thus in need of a total overhaul, Hume is deeply suspicious about the puffery, the REALLY BIG IDEAS, deployed by the professors. To deflate their conceit, he demands they too pass his test:

> When we entertain, therefore, any suspicion that a philosophical term is employed without any meaning or idea (as is but too frequent), we need but enquire, from what impression is that supposed idea derived? And if it be

impossible to assign any, this will serve to confirm our suspicion. ***By bringing ideas into so clear a light, we may reasonably hope to remove all dispute***, which may arise concerning their nature and reality. (13)

Again like Descartes, Hume is out to defuse the seemingly endless disputes that have characterized traditional philosophy. (As a result, both would likely find the book you are presently reading, whose hero is Socrates and which celebrates rather than recoils from dispute, uninteresting.) He thinks that philosophical competition and disagreement, intractable for so many centuries, has arisen through carelessness. Intoxicated with fancy words like "substance," "essence," "mind," "existence," "nature," and "soul," philosophers forget to ask what they mean. Which is to say that they lose sight of the fact that all the ideas these words label originated in sensory experience. As a result, they end up arguing about what finally is no more than confused figments of their imagination. Their beloved ideas have no more reality than that of a golden mountain.

To sum up the disagreement so far: for the rationalist Descartes a proper analysis of ideas such as the "I" and God certifies their very existence. Even if I'm sitting in a dark and soundproofed closet I can think my way outside of my own head and into real existence. For the empiricist Hume ideas have no such power. They are rooted in sensory impressions, and the human ability to combine and reflect upon them, without which they would never even arise.

To elaborate, consider Hume's treatment of the idea of God. He agrees that it is of a being "infinitely intelligent, wise and good" (11). But unlike Descartes, he is ruthless in his deconstruction of it. By his lights, the idea of God "*arises from reflecting on the operations of our own mind, and augmenting, without limit, to what length we please*" (11). In other words, it's just like the idea of a golden mountain, which means that careful introspection will reveal its component parts.

I notice that I have the power to stand up from my chair, that I can solve an algebraic equation, and that I occasionally try to be kind to others. By inflating these observed qualities to the highest possible level, I come up with the Idea of God, a supremely powerful, all-knowing, and benevolent being. No wonder some of Hume's contemporaries suspected he was an atheist.

Principles of Association

Hume's empirical framework is now roughly established. More work, however, is needed before he can explain knowledge acquisition, and for one reason: impressions by themselves don't add up to much. In fact, were our cognitive lives composed only of them (or of ideas that correspond only to them), there would be total chaos.

Right now I am aware of light shining above me, cool air on my skin, green patches out the window, and an itching in my throat. I see a bright rectangle in front of my eyes, hear clicking sounds, feel my fingers moving. The list could go on. On the one hand, these impressions, received through different senses, are disconnected from one another. On the other, that's not how I actually experience them. Instead, the bright rectangle, my moving fingers, and the clicking sounds are apprehended as a single event: typing on a computer's keyboard. If this sort of amalgamation did not occur, if impressions remained isolated from one another, they would make no sense and quickly would become overwhelming. There would be chaos. But impressions are not apprehended as detached from one another, and they do make sense. Therefore, Hume reasons, what he calls "*principles of association*" (14) must be at work connecting them.

When I hear a low roar and see a large squarish object rolling through my field of vision the two impressions, apprehended through two different senses, merge into one. I take the first to have been caused by the second. That was a truck driving by. The clicking sounds and the dark marks appearing on the bright screen are similarly connected. My fingers hitting the keyboard causes them to appear. *Cause and effect*, then, is a principle of association. It is the connective tissue that holds together what otherwise would be a crazed cascade of fleeting impressions.

I see two objects in front of me. One is black and the other, somewhat smaller, is green. There's about a foot between them. Both are sort of cylindrical and have half-circles protruding from their sides. Despite their differences I don't see them as two entirely distinct objects. Instead, I see two coffee mugs. The *resemblance* – Hume's second principle of association – is sufficiently strong for the two impressions to merge into a single tableau.

Turning my head to the left, I see the black object and a brown surface. But that's not quite right. What I really see is a coffee cup, which is on the table. Because they are touching each other, because they are *contiguous* – Hume's third principle of association – the two impressions are coupled and become one.

These principles organize our experience of the world. Without them we would be continually bombarded by stimuli – brown shape, roar, clicks, flashes – and quickly become unhinged. With them at work impressions are rendered intelligible. Life makes sense.

Skeptical Doubts

So far, Hume's theory may seem attractive and perhaps even commonsensical. But pay close attention to the title of the next section of his book: "*Sceptical Doubts* Concerning the Operations of the Understanding." What seemed to be a straightforward, and perhaps reassuring, empiricist framework is about to get complicated. Hume's explanation of why needs to be presented in stages (which at first may not seem quite connected).

First, he divides all our reasoning, all our thinking and attempts to gain knowledge, into two categories: there are "*relations of Ideas*" and "*matters of fact*" (15). Here's an example of the former. You have an idea of a man named Bob, whom you've never met. Someone tells you that he's a bachelor. Now, think about this sentence: "Bob is not married." You know it's true. Why? Because that's what a bachelor is, what the word "bachelor" means. Even though you've never laid eyes on Bob, and you never will, you know that this sentence about him not only is but must be true. This is because you know that the sentence "Bachelor Bob is married" must be false. It must be false because it is equivalent to saying a "Bob is both unmarried and married." This is a *contradiction*, an assertion that two opposites belong to the same subject, which in logical fact they cannot do. As Hume puts it, a contradiction can "never be distinctly conceived by the mind" (16). Trying to grasp the sentence "an unmarried man is married" brings the mind to a halt, for a contradiction cannot possibly be true. As a result, simply by inspecting the ideas contained in the sentence "Bachelor Bob is unmarried" you can determine that without doubt it must be true. You don't have to do any empirical research since its truth is "*discoverable by the mere operation of thought*" (15). Even if you are alone in Descartes's dark and soundproofed closet, even if you never have met Bob, you can determine that without doubt he is unmarried. The problem – and this is the decisive break between the empiricist and the rationalist – is that such reasoning, however logical, discloses *only* relationships that obtain between two ideas, and nothing about the world.

The story is totally different with a statement like "it's 64 degrees in the room right now." Think about this sentence as long as you want, analyze its component ideas, be as logical as you can, and you still won't know whether it's true or false. The only way to find out is to use a thermometer. If it reads 64, the statement is true. In other words, empirical observation is required to determine whether it is 64 degrees in the room. For this is a matter of fact and not merely a relationship between two ideas.

On its own no "operation of thought" can determine whether a statement concerning a matter of fact is true or false, and for one reason: the contrary of such a statement is not a contradiction and so is logically possible. Saying "it's 62 in the room" is as equally intelligible as saying "it's 64." Hold on to this thought.

The second stage of Hume's argument reinforces a point made earlier. Reasoning about matters of fact – or we might also say, about the world – is "*founded on the relation of Cause and Effect*" (16). Only by putting this principle of association to work can we weave our impressions into a coherent unity. Without it we would be overwhelmed by stimuli isolated from one another – brown shape, roar, thing moving, instead of a truck passing by and making noise – and life would quickly become untenable.

Hume's central point is that by itself thought can discover nothing about causal relations. When a two-year-old child sees a candle on her birthday cake, she might squeal in delight and touch the flame. Naturally, it will hurt. The child had, thinks Hume, absolutely no way of knowing in advance that pain would follow upon her touching the flame. He explains:

> Let an object be presented to a man of ever so strong natural reason and abilities; if that object be entirely new to him, *he will not be able, by the most accurate examination of its sensible qualities, to discover any of its causes of effects*. ADAM, though his rational faculties be supposed, at the very first, entirely perfect, could not have inferred from the fluidity and transparency of water, that it would suffocate him. (17)

Even if the child were a genius, merely by observing a flame for the first time she could not infer that touching it would hurt. For this reason, having done so once she might even touch it a second time. If her memory is functioning properly, she will quickly associate the two impressions – flame and pain – and likely not go back for a third try. Hume's general point is this: "*causes and effects are discoverable, not by reason, but by experience*" (17).

Even without in any way observing bachelor Bob, I know that the statement "Bob is unmarried" is true. I do so because its contrary, "Bob is married," is a contradiction, which must be false. In slightly more technical language, I can discover the truth here by means of "*a priori*" (17) reasoning. This Latin phrase means "before" or "prior to." A priori reasoning takes place independently of experience. That bachelor Bob is not married I know before meeting him. For it is logically impossible that he be married.

By contrast, there's nothing contradictory about the statement "the flame does not cause pain." We can easily imagine situations in which flame does not cause pain: when someone is wearing a fireproof glove or has an artificial hand made from titanium, for example. That fire causes pain to a normal, unprotected finger is discoverable only by the repeated experience and then the conjunction of two disparate impressions. Causal connections, then, can only be discovered *a posteriori* – through reasoning that comes after, is posterior to, experience.

The third stage of Hume's argument follows directly from the second and takes us to the phrase found in the title of this section: "skeptical doubts." Because the contrary of every matter of fact is logically possible, it follows that knowledge of casual connections cannot be obtained through a priori reasoning. Furthermore, only a priori reasoning can issue in completely certain knowledge. The best that a posteriori reasoning can achieve is probable predictions. (It is quite likely, but not absolutely certain, that touching the flame a third time will again cause pain.) Therefore, Hume concludes, we can never be completely certain about causal connections. Since causal connections are the glue that holds together our experience of the world, we can never really be absolutely sure about the world we are experiencing.

The sun will rise tomorrow. About this we feel entirely confident. However, because the statement "the sun will not rise tomorrow" is fully intelligible – that is, it is not a contradiction – we cannot prove with absolute certainty that the sun will in fact rise tomorrow. Of course, you would be extremely foolish to bet against this happening. On the other hand, there are any number of intelligible, even if far-fetched, scenarios that result in the sun not rising. Perhaps a giant asteroid will hit the earth and produce so much dust that the sky will no longer be visible. Perhaps the sun will run out of gas and go dark. This is silly, I know, but Hume's point here is that the only basis we have for believing that the sun will rise tomorrow is our association of early morning and seeing the sun, two events that we have repeatedly experienced and then associated over the years. It is therefore not 100 percent certain – it is not a priori demonstrable – that this pattern will continue into the future. Such is the basis of Hume's skeptical doubts.

Or think of it this way: our confidence that the sun will rise tomorrow is based upon an assumption whose truth we cannot demonstrate: "*that the future will be conformable to the past*" (23). Of course, most of the time this principle seems to hold. On the other hand, life is full of surprises. The next time you put your finger to a flame there might be no pain. Perhaps someone slipped a fireproof glove onto your hand when you were sleeping. Unlikely, to be sure, but logically possible.

In short, Hume is a skeptic.[5] By his lights, human beings cannot achieve certain knowledge of the world. Be clear: it is his empiricism that leads to his skepticism. The world only makes sense to us because of our awareness of causal relations, and these are dependent on our ability to associate disparate events – touching the flame, feeling pain – that we repeatedly experience (and then remember), and on our (unprovable) assumption that the future will be like the past. No causal relation, then, can be secured through a priori demonstration. Hume generalizes:

> *The ultimate springs and principles [of the world] are totally shut up from human curiosity and enquiry* ... The most perfect philosophy of the natural kind only staves off our ignorance a little longer ... Thus *the observation of human blindness and weakness is the result of all philosophy*, and meets us, at every turn, in spite of our endeavours to elude or avoid it. (19)

Skeptical Solution of Skeptical Doubts

At first blush, the title of Section V is, or at least should be, puzzling: "*Sceptical Solution of These Doubts*" (25). How can skepticism solve anything?

Let us join Hume and grant that we cannot know with certainty that the sun will rise tomorrow. Similarly, I cannot prove that it will not snow in Boston in July of next year or that the sidewalk on Commonwealth Avenue will be intact when I leave my building this evening. So what? Lacking this sort of knowledge will not affect my plans for the future. Bereft of a priori knowledge of the world I still get along fine, and for one reason: I am guided by "*custom or habit*" (28):

> For wherever the repetition of any particular act or operation produces a propensity to renew the same act or operation, without being impelled by any reasoning or process of the understanding; we always say, that this propensity is the effect of custom. (28)

For as long as I can remember, the sun has risen every morning. Without giving it a moment's thought, I fully expect to see light outside of my window when I wake up. This is not because I have an a priori scientific theory at my disposal that predicts this event – after all, I am ignorant of astronomy – but because I'm so used to seeing light in the morning. I effortlessly move toward the future based on what I have experienced in the past, and the implicit assumption that the future will be like the past. In short,

> *Custom is the great guide of human life*. It is that principle alone, which renders our experience useful to us, and makes us expect for the future a similar train of events with those which have appeared in the past. Without the influence of custom, we should be entirely ignorant of every matter of fact, beyond what is immediately present to the memory and senses. (29)

Hume's point here is that even without firm or assured knowledge, human beings get by just fine. You cannot prove that your coffee machine will work tomorrow morning. Nonetheless, when you awaken and have gotten dressed you will head to the kitchen to fire it up. Very likely the machine is in the same place that it has been for years, as are the coffee bag and the measuring cup. Making coffee, then, will require almost no thought or attention on your part. It's just what you do, and have been doing for years. As a result, the entire process will feel almost automatic. This, however, it is not, for you are not a robot programmed to make coffee. After all, should you choose to do so, you can skip the coffee and go straight to work. This would probably make you feel a little weird. Habits so powerfully organize or structure our lives that they come to feel like "second nature." Breaking them thus tends to be difficult, but not impossible.

To reiterate the metaphor suggested in our earlier discussion of Aristotle (Chapter 4), habits occupy a cognitive gray zone. They lie in between actions exposed to the bright light of conscious deliberation, and mechanical ones over which the mind has no visible role to play. So, for example, your heart is beating now. You can't do anything about that (except, of course, blowing your brains out and making it stop). By contrast, raise your right hand and ask yourself, do I want to scratch my ear? There are reasons to do so, and countervailing ones to refrain. Which do you prefer? Whatever the answer, your next step will be guided, illuminated, by this deliberation. Going to the kitchen in the morning is not like this. Making coffee is just what you do. And yet the action is not mechanical. You can skip coffee just this once.

For Hume, habits extend far more deeply into our lives than we might suspect (or Aristotle would acknowledge). That I fully expect the flame to hurt when I touch it is the result of my having experienced the two events so frequently that, even if a causal connection between them cannot be proven, I nonetheless take to be connected. Touching a flame is followed by pain, just as awakening in the morning is followed by walking to the kitchen. No fuss, no muss, just custom, the great guide of life, doing its thing. Hume's point is that habit explains why we transact our lives with reasonable ease even though we do not possess certain knowledge. I cannot be absolutely sure that the coffee machine will be in the same place tomorrow that it was yesterday, but that doesn't cause me any grief. I still walk to the kitchen after I get dressed. Habit is so effective that it provides a *skeptical solution* to the *skeptical doubts* that Hume himself had uncovered when he was analyzing the possibility of acquiring knowledge of matters of fact. On the one hand, we cannot acquire a priori knowledge of the world. Nonetheless, we get by just fine.

Their divergent views concerning skepticism provide a convenient way of encapsulating the competition between Descartes and Hume. The former invokes skeptical doubts, but only as a tool that will allow him to overcome skepticism itself. He uses methodical doubt in order to arrive at an indubitable bit of certain and a priori knowledge that functions as the foundation of his epistemic edifice. Hume, by contrast, does not believe that skepticism can be overcome. Instead, his view of knowledge accommodates it. He transforms skeptical doubt into a solution. To clarify and elaborate his train of thought, let's turn to a contemporary issue, and see if we can imagine Hume's response to it.

Hume on Global Warming

As mentioned in Chapter 4, most scientists today agree that emission of greenhouse gases has contributed to global warming. In turn, they argue, global warming has caused sea levels to rise and more powerful and destructive storms to occur, a trend they predict will continue, and will ultimately have a negative impact on human civilization. There are, however, dissenters or "climate skeptics." These are people – some of them (usually politicians) bombastic fools; others (like Freeman Dyson) serious thinkers – who call these arguments into question.

While it is an observable fact that average temperatures have risen in recent years, that glaciers are shrinking and the sea level is rising, it is not absolutely certain that carbon in the atmosphere is the cause. That these different events are occurring (and measurable) is clear, but determining the causal relationship between them is another matter altogether. Perhaps glacier melt is the result of cyclical changes in the climate that would have taken place even if human beings had never started to burn coal and petroleum. In a similar fashion, one may doubt that the effects of global warming will be as dire as conventional wisdom takes them to be. Since plants utilize carbon, having more in the atmosphere might make crops grow bigger and faster. Perhaps a warmer planet will mean longer growing seasons in northern regions, which in turn will result in the production of more food. Even if these hopeful scenarios don't come to pass, it is conceivable that human ingenuity will engineer solutions to the rising tides, and civilization will continue to progress.

The Humean point here is that in the case of global warming – indeed, in every bit of reasoning concerning matters of fact – we cannot know for certain the casual connections that are at work. As he puts it,

> We are never able, in a single instance, to discover any power or necessary
> connexion; any quality, which binds the effect to the cause, and renders the
> one an infallible consequence of the other. We only find, that the one does
> actually, in fact, follow the other. (41)

In other words, correlation does not imply causation. Yes, glacier melt has
accelerated, and perhaps even at a rate proportional to the increased
amounts of carbon that have been deposited into the atmosphere. By
itself, however, this does not mean that the latter caused the former.

The big question is this: even if we agree with Hume that a necessary
connection between carbon increase and glacier melt cannot be demon-
strated, does this mean we should do nothing about climate change?
Because we cannot prove that burning more oil and coal will have disastrous
consequences, should we abandon the attempt to reduce our dependence
on fossil fuels? Does Hume's dictum that "the ultimate springs and principles [of the world] are totally shut up from human curiosity" imply that
we should stop doing research on global warming?

Imagine a law were proposed by the President of the United States that
mandated all coal-fired power plants to be shut down, and petroleum-
fueled automobiles be outlawed, three years from now. Less drastically,
imagine that in order to lower the amount of carbon that was released the
President proposed a hefty tax on all fossil fuels in order to discourage
their use. The climate skeptic might well say that these are really bad ideas.
It is likely, she could argue, that enacting such proposals would have
significant economic consequences in the short term. Jobs would probably be lost, productivity would go down, there could be social disruption.
Therefore, reasons the skeptic, because the long-term benefits of such
policies are impossible to predict with certainty, while the short-term costs
are more readily conceived, it is best not to shift away from oil.

Despite being a skeptic himself, it's not obvious that Hume would join
in the chorus arguing against climate research or environmentally conscious
political policies. First, you can be a Humean and still be a scientist. You
can't be an a priori scientist; for example, a theoretical physicist who does
nothing but scribble mathematical equations on the blackboard in the
hope of penetrating the depths of the universe. But you can still be an
empirical scientist, one who takes her bearings from observable data.
Empiricists, as Hume has shown so well, cannot achieve certainty. Nonetheless,
through meticulous attention to patterns of correlation they can make
predictions about the future. It is quite likely, for example, that the sun
will rise tomorrow. Therefore, it is reasonable for me to plan my day

around this expectation. As long as the scientist articulates her results with this sort of *epistemic modesty*, she can continue her work in the lab.

A great, perhaps even an overwhelming, number of climate scientists now agree that the atmosphere and the oceans are warming, that this trend will continue, and that it is caused by carbon being released by the burning of fossil fuels. Furthermore, many of them believe that the consequences of global warming will harm a lot of innocent people. None of them can prove that they are absolutely right. As a result, there is conceptual room for the skeptic to enter the fray. Nonetheless, just as we expect the sun to rise tomorrow even though there is no a priori demonstration that it will do so, a Humean scientist might argue that we should be prepared for, and try to lessen, what quite possibly will be the significant impact of climate change. Even though there will be short-term economic dislocation, which itself is difficult to predict, the Humean might argue that the potential for future disaster is strong enough to warrant taking action now. Once again, as long as scientific arguments are couched in the language of probability rather than necessity, and are accompanied by epistemic modesty, they can be legitimately promulgated even within the constraints implied by Hume's skepticism. In other words, his skepticism doesn't lead to paralysis or fatalism.

The same goes with political policies. Caution is surely needed. On the other hand, because the correlation between carbon increase and glacier melt is so well documented, and because predicted consequences are so dire, it might well make good sense for governments to act sooner rather than later. They probably won't. After all, long-term planning is not a strong suit of most governments. So we may just have to wait and see how bad it all gets. Then it might be too late.

Resolving the Dispute: Rationalism or Empiricism?

The issue is knowledge. Most of us think that we have some, at least once in a while. Few of us bother to think about how we get it, or what having it actually means. Both Descartes and Hume hold extreme positions, and so thinking through their competition can be philosophically fruitful indeed. For Descartes, knowledge obtained through pure or a priori reasoning – such as that secured by the *cogito* and the proof of the existence of God – gives us supremely valuable information about reality. For Hume, experience that begins with our eyes and ears is the source, but also the abiding limitation, of the epistemic enterprise. Descartes is extraordinarily ambitious. Inspired by the power of the human mind, he dreams about unleashing spectacular new technologies upon the world. Hume is modest and deeply chastened by the thought that many of our big ideas are really like that of a golden mountain. He's every bit as intellectual as Descartes, but he insists that our claims to knowledge must be rooted in experience, which itself can never yield to certainty.

Where do you stand? And how do any of us even begin to navigate such a monumental dispute? Perhaps the following question, which at first blush will seem to come from nowhere, might help: what do you think about **mathematics**? Do you find it beautiful and compelling, or hopelessly abstract and lifeless? More simply, do you like it or not?

I ask this question because in the history of Western philosophy the divide between empiricists and rationalists has often been marked by their divergent interpretations of mathematical knowledge. Hume, for one, thinks that arithmetic is no more than reasoning about relations between ideas. Knowing that "7 + 5 = 12" is on the same conceptual level as knowing that "Bachelor Bob is unmarried." These are analytical truths that tell us nothing about matters of fact; they give us no new information about the world. So, while arithmetic may be crystal clear and extraordinarily precise, it does not provide us insight into the nature of reality. A later rationalist (although he would reject this label) is Immanuel Kant. He thinks that "7 + 5 = 12" is not merely an analytical truth, but what he calls a "synthetic" one. What exactly this means is not important here. Suffice it to say that for Kant the ideas contained in "7 + 5" are different from the idea of "12." Something new is gained when the mind moves from the left to the right of the "equals" sign. For him, a mathematical truth does more than state a relationship between two ideas like "bachelor" and "unmarried." Kant holds a similarly positive view of our knowledge of causal relations. It too has an a priori basis, and so for him features of the world can be discovered by using pure thought and thus be known with certainty. He was a great fan of Newton's mathematical physics.

Plato is regularly identified as a rationalist. Like Kant, he was enormously impressed by mathematics. In the school he founded, called the "Academy," Plato required entering students to have studied geometry. He was confident, or at least hopeful, that pure reasoning could attain robust truth about all aspects of the world. By contrast, his student Aristotle was far more interested in biology than mathematics, and was far more of an empiricist. Like Hume, he insisted that the epistemic endeavor had to begin with simple sense perceptions, which he took to be the source of even the most sophisticated theories about the world. Indeed, he regularly criticized other thinkers for giving into flights of fancy and losing sight of the ground beneath their feet. One of his most succinct criticisms of Platonists is that for them philosophy had become far too similar to mathematics. For Aristotle, this is bad epistemic news for it is sure to lead to exaggerated claims and a loss of contact with reality.

Perhaps, then, the first step you should take before entering this dispute is to ask, does mathematics seem attractive and to promise great things? Or is it a drag? Are you skeptical about its applicability to other features of life? Of course, by itself such introspection will reveal no more than bits of information about yourself. Still, it can function as the first step in a long train of thought. Why do you admire mathematics? Is it the formal beauty, the clarity, the fact that a rock-solid yes or no can be discovered to its questions? Is it that mathematical equations can be used to predict the movement of physical bodies? Are you convinced that the scientific study of the world requires mathematics as its most basic tool, even its language? Does this lead you to suspect that at bottom the world has a structure that we, using pure reason alone, could access even if we were trapped in a dark and soundproofed closet? Or must we enter the messiness of sensible particulars, get our hands dirty, and then slowly work our way up from that? Is the dream of crystalline truth a pernicious illusion?

These are monumental questions indeed. Fortunately, we will return to them in our next chapter.

Notes

1   In the *Discourse on Method* Descartes formulates the *cogito* as "I think, therefore I am." But this is an inference, not an immediately apprehended truth. In the *Meditations* he reformulates it as "I am, I exist."

2   This argument has inspired what is now known as "the mind–body problem"; that is, how is the thinking thing related or connected to the body? Arguably, it is the most discussed topic in contemporary philosophy. For a good overview, see the entry "Dualism" in the *Stanford Encyclopedia of Philosophy* (http://plato.stanford.edu/entries/dualism/).

3   Saint Anselm's treatise *Proslogion* (1078) contains one of the first versions of the ontological argument. See http://www.stanselminstitute.org/files/Anselm Proslogion.pdf, chapter 4.

4   This may seem puzzling given that, when struggling with the *cogito*, Descartes became entangled in the mind–body problem. Do remember, however, that after the proof of the existence of God, he thinks he has the epistemic tools to solve it.

5   A challenge facing the Hume scholar is to explain the relationship between his *Enquiry Concerning Human Understanding*, the focus of this chapter, with his *Treatise on Human Nature*. The former puts great emphasis on his skepticism, while the latter (published earlier in 1739) itself makes claims to be a science, albeit a thoroughly empirical one.

7

Being in Time

The Question

When you're eating your pasta, are you already thinking about dessert? Do you make plans and tightly map your day? Are you restless, always anticipating your next move? Or does the past draw you like a magnet and do your memories, laden with regret, keep you up at night? Do you lose sight of where you are because you are preoccupied with where you've been? Or are you someone who can simply appreciate what's standing before you without measuring it against either what has been or might be?

How we orient ourselves in the flow of time shapes what kind of people we become. It may even be instrumental in shaping our philosophical views. In fact, the options we have examined in this book so far can themselves be mapped upon a temporal grid. Consider, for example, how the following philosophers give pride of place to the present:

1 Rousseau's critique of socialized man depends on his story of our "fall" from the state of nature. There the "savage" was spontaneous. His desires did not go beyond the immediacy of his physical needs. He ate when he was hungry, hooked up when he felt the need for sex and had an available partner, and took a nap when he got tired. Bereft of imagination, he was oblivious to how he appeared to others, and to the consequences of his actions. Like a child, he lived largely in the present. By sad contrast, in society our hyperactive imaginations keep us perpetually ill at ease. We worry, especially

Thinking Philosophically: An Introduction to the Great Debates, First Edition. David Roochnik.
© 2016 John Wiley & Sons, Inc. Published 2016 by John Wiley & Sons, Inc.

      about death and how we stand in relation to others. We live in the projected future, and so are invariably outside of ourselves.

2   In a similar vein, Lao-Tzu finds inspiration in the child. Immersed in the present, aimless, not contending, the child goes with the flow, and thereby instinctively practices *wei wu wei,* action non-action. "Sages," he tells us, "become the world's children."

3   For Nietzsche, the archaic mode of valuation, that of the good–bad distinction, privileges spontaneous, joyful, healthy action. By contrast, the moral dichotomy between good and evil, animated by resentment and the repressed desire for power, is forever chained to an agenda. Again, and as we will see more clearly at the end of this chapter, a child who lives in the moment, rather than a moralistic, socially responsible, God-fearing adult, exemplifies human being at its best.

Other philosophers invest heavily in the future:

4   Mill's moral theory is consequentialist. For him the measure of a good act is whether it will produce more happiness for more people. Trying to do the right thing requires us to get ahead of ourselves. He is at heart a progressive.

5   Aristotle is a teleologist. For him, living beings drive themselves forward toward a goal or purpose. When it comes to human beings, that *telos* is happiness, which means the full actualization of our rational capacity. Such an achievement is only available for someone advanced in years who has gained practical wisdom. But even having reached that goal, such a person does not cease looking to the future. As we saw in the *Politics,* for Aristotle human beings are by nature political. In order to be most ourselves we must assume responsibility for the well-being of our community. This requires planning and "projects," a word derived from the Latin for "throw" and "forward." The political person, then, is prepared for what's coming down the road. While it's perfectly okay for a child just to have some fun, a mature adult, the pinnacle of human development, is oriented to the future.

6   Like Aristotle, Confucius is a teleologist who thinks human development peaks at an advanced age. Young people should aspire to a future when they will become mature. And yet Confucius is also a serious conservative who takes his bearings from tradition and ritual. In this regard, he advises us to look to the past for models of character and behavior.

Even our epistemologically minded philosophers can be categorized in terms of their orientation to time:

7 For Descartes, the truth of the *cogito*, "I am, I exist," is self-certifying. It requires no experience or sequence of steps. Instead, it immediately presents itself to the bright light of reason. And his a priori proof of the existence of God purports to demonstrate that a Being stands forever present, outside of time itself.

8 By contrast, Hume believes that knowledge of the world is derived from experience. Touching the flame of a candle once will hurt you, but after touching it two or three times, a causal relationship will be forged, and you'll know better. Gaining knowledge takes time.

These miniscule sketches do no more than make a suggestion. Just as someone's orientation to (or in) time can decisively shape her character – or perhaps it's the other way around – so too might a philosopher's view of the world be illuminated by pegging it to one of our three time frames: future, present, and past.

There is another sense in which our relationship to temporality tells us who we are. For there are some people who despise the flow of time, and seek to escape it altogether.

You have a friend who is seriously religious. She believes that God is absolutely real and good, and that because all the things of this world (her body, phone, dog, pasta, friends, and memories) pass away, they pale in comparison with the permanent being of God. For her, it is only by turning away from the temporal flow and toward God that she finds herself properly oriented in time.

Another friend couldn't disagree more. For him the religious person is an escapist animated by fear. Of course nothing in this world lasts. When living beings die, he thinks, the particles composing their bodies disperse, and that's it. But he believes that temporality is to be affirmed rather than shunned. We live in time, that's all we've got, and our job is to make the best of it. Your religious friend, by contrast, disagrees entirely. She is convinced that at bottom ordinary life does not suffice. Something, she is sure, must endure.

Who are you? Someone acutely aware of how relentless time steals everything dear? Do you feel, in your bones, the insubstantiality of temporal being and therefore long for what is permanent? Or are you someone willing and able to go with the flow?

The last topic in this book – and likely the most fundamental – is what it means to be in time. Before beginning, be clear about this. What's at issue here is not the time studied by the physicists. Instead, it is the future–present–past flow as experienced by normal people in their everyday lives. As such, our question is perhaps better labeled as that of "time consciousness." On the one hand, this is something with which we feel deeply familiar. And yet few of us have ever paused and tried to figure it out. As Saint Augustine, the next thinker we will meet, puts it, "*What is this time? If no one asks me, I know; if I want to explain it to a questioner, I do not know*" (XI.14).[1]

Saint Augustine's Answer

 Augustine, *The Confessions*

Time and the Eternal

Augustine's analysis of time, found in Book XI of his book *The Confessions* (written around 400 CE), begins with him talking to God. Or you might say, with prayer. "But, Lord, since *You are in eternity*, are You unaware of what I am saying to you? Or do you see in time what takes place in time?" (XI.1).

Augustine's God is without qualification, and so is absolutely different from all finite beings. That is to say, He is *eternal*. This word needs clarification. A Greek god like Zeus is immortal and so does not die. Like us, though, he was born, grew up, and then reached maturity and the fullness of his power. Because Greek gods never get old, Zeus stayed at the top of his game forever. But he wasn't eternal and he regularly interacted with mortal beings. Augustine's God, by contrast, was not born. He is outside of, immune or impervious to, the temporal flow. To put the point in grammatical terms, when we speak about Zeus we use verbs in the present, past, and future tenses. But God requires only the first. HE just IS.

For this reason the stories we read about Him in the Bible are profoundly puzzling, even mysterious. How can an eternal Being, one who is exclusively present, enter into history or interact with a world in continuous change? How, as Augustine just asked above, can an eternal being even "see what is in time?" Wouldn't such seeing itself need to be "in time," which God is not?

The temporal and the timeless are two radically or ontologically distinct realms and thus, as Augustine puts it, they are "*not comparable*" (XI.11). ("Ontological" is derived from *on*, the Greek word for "being.") Being-in-time implies the continuous flow of a future passing through a present and into a past, while "*in eternity nothing passes but all is present*"

(XI.11). But the Bible is precisely the story of God's entrance into the temporal world (or history) where everything passes. How, Augustine wonders, can this possibly make sense?

He pursues this question, which all biblically based religions must confront, by pondering the first words of Genesis. "Grant me to hear and understand what is meant by *In the beginning You made heaven and earth*" (XI.3). How, he asks, could God have created the world? On the one hand, the biblical text supplies an answer: "You spoke and heaven and earth were created" (XI.5). But this cannot be literally true. For speaking requires the enunciation of a string of distinct but connected syllables, and thus takes time. An eternal God cannot speak in this sense because that would take time. His "speaking" of the Word – and this is the mystery – is thus "uttered eternally" (XI.7):

> Thus it is by a Word co-eternal with Yourself that in one eternal act You say all that You say, and all things are made that You say are to be made. You create solely by thus saying. (XI.7)

Strikingly, the theological conundrum of the eternal Word, of a saying that takes no time, that takes places in one undivided "act," parallels the fundamental human problem as well:

> Who will understand this? Who will relate it? What is that light which shines upon me but not continuously, and strikes upon my heart with no wounding? *I draw back in terror: I am on fire with longing: terror insofar as I am different from it, longing in the degree of my likeness to it.* (XI.9)

Augustine feels infinite distance between himself, a man aware of being irrevocably implicated in the flow of time, and the eternal presence of God. And this is terrifying, for it means that everything that belongs to us – our bodies, minds, devices, money – are nothing when compared to God. Nonetheless, we also bear, he says, some "likeness" to God. For we can think about Him. Regardless of whether we are believers or not, we can, at least through a process of negation, arrive at the concept of the eternal. It is that which suffers **no** change, is **not** temporal, has **no** truck with past or future tenses. It is completely **un**like ourselves and everything we encounter in this world. This cognizance of the eternal constitutes, however minimally, our likeness to it. And it is also what makes us so fully conscious of our own quick passage. Because we can somehow think (or imagine) the eternal, we feel ourselves coming up radically, poignantly short.

The theological problem sparked by the first words of Genesis remains. How did God create heaven and earth? How did the eternal enter into the temporal flow? To find an answer, Augustine gets to work on his analysis of time.

His first observation might seem trivial. Temporality is triadic for it is constituted by past, present, and future. His second seems equally straightforward, but implicit within it is a germ that will explode into full view as the analysis develops. "*The past is no more, and the future is not yet*" (XI.14). And the present is what it is only because it becomes the past. As such, the present "*is only because it will cease to be. Thus we can affirm that time is only in that it tends towards non-being*" (XI.14).

If this is true, then our hold on time, and thus on our own lives, is worse than precarious. What is now is only because it will not be. What is here today is only because it will be gone tomorrow. Augustine forces his reader to face the possibility that human experience, which is essentially temporal, is riven with the very nullity that characterizes the passage of time itself.

Fortunately, this analysis, so far entirely negative, doesn't quite hold up. Time can't be nothing because "we speak of a long time or a short time" (XI.15). Because we *measure* it, it must have some reality. But what exactly is being measured? If in meeting a childhood friend, I say, "It's been a long time since I've seen you," what am I calling "long?" It cannot be the past, for that "is no more." Because it is not, the past cannot be measured, and so cannot be long. Perhaps then, "a particular time was long while it was present" (XI.15). Augustine quickly reveals the failure of this answer. Is, he asks, a hundred years a long time? It certainly seems so. However, if only that-which-is is measurable, and if time is only insofar as it is present, then describing a hundred years as a long time implies that "a hundred years can be present" (XI.15). But this is absurd. For a temporal segment of measurable length is divisible and so contains within it past, present, and future times. "Thus a hundred years cannot be present" (XI.15). Of course, neither can a month, or an hour, or even a second. The only possible object of measurement is thus that "*which cannot be divided* into even the minutest parts or moments, for that is the only point that can be called present" (XI.15). The true present, or the "now," must be an indivisible moment. But there's a problem, and it's decisive. If the now is indivisible then it "*has no extent of duration at all*" (XI.15). Like a geometrical point, it has no magnitude and so cannot be measured. We do, however, measure time.

Faced with this predicament Augustine, no slouch as a writer, plays a little trick. He personifies the present and transforms it into the subject of a verb: "*the present cries aloud that it cannot have length*" (XI.15).

The present, the single time-frame on which all hope for being is staked, calls out to us. It declares its own absence. It has no duration, and so even the phrase "here today, gone tomorrow" understates the case. For nothing is really here today, since the true present is no more than an indivisible gateway between future and past, neither of which is.

This cry of the present echoes the problem Augustine uncovered in his reading of Genesis. God created the world by "speaking." God, however, cannot utter a string of syllables, for that would take time. So too the present cannot really cry out to us (for that would take time). It must, then, somehow make its absence felt even while remaining absent. It magnetically attracts, even as it eludes. Since the past is no longer and the future is not yet, only the ever-absent present can possibly be. And so we are "*on fire with longing*" for being-present.

The Cry of the Present

What Augustine has uncovered in this analysis is a basic feature of human experience. In our bones we sense that our temporal existence, our transience, might well be fundamentally unsatisfying. Aware of the slipstream that is our life, we seek refuge. We long for the present even if, or perhaps just because, it is what we lack. Here are some examples to explain.

Many of us can't sit still. Our bodies just won't do it. So too with our thoughts. They hop around like crazed rabbits and we think about dozens of things in rapid succession. We repeatedly check our e-mail and favorite web sites even when we're on the job. We fidget and itch to be somewhere else. We change the channel a lot. Another cliché makes sense here: "the grass is always greener on the other side." Never quite content with what we have, we always look elsewhere. Pulled by projects and possibilities, we throw ourselves forward into the future where we hope to gain a foothold. We cannot rest.

As his *Confessions*, his spiritual autobiography, makes clear, Augustine himself was a terribly restless person. It required decades of struggle for him to realize (understand, decide, believe) that only the eternal presence of God could pacify his restive existence. His book, which describes his journey, thus begins with this declaration: "*our hearts are restless till they rest in Thee*" (X). But Augustine's readers don't have to join him in the ranks of the faithful in order to take his analysis seriously. For chances are that, whatever your religious beliefs may be, you too are restless and much of what you do is an attempt (however unreflective) to repair your condition by heeding the present's cry.

Consider this question: why do so many people drink? What exactly is the lure of intoxication? There is, of course, the pleasurably warm sensation permeating the body. But deeper than this is the release that drinking brings. It frees us from the constraints of self-consciousness, of time-consciousness.

Why do you have a few drinks before going to a party? You're deliberately engineering a suspension of the everyday. Normally you're shy and insecure, and you don't talk easily to strangers, especially those you find attractive. You're worried that you will say something stupid and be rebuffed. When you're particularly self-conscious you tighten up and feel even more awkward. No matter how many times you tell yourself, "don't worry, just be yourself," you can't stop. But when you're smashed you can let loose and approach others without hesitation. You can speak without fearing the consequences.

The enormous lure of intoxication, and the source of its nearly universal appeal, is that it liberates us from the constraints of ordinary consciousness. Too often we worry about what we're going to do today because we're afraid to screw things up as badly as we did yesterday. But roaring with wine or drugs, we feel unified and concentrated. Caring not a whit about consequences, or about how we look or sound, we ignore the possibility of failure. We talk freely, sing, dance, twist and shout. We revel in the present. No wonder intoxication is at the root of both great fun and terrible violence.

Another example to illustrate the power of Augustine's insight is found when we're lucky enough to have some leisure, or free time. Unburdened by external demands, with no need to look at the clock, we can do just what we want. Frequently this is when we play. And when we're playing we're not trying to achieve a specific goal; we're just having fun.

What is striking about play, mental or physical, is how fully it absorbs the player. In a sporting event, for instance, the athlete is oblivious to anything beyond the limits of the court or field. Untroubled by the past and not worrying about the future, she operates within a world reduced to the tightly restricted space in which she plays. And therein the physical demands of her sport concentrate her on the task at hand. She is thoroughly immersed in the action.

What sport offers to the athlete, then, is a taste of eternity. This metaphor does not allude to anything mystical. Instead, it does no more than describe what it feels like to play. The player's heart is beating, and so as every moment passes she is one step closer to the grave. And yet, because she is so fully absorbed by her play, she is unaware of the flow of ordinary time. This is not to say that play is without duration, for of course it is. Nor is it to deny that within the play activity there is no perception of time, for especially in athletic competition, which requires a finely tuned awareness of an action as it unfolds into the future, there surely is. Instead, as in experiences of intoxication or intense bodily pleasure, when a player is maximally engaged she pays no attention to anything else. As experienced from within the activity, even if not in an externally measurable sense, she has broken free from the ordinary passage of fractured time. This is why both fans and players so passionately love their sports. They provide refuge from the bruising lives most of us have in the so-called real world, a world which, if Augustine's analysis of time holds up, isn't so real after all.

War exerts a similar appeal. Every object on the battlefield potentially threatens the soldier's life, and so demands his maximal attention. There-fore, despite its terrible brutality, war has invariably been attractive. In the fight everything matters, nothing is boring, there is no distraction, no regret or anxiety. This point is beautifully illustrated near the end of the film *The Hurt Locker*.[2] The hero, who was on a bomb squad in Iraq and whose life there was regularly at risk, returns home to his wife and child. Near the end of the movie there's a scene in a supermarket when he is contemplating a long row of breakfast cereals. He seems paralyzed. It is clear that this man cannot endure the peaceful tedium of domestic life. The camera then quickly cuts to Iraq, to which the hero has voluntarily returned in order to resume the absurdly dangerous work of defusing bombs. The present cries so loudly that some people – call them "adrenaline junkies" – put them-selves into life-threatening situations in order to heed its call.

A while back my wife was hospitalized with a serious illness. (She's better now.) During those days, one of which involved an ambulance and a visit to the emergency room, my life became narrowly focused. I spent hours with my wife who needed my help and attention. Despite this being a chal-lenging stretch, I didn't feel agitated. Instead, while I was sad, I also felt calm. Rather atypically, I moved slowly and deliberately, and felt almost peaceful. Something serious was going on and it demanded my attention. The immediate situation rather than frivolous worry or regretful memory took a commanding position on center stage. I had a job to do, and little else mattered. Strangely enough, the feeling wasn't all bad.

These days many people heed the cry of the present by practicing various forms of "mindfulness," a word now in wide circulation. They aspire to an acute awareness of the present; of their breathing, for example. Most of all, they seek release from the pressure of everyday life. Hoping to relieve stress, they make sure to go to their yoga class every week. Or, if their anxiety is severe enough to send them to a doctor, they may there be introduced to mindfulness-based cognitive therapy. They will be trained to sit and pay attention to what is in front of them, rather than allow their minds to scamper to a future unknown. They will be trained to calm down.[3]

These activities, and many more, can be interpreted along Augustinian lines. Human beings, aware (even subliminally) of the nullity of temporal existence, are magnetically attracted to presence and those activities that narrow our focus, force us to pay attention, and thereby make us feel alive. We relish those times in which we are (or seem to be) in the moment. Now, for Augustine, a man of the Church, the only true fulfillment of this longing-for-presence can be found in the worship of God.

The Subjective Reality of Time

"The present cries aloud ... that it cannot have length." Since it has no duration, and since both past and future are not, the human animal, arguably the only one with a highly developed sense of internal time-consciousness, is aware of its own passage toward non-being. For Augustine, however, this negative pole of the argument cannot have the final say. For "we compare one period with another and say that some are longer, some shorter" (XI.16). Time is measurable, and "we cannot measure what does not exist" (XI.21). The future and the past, there-fore, must somehow be. However, since being is located only in the present, *"whatever they are, they are only as present"* (XI.18). For past and future to be – and be they must since they are measurable – they must somehow be brought into the present. And this transportation, as we will see, requires an act of the mind. More specifically, it occurs through *memory and expectation*. Augustine explains:

> My boyhood ... no longer exists, is in time past, which no longer exists; but
> the likeness of my boyhood, when I recall it and talk of it, I look upon in
> time present, because it is still *present in my memory*. (XI.18)

Memory is the presencing of the past. I recall that yesterday I had a cheese sandwich for lunch, and an image of it appears in my mind. There were any number of events that occurred yesterday, but unless I recall them they are lost in darkness. Only by bringing a select few into the light of memory do they spring back to life. Such recollections are somehow brought into here and now. They are re-presented.

In remembering my childhood friend, whom I have not seen in dec-ades, what I bring to mind is not an external or objective being, but the *"impress"* (XI.27) made by him on my mind; something "which remains engraved in my memory" that I can retrieve. When I think of my grandfa-ther, who has been dead for decades, he is not gone or past. Instead, he is somehow present as the vibrant old man whom I knew well. I can, it seems, measure the length of his life because memory makes the past present and thereby gives it extension.

A similar operation occurs with the future:

> When we speak of seeing the future, obviously what is seen is not the things which are not yet because they are still to come, but their causes and signs do exist here and now. Thus to those who see them now, *they are not future but present*. (XI.18)

When I imagine myself at the meeting that's on my calendar for tomorrow, what comes to mind is not a future-which-is-not but an event that is now … in my mind. I'm sitting around a table with a bunch of other professors, bored silly. Like the past, the future is accessible only insofar as it is somehow made present.

To sum up this line of thought: because it is measurable, a period of time must have extension. Since it is extended it is divisible, and since it is divisible it is composed of the past and future. The measurable reality of time, therefore, depends upon the work of the mind, for only through memory and expectation can past and future be brought into the present, given extension and thereby made measurable. Augustine tentatively encapsulates this line of thought: "*I do not know what [time] is extendedness of; probably of the mind itself* (XI.26)." He elaborates:

> It is now quite clear that neither future nor past actually exists. Nor is it right to say there are three times, past, present and future. Perhaps it would be more correct to say: there are three times, *a present of things past, a present of things present, a present of things future*. For these three exist in the mind … the present of things past is memory, the present of things present is sight, the present of things future is expectation. (XI.20)

At this juncture, in another masterful writerly move, Augustine addresses his own mind: "*It is in you, O my mind, that I measure time*." An inward turn is required to discover the reality of time, and thereby the glue that holds our lives, irrevocably temporal, together. We find ourselves only within ourselves.

Reason to Pray

The operations of time-measurement and consciousness are exceedingly complex. (One twentieth-century philosopher, Edmund Husserl, devoted a significant number of pages to trying to figure them out.)[4] Fortunately, they do not need to be addressed here. For our purposes, what is of paramount importance is simply the fact that, even if the mechanics by which time's subjective reality is constituted were explained, awareness of our own transience would hardly become easier to bear, and for at least three reasons.

First, if Augustine is right that the past is an extension of the mind – that is, it lacks reality until memory works on it and makes it measurable – then it depends on the mind. And the mind depends on the brain. This means that if the brain is damaged and memory erased then the past disappears. When this happens to someone he becomes altogether lost to himself. You need only think of the old man suffering from Alzheimer's. He has almost no memory, and so in a terribly real sense he is no longer himself. For to be a self requires a meaningful connection between past and present. Indeed, the very possibility of personal identity requires memory. This implies that our hold on life, on ourselves, is stunningly fragile. One blow to the noggin and you're a goner.

The second problem is this. The processing of time depends upon the present. Recall Augustine's statement: "nor is it right to say there are three times, past, present and future. Perhaps it would be more correct to say: there are three times, a present of things past, a present of things present, a present of things future." And yet even if this saves the past and future from non-being by attributing to the mind the power to extend itself in both directions, the present remains as elusive as it has been throughout the analysis. It still has no duration and so it remains unclear how any segment of the past or future can be measured. "It was 40 years ago to the day that I last saw my friend." The day, however, is not a simple point, for it can be divided into hours, minutes, seconds, and so on. If the present is absent, then how can the past be "the present of things past?"

The third problem is that the past, whose "impress" is brought into the present by memory, can never be experienced as genuinely past. If I recall my long gone grandfather, he appears in my mind as a vibrant old man, even though I know he's no longer here. Because it isn't very different from the images I summon of friends who are alive and well, my memory-image of my grandfather requires interpretation. It is not just seen by the mind's eye, it is seen *as* the image of something past. As a result, it becomes very difficult, and perhaps impossible, to genuinely experience temporal distance between present and past.

Bring to mind a recollection of the vacation you took last summer. You got it. It's in your mind. As Augustine says, it's present. For precisely this reason it doesn't feel like much if any time has passed between now and then. After all, if the past has been made present then the interval between the two has been obliterated. In recollecting the past it thus feels as if no time has passed at all. "Time flies," we regularly say, and this is precisely the point. The past, when it is retrieved by memory, flies into the present at lightning speed.

When you think of last summer, the interval between now and then doesn't feel like much at all. When you think of being in high school it's the same deal. Now imagine that you're 88 years old and on your death-bed. You're looking back on your life. What do you think that's going to feel like? No wonder people are unnerved by the passage of time. Whatever the objective status of time may be (whatever the physicists may tell us), the subjective experience of it will always be that of flight.

Augustine understands that his analysis of time-consciousness leads to precisely this dire predicament, and so he cites a line from Psalm 31: "*But now my years are wasted in sighs*" (XI.29). He may be playing here, for in reality there is no "now" to which memory brings the past. Nonetheless, his point holds. Within the temporal flow there is nothing but fading shadow, and so there's every reason for us to sigh.

How to respond? We may flee from this terrible realization by getting smashed, or playing basketball, or practicing mindfulness, or augmenting our sexual pleasure. We may risk our lives paragliding or trying to scale Mount Everest. Or we may head to the poker table and the furious adren-aline rush of having money on the line. Or to the battlefield. Anything that grabs our attention fully and gets our heart beating by concentrating us on (what seems to be) the present. Anything that keeps our awareness of transience at bay. While such activities are intelligible as responses to the cry of the present, none of them, Augustine believes, adequately responds to the intrinsic unsustainability of temporal experience.

My years are wasted in sighs. The only truly appropriate or even reason-able reply, Augustine thinks, is to pray. For him, only a devotional relation-ship to the Eternal properly captures who he is as a temporal being. By saying, "*Thou, O Lord, my eternal father, art my only solace,*" he acknowl-edges his longing for the absent present. For God, who is eternal, who just IS, is the presence he craves but can find nowhere on earth. By his lights, then, we must orient ourselves to Him in order to make best sense of our-selves. In other words, for Augustine there are good reasons to pray. Doing so properly (accurately) acknowledges our temporality. It tells us who we really are. Creatures of a passing day, we long for the present.

The Nature of Sin

Religious thinkers who take their bearings from the Bible inevitably face a challenge. If God is absolutely good, and He created the world and all its creatures, why is evil all around us? On this question many a soul has foundered. As he reports in the *Confessions*, Augustine too suffered long and hard with it. He tells us that, until he became a fully committed (believing) Christian, he was "*on fire with the question whence comes evil*" (115). Finally, in Book VII, he explains the answer at which he arrived.

Augustine begins with the proposition that everything in God's creation, everything there is, is good. They have to be. After all, God created them. But some things are better, or "higher," than others. Inanimate things like rocks or trees, however beautiful they may be, are inferior to living beings. Because they can perceive the external world animals are superior to plants. And human beings, who alone possess the power of reasoning, are superior to all other animals. Since reason can apprehend immutable truths – such as "seven plus three equals ten" – it is the highest of all human capacities. In short, the created (finite) world forms a kind of ladder, an ontological hierarchy. Above it all stands God.

With this set-up Augustine can assert both that there is nothing in God's creation that is in itself evil, and that evil-doing, iniquity or sin, nonetheless exists. He explains:

> When I now asked what is iniquity, I realized that it was not a substance but a *swerving of the will*, which is turned towards lower things and away from You, O God, who are the supreme substance. (121)

The key word in this passage is "*will*" (which, you recall, is also crucial in Kant's moral theory). Human beings can freely make choices and then through force of will *turn* toward objects they deem worthy. Whether our lives are good or we become sinners depends on what those objects may be and how we orient ourselves toward them. So, for example, because God created them, the food and drink that nourish our bodies are good. These items, however, pose a risk. They can assume a significance disproportionate to their actual level of goodness. They're good, but not that good. Thus, if someone devotes himself to the pursuit of food, he becomes a glutton. If above all else he longs to drink, then he's a drunk. And if all that matters to someone is sex, he's a fornicator. Again, food, drink, and sex are not bad. Indeed, in God's creation nothing is intrinsically bad. To ⸱ Augustine's term, evil is not a "*substance*," a positive being in itself. ⸱theless, evil-doing among human beings is commonplace and per- ⸱ᵼ the default mode of human existence.

ʰor is useful here. Things of this world, especially our bodies, ⸱ational pull on the human will. They attract and drag us ⸱ᵐ. They do so precisely because they are good. (Perhaps ⸱Mill's distinction between higher and lower pleasures.)

Unfortunately, it's easy to forget that they are not that good, and shrivel when compared to God. What is required, then, is to acknowledge and appreciate finite things of the world for what they really are – pretty good or not bad – and to keep them in their proper place within the ontological hierarchy, or what medieval philosophers called the *scala naturae*.[5] We should enjoy our dinner, but before eating we should thank God for the food on our table. Doing so is a reminder that God, absolutely good and permanent, is ontologically superior to what's on the plate, which is nice but temporary. We should enjoy having sex, but only within the consecrated institution of marriage. Wine should be drunk but only after saying a blessing. These exercises keep our eyes on the prize. Only God truly IS. Saying our prayers brings reality into better focus and reminds us of who we are.

Evil-doing occurs when people fail to resist the gravitational force exerted by items lower on the ontological totem pole. Instead of taking them for what they really are, the sinner swerves toward and absolutizes them. As Augustine puts it in another book, *On Free Choice of the Will*,

> Sins come about when someone *turns* away from divine things that truly persist and toward changeable and uncertain things. These things do have their proper place, and they have a certain beauty of their own; but when a perverse and disordered soul pursues them it becomes enslaved to the very things that divine order and law command it to rule over. (27)

Augustine's account of evil-doing can be reviewed through the lens of his analysis of time-consciousness. Tonight's elegant dinner and delicious wine, as well as the tumble in bed we look forward to soon thereafter, are transient. Like everything else on the menu, they are only insofar as they tend toward non-being. Awareness of this overwhelming fact drives us to seek what is present, and we do this in any number of unreflective ways: getting smashed, playing basketball, and so on. By contrast, Augustine recommends **conversion**, a word whose Latin root is *vertere*, "to turn around." Indeed, the *Confessions* tells the story of how he himself, after decades of struggle, finally turned to God. Weaving together philosophical reflection with prayer and autobiography, this book makes the case that such an orientation to the eternal, to God, is the only reasonable stance for a self-consciously temporal creature to take.

From all this it follows that the great threat to human existence is **perversion**, whose Latin root means "turn away." By swerving away from God and identifying ourselves with smaller things we sin – not because those things are bad, but because they are temporal.

Augustine's ideas may seem congenial to some of you. To others they may sound like total rubbish, and you're itching to ask, "but what if God doesn't exist?" Perhaps surprisingly, the strength of his analysis of time-consciousness, and his conclusion that prayer is a logical response to it, isn't entirely compromised even if God is merely a fantasy. For if he's right about the subjective reality of the temporal flow, then it becomes reasonable for us to direct our attention beyond the temporal; that is, to turn to what is eternal, to what is present (even if it doesn't exist). As suggested above, many of us unreflectively do this when we drink or play basketball. There is also another possibility: namely, that the search for the eternal take place in the domain of the theoretical. To explain, let us take two abrupt but brief digressions, both of which were prefigured at the end of Chapter 6.

Digression 1: Pythagoras

Scholars tell us that Pythagoras was born in approximately 570 BCE. None of his writings, if there were any, survived, and so he really is more of a legend than a historical figure. Nonetheless, there was a school of thinkers called "Pythagoreans," and about them we do know a little.

First and foremost, the Pythagoreans believed that numerical relations or ratios constitute the intelligible structure of reality. "*They supposed the elements of numbers to be the elements of all existing things*" (19). At its core the world is mathematical. A prime example of this, one that may even have inspired Pythagoras himself, is music.

Imagine the following (entirely fictional) scenario. Young Pythagoras comes upon a musician preparing to give a performance on the lyre, the ancestor of the guitar. He watches him tune his instrument. The player strums all the strings and then tightens or loosens each one individually until the chord sounds right. His instrument has produced a harmony and so he begins to play. Pythagoras is enjoying the music when he suddenly has an epiphany. Strings of different lengths result in sounds at different pitch. The lovely tune he is listening to has thus been produced not just by the strings, but by the relationship between their lengths; in other words, v a *ratio*. Even though a physical object generates the sound, which in ˙ is perceived by the ears, it is grounded upon a mathematical relation-ʰich itself is neither physical nor can be heard.

ʰras then notices that a very similar sound or harmony is pro-
ˑcond lyre tuned by another musician. When a third musician,
ˑument closely resembling the first two, steps on stage and
same tune, he realizes that the three chords, produced
ˑsical objects, are in one sense identical. They are each

sensible manifestations of the same one numerical ratio embodied in the strings of the instruments. The strings by themselves are not responsible for the music he enjoys. Instead, it is the relation between them, or ratio, they share.

Stunned by his realization, Pythagoras entertains a radical thought. What if everything we hear, see, smell, taste, and touch, what if the entire sensible world, is organized around just such ratios? What if, to borrow a metaphor used much later by Galileo, *"the book of nature is written in mathematical characters?"*

For the Pythagorean, nature, like a book, can be read; that is, it is intelligible and can be comprehended by the human mind. But the surface sheen of natural things, the ones we detect with our eyes and ears, doesn't reveal their deepest reality. For that is found only in the mathematical relations, themselves imperceptible, that somehow lie behind, structure, and make possible all sensible phenomena. Such ratios can be apprehended only by the mind. As one Pythagorean saying has it, *"all things that are known have number. For without this nothing whatever could possibly be thought of or known"* (19).

The next step in the scenario is this. The first of the lyre players carelessly leaves his instrument on the ground, and someone steps on it. Shattered into pieces, it is ruined. The second musician, however, has no problem reproducing the same chord on his instrument. Unfortunately, he too leaves his lyre unprotected and it too is stepped upon. The third musician can still play the chord. Witnessing this sequence of events, Pythagoras realizes that the ratio underlying the production of the harmony endures even though the physical objects generating the sounds he hears are transient. They come to be and then pass away, but the numerical structure of the chord remains. Purely intelligible, accessible only to thought, permanent and changeless, numbers are more stable, more real, than the physical manifestation of ratios in the music produced by a well-tuned lyre.

Like Augustine, Pythagoras takes reality to be like a ladder; it is ontologically stratified. Some beings, such as the lyre and the music we hear with our ears, are lower than others. They are physical, come to be and pass away, and change all the time. By contrast, the ratio responsible for the chord, composed of numbers alone, just is and will never be otherwise. Only its sensible and therefore temporary manifestation is heard when the musician plays his instrument. The ratio itself, by contrast, can be accessed only by the rational mind. (The Greeks would have used the word "soul," which in Greek is *psuchê*, the root of our words "psyche" and "psychology.")

The next step in the argument goes thus: since the soul apprehends the ratios, there must be a basic affinity between the two. Since the ratios are non-sensible and permanent then, the thinking goes, so too is the soul. Indeed, this is precisely what the Pythagoreans believed. They held the doctrine of metempsychosis or reincarnation. On their view, the soul/ mind was not physical and did not die.

The point here is only this: a philosopher need not be a believing Christian to think that there is a non-sensible, changeless, and eternal reality toward which the human mind should turn. Many thinkers imbued with the spirit of Pythagoreanism – and this includes rationalists like Descartes and physicists like Galileo, Newton, and Einstein – take the world to be grounded on a mathematical infrastructure accessible to rational thought. Some of them also held the corresponding belief that the soul or mind apprehending such immutable truth itself neither comes to be nor passes away. You don't have to agree with this cluster of ideas to see that at least they make some sense.

Augustine himself has a Pythagorean streak, to which he gives full voice in *On Free Choice of the Will*. Here he creates a dialogue between himself and a character named Evodius. His first task is to persuade Evodius that human reason is the best or highest of all human capacities. He does so by citing arithmetic as his example:

> When I perceive something with the bodily sense, such as the earth and sky and the other material objects that I perceive in them, I don't know how much longer they are going to exist. But I do know that *seven plus three equals ten, not just now, but always.* (44)

An arithmetical fact is true for all time. It does not change in the slightest and is the same for all who apprehend it through the "inner light" (46) of their minds. Augustine wants his friend to understand that the rational capacity of the mind to apprehend the immutable truth of arithmetic is higher than, ontologically superior to, the body and its senses. Unlike this or that perception, rational truth is indisputable, inexhaustible, and universal. Therefore, the mind that apprehends such truth is higher than physical things. As he puts it, "when I contemplate within myself the unchangeable truth of numbers ... I am far removed from material objects" (52).

The hierarchy, the *scala naturae*, is set. There are physical things such as rocks, then bodily senses that apprehend them. Then there is the human soul that, through the use of reason, can apprehend the intelligible reality of number. Then there are numbers themselves. Infinite and unchangeable, they are permanent fixtures of the universe that, just as the Pythagoreans thought, are responsible for the intelligibility of the sensible world.

In the next passage, Augustine introduces a crucial new term:

> Consider the heavens and the earth and the sea and everything in them that shines from on high or crawls here below, everything that flies or swims. They have *forms* [they are intelligible] because they have numbers; take away their *form* and number and they will be nothing. (60–61)

In trying to convince Evodius to "convert," to turn away from what is sensible or transient – that is, everything found in the temporal world – and toward the intelligible-eternal, Augustine asks him to pay strict attention to *forms*. The next digression will elaborate and try to explain. Before moving to that, however, consider these last words from Saint Augustine. He exhorts Evodius to *"cast aside all attachments to times and places and apprehend that which is always one and the same"* (60). He is trying to pry his friend away from particulars – that is, from this house or that painting or person – and instead turn his attention to what is universal, eternal, and self-same; to, in other words, God. Here the key point of this digression is laid bare. A Christian thinker like Augustine and a mathematical-ontologist like Pythagoras have something in common. Both subordinate the sensible world, which is always particularized, to the eternal. One does it through prayer while the other does it through mathematical physics. Both are coherent responses to the structure of time-consciousness. Here today, gone tomorrow. Time flies. But not number, not being, not God, not *forms*. This last word is all-important to yet another great thinker: Plato.

Digression 2: Platonic Forms

In our daily lives we typically don't have much trouble getting by, and for one big reason. Things out there have a shape or form. Walk into a classroom and you know where to sit: on a chair. There are dozens of things scattered around, but you ignore the podium and head straight for a chair. Regardless of what color they are, or whether they're made of metal or wood, chairs all look roughly the same. Their visible shape tells you that any one of them is suitable for sitting. You don't have a problem navigating the room because chairs share a distinctive "look." (The Greek word *eidos*, translated as "form," is derived from the verb "to see.")

In the history of Western philosophy, the word "form" is most closely associated with Plato. To get some sense of why, we will briefly discuss a short passage from the *Phaedo*. We must do so, however, in tandem with an idea closely related to it: what Socrates calls "recollection."

If you recollect something, you must have known it before. So, for example, if your friend Bob plays the guitar, and you see a guitar, you might think of or recollect Bob. More directly, if you see a reasonably good picture of Bob on your phone, the real Bob will come to mind. Both the guitar and the picture are reminders, but in different ways. One of them is unlike, while the other is like, the recollected item, which we can call the "original."

If the reminder is like the original, it must also be unlike it. In seeing Bob appear on your phone, you are aware that, however close the resemblance, what's on the screen isn't Bob himself. Instead, it's *only an image*. This you know because the image falls short of the original in some way. In this case, it is two-dimensional, while the real Bob is three-dimensional. Seeing an image, then, is actually a kind of double-seeing. In looking at your phone you see both what's on the screen and what it reminds you of: the real thing, old Bob himself. In other words, you see the picture as a picture of, *as an image of*, the original.

With these notions on the table, Socrates continues. He asks you to imagine that you are holding two sticks. They seem to be of equal length, but you're not sure. So you pull out your ruler. Both measure at five inches and so you say with confidence, "yes, they're equal." True to form, Socrates challenges your claim. He grants that the two sticks are equal in length (even though they are not perfectly so; after all, your ruler is a rather imprecise measuring device). But he then demands that you put both of them on a scale. One weighs three ounces, the other four. The sticks are unequal in this respect. Socrates makes much of this fact. "Do not equal stones and sticks sometimes, while remaining the same, *appear to be equal in one way and in another way to be unequal?*" (74b). He elaborates. The two sticks you're holding in your hand, as you now realize, are only imperfectly equal; that is, they are both equal (in length) and unequal (in weight). But this realization contains within it another. To determine that something is imperfect you must invoke a standard in comparison to which it falls short. The realization that the equality of the two sticks or two stones is imperfect thus requires you, however implicitly, to invoke an idea of pure and perfect equality; that is, equality that is in no way contaminated by inequality. This Socrates calls this "the Equal Itself" or the "Form of the Equal."

> Consider, Socrates said, whether this is the case: we say that there is something that is equal. I do not mean a stick equal to stick or a stone to stone, or anything of that kind, but something else beyond all these, *the Equal Itself.* (74a)

He continues:

> Whenever someone, on seeing something, realizes that that which he now sees wants to be like some other reality but *falls short and cannot be like that other reality since it is inferior*, do we agree that one who thinks this must have *prior* knowledge of that to which he says it is like, but *deficiently* so? (74e)

I'm not a great basketball player. One reason I'm confident in this self-assessment is that I know that LeBron James could score against me at will and prevent me from even releasing a shot if he chose to do so. Without being aware of his superiority, how would I know that I'm way down on the basketball scale? Awareness of imperfection requires a corresponding awareness of a standard against which the imperfection is detected. As such, it is a reminder of perfection. The equality (in length) of the two sticks that I detect with my senses and my ruler is similar to the Form of the Equal. It is also different, for like everything else that we see with our eyes or touch with our hands it is deficient. After all, the two sticks are unequal in weight and only approximately equal in length. But the Form of the Equal, which is what we invoke in our measurements, has not a smidgen of inequality associated with it. Even if we aren't thinking about it, it must somehow be present in order for us to become aware of the imperfect equality of the two sticks I'm holding in my hands. In short, the sensible and measurable equality of the two sticks is but an image of an original: the Equal Itself.

This argument can be generalized. Aware that our lives are shot through with imperfection from start to finish, we are restless, dissatisfied creatures who move forward, eager to improve. For Plato, such awareness is the motive force that energizes our lives. Our experience, so impressive in its deficiency, is a reminder that there must be something more, something perfect, and an incentive to seek it. We are surrounded by images but long (or should long) for originals.

This train of thought is similar to that which animates Augustine as he speaks with Evodius. Everything "that shines from on high or crawls here below, everything that flies or swims," everything that we can apprehend through our senses, is deficient. But it can serve as a push toward what is eternal and unchanging; what is perfect. Such a realization can and should be transformative.

Another example: you and I are having a heated discussion about the American practice of using drones to kill terrorists. While we agree that it is just to kill terrorists who are planning to kill us, I maintain that drone strikes are unjust because innocent people regularly die in such attacks.

You counter by saying that the policy is a good one, for with their great accuracy drones limit civilian casualties. But how, I ask, can the military be sure that the target is actually a terrorist who plans to do harm?

In entering this debate we assume that, at least in principle, it can be resolved. If you and I really believed that it was impossible to answer the question, "what is just?" then there would be no point in us debating whether it is just to use drones to kill terrorists. Our disagreement would have to be chalked up to our personal preferences, and left at that. But we do converse and so we must believe that there is a point; that, in other words, in principle the debate can be resolved. And what would resolve it is an answer to the question, what is just? According to Plato, such an answer would require an articulation of the Form of Justice. For him, our ordinary conversations, especially those in which we disagree but keep talking, are evidence of the presence of the Forms, the ultimate adjudicators that we assume must be there, even if we are unsure of what they are.

For Plato, what makes someone a philosopher is the desire to figure out what these Forms are; that is, to pursue questions like, "what is justice?" By his lights, the world we encounter with our senses, and that we talk about in ordinary conversation, is ultimately no more than a reminder or an image of a higher reality, that of the Forms.

The next move Socrates makes in the *Phaedo* is to identify where this knowledge of the Forms might come from. The Form of the Equal is perfect, universal, and objective. By contrast, nothing we see with our eyes or touch with our hands is perfectly equal. Therefore, we could not have acquired knowledge of the Form through our senses. As he puts it,

> Whence have we acquired the knowledge of it? Is it not from the things we mentioned just now, from seeing sticks or stones or some other things that are equal we come to think of [the Equal Itself], which is *different* from them? Or doesn't it seem to you to be *different*? (74b)

The sensory apprehension of the two sticks, whose equality is tarnished with inequality, is a reminder of perfect equality, or the Form of the Equal. This awareness of the Form cannot itself be derived from sensible experience, which always fall short. Instead, it must be "prior" to sensible experience:

> We must then possess knowledge of the Equal *before* that time when we first saw the equal objects and realized that all these objects strive to be like the Equal but are deficient in this. (74e)

The Forms are prior to and make possible our experience of the sensibles. Here we should be reminded of our earlier discussion of Hume (in Chapter 6). He used the Latin phrase *a priori* to describe the sort of knowledge that is independent of experience. His example was 7 + 5 = 12. For him, this statement articulates a relation that obtains between ideas and needs no experience or empirical data in order to be confirmed as true. My own example of an a priori truth was the sentence, "bachelor Bob is not married." We do not need to examine the flesh-and-blood man in order to determine that this statement not only is but must be true. By contrast, the statement "the flame caused my finger to hurt" is one that can only be derived, and so is dependent upon (or posterior to) experience. Only through my memory of repeated experiences of the flame and pain in my finger do I associate the two and make this inference. On Hume's view, all our knowledge of the world, of causal relations, is like this. It is, to use another Latin phrase, *a posteriori*; that is, dependent upon and so "after" experience. He is an empiricist.

Plato, like Pythagoras, disagrees. He's a rationalist. For him the mind itself affords us access to the basic structures or Forms that make our experience of the world intelligible. Our encounter with the sensible particulars is not the source or origin of knowledge of the Forms, but only a reminder that they are there.

Like Augustine, Plato too is in the "conversion" game. Remember, this word is derived from the Latin *vertere*, "to turn around." Augustine wants Evodius to "cast aside all attachments to times and places and apprehend that which is always one and the same"; that is, to turn away from particulars and to redirect his longing toward the eternal God. Plato wants us to conceive of sensible things as reminders that propel us into the greatest of all rational enterprises; namely, comprehending the Forms. We are aware that the two sticks, equal in length, are also unequal. Such equality falls short of perfect equality. And so we must ask, "what is equality?" In doing so we assume that the question can be answered. We assume we have a priori access to the Form of Equality. A full articulation of the Forms then becomes the object of our longing. We become philosophers, lovers of wisdom.

Next, Socrates takes the same leap as the Pythagoreans. Because there must be intelligible Forms that make our sensible experience possible, and because our mind has a priori access to them, there is a fundamental affinity between our soul and the Forms. They are both non-sensible and independent of the changing world. In short, Socrates argues in the *Phaedo* that the soul is immortal. Whether his arguments are any good is another question, one that you should pursue on your own by reading the whole dialogue.

To sum up: Augustine, Pythagoras, and Plato belong in the same camp. They are uncomfortable, restless souls, dissatisfied with ordinary (sensible) things that come and go. They strive for what is timeless, whether that be God, mathematical structure, or intelligible Form. They are human animals who rebel against their own animality. They are in time but long to go beyond. They want what seems impossible: to jump out of their own skin.

No thinker in the history of Western philosophy has been more hostile to this way of thinking – this way of living – than Friedrich Nietzsche. To him we turn next.

Nietzsche (on Heraclitus) on Time

 Friedrich Nietzsche, *Philosophy in the Tragic Age of the Greeks*

Becoming

One of Nietzsche's more interesting works is a little book titled *Philosophy in the Tragic Age of the Greeks* (1873). In it he discusses a group of early Greek philosophers, now known as the "pre-Socratics," who lived before or during the life of Socrates (469–399 BCE). Most striking are his comments on Heraclitus (535–475 BCE), a thinker with whom Nietzsche feels the deepest affinity.

Heraclitus' most famous saying is, "*It is not possible to step twice into the same river*" (#40).[6] Here he is not stating a fact about the properties of water molecules. Instead, he is deploying a metaphor in order to express a fundamental thought. Just as the river never ceases to flow, nothing in the world (or outside of it) abides. All is in flux, in continual change. In academic terminology, Heraclitus holds that there is no ***Being***, nothing that just is. Instead, all is ***Becoming***: here today only because gone tomorrow.

Nietzsche feels so close to Heraclitus that he speaks on his behalf:

> Heraclitus proclaimed: "*I see nothing other than becoming*. Be not deceived. It is the fault of your *myopia*, not of the nature of things, if you believe you see land somewhere in the ocean of coming-to-be and passing away. *You use names for things as though they rigidly, persistently endured*; yet even the stream into which you step a second time is not the one you stepped into before." (52)

If you think there is a permanent and immutable reality – the mathematical structure of nature, or the soul, or God, or a Platonic Form – you suffer from myopia, weakness of vision. If you cling to the belief that the solid ground of Being exists somewhere in the ocean of Becoming, you aren't seeing clearly, and you will be easy prey for philosophical seducers like Augustine and Plato.

What occludes our view of the world, Nietzsche proposes, is "names"; more generally, language. Consider the word "tree." We use it to label that tall thing growing in our backyard as well as the trees in the forest and the one on the street. All these particulars are in the realm of Becoming. A while back they were merely seeds. Then they became saplings and grew to maturity. Eventually they will die. They are irrevocably implicated in a continuous process of coming-to-be and passing away. By contrast, the word "tree" is a universal that somehow refers to, but is distinct from, all of the particular items it names. We repeatedly use this same one word even as the old ones die and new ones grow. It is thus tempting to believe that "tree" refers to something that, unlike the many individual (sensible) trees, does not change. Perhaps, this line of thought runs, the word we use refers to some Essence or Form of tree that stays constant even as all the trees we see with our eyes continuously change. Perhaps it is ontologically superior to and even responsible for the particular trees being what they are.

Or think of the Platonic example cited in the previous section. We regularly say that two sticks or stones are "equal." Realizing, however, that the "equality" we can measure with a ruler is imperfect and polluted with inequality, we may then suspect that behind this word stands a concept or Form of Equality that has no truck whatsoever with inequality. In its purity, it is above and beyond the sensible items we hold in our hand. We may then follow Plato's lead and hopefully imagine a permanent Essence of things that stays the same even as particulars change; one that is properly assigned to the realm of Being rather than Becoming. From Nietzsche's perspective, such thinking typifies the seductive lure of language.

Nietzsche acknowledges that Platonism is tempting indeed. For it is terribly difficult to face up to the possibility that nothing abides and is exempt from the ravages of time. He explains:

> The everlasting and exclusive coming-to-be, the permanence of everything actual, which constantly acts and comes-to-be but never is, as Heraclitus teaches it, is a ***terrible, paralyzing thought***. Its impact on men can most nearly be likened to the sensation during an earthquake when one loses one's familiar confidence in a firmly grounded earth. (54)

Nothing firm to grasp and the ground beneath our feet shaking: the absence of Being can be terrifying. To take only the most personal example: if everything flows, then nothing fixed stands behind our names (David, Gina, Bob).

There is no stable "self," no unwavering "I" that unites or accompanies the ceaseless flow of "my" conscious experience. Instead, the name I attribute to myself, and take to refer to something real, is no more than wish projection and a desperate stab at halting the flow of ideas, images, perceptions, feelings that pass through my mind at lightning speed. If all is Becoming, then no stable "I" remains identical to itself through the passage of time.

Why, then, bother getting out of bed in the morning? If nothing abides, including myself, then nothing matters. Does Nietzsche counsel despair?

Not at all. Speaking as much for himself as for Heraclitus, he tells us this: although "it takes astonishing *strength*," it is possible to transform the potentially paralyzing thought of Becoming "into its opposite, into sublimity and the feeling of blessed astonishment" (54). For Nietzsche the goal is not only to affirm Heraclitus' insight, but to transform it into an occasion for celebration.

Play

Another statement by Heraclitus also made a deep impression on Nietzsche. "A lifetime," the old Greek said, "is *a child playing ... the kingdom belongs to a child*" (#103). Heraclitus indulges in some wordplay here. The Greek words for "child" and "play" are closely related. "A child playing" translates *pais paizôn*.

To grasp what he is getting at, we need only recall our brief visit to Lao-Tzu. A child at play is spontaneous, purposeless, free flowing, and imaginative. Most important, he is not bounded by a set of rigid rules. Child's play, then, is radically different from adult play, which typically takes the form of tightly structured and goal-oriented games. In basketball, for example, players are not permitted to use their feet to move the ball, and a referee is employed to make sure this rule is enforced. By contrast, when young children play there is no referee and either no rules or ones that keep changing. The child uses his feet, hands, or nose to move the ball any way he likes. Constrained by no predetermined goals, oblivious to the clock, unburdened by demands, the child does not contend. Instead, he flows aimlessly and with high spirits.

Like the river, a child at play represents not only Heraclitus' conception of a world in which all things come and go, but also the best (most truthful) way to respond to it. Nietzsche explains:

> *In this world only play, play as artists and children engage in it, exhibits coming-to be and passing away, structuring and destroying, without any moral additive, in forever equal innocence.* (62)

Children do not play because they *should*. Acting on deeply felt impulses, they're just having fun and they care not at all about the physical or social consequences of what they're doing. Fully absorbed in the activity, they just flow. Many adults have watched with envy and sensed that only by somehow reclaiming this state of childhood innocence will they spring fully back to life.

The painter facing a blank canvas must be open to surprises, willing to experiment, fool around, try this or that. She must make psychological room for impulsive stabs of the imagination by not locking herself into a rigid preconception of what she will paint. How else will she create something new and exciting?

The biologist is captivated by the gorgeous complexity of organisms. Wonderstruck and intensely energized, he plays with ideas and hypotheses, and ways of testing them in the laboratory. Only by being immersed in such pure research, whose results are unpredictable, might he stumble onto something interesting. Many a discovery in the history of science has been made by someone who did not set out looking for it. Instead, he was just looking.

The following passage from Nietzsche's *Thus Spoke Zarathustra* encapsulates this line of thought:

> The child is *innocence and forgetfulness, a new beginning, play, a self-propelling wheel, a first motion, a sacred Yes.* Yes, a sacred Yes is needed, my brothers, for the play of creation. (32)

Bound by no pre-given rules or moral imperatives, and with nothing written in stone, animated by neither goals nor ambitions, but only by the energy coursing through his body, the child at play just goes forward. Play is thus a way of saying "yes" to the reality of Becoming. By sad contrast, serious philosophers like Plato and Augustine lead us astray. In counseling us to seek Being and Eternity they are deceivers, myopic pipsqueaks who can't stomach the fact that nothing abides. And they tend to be self-righteous about it. Instead of escaping to the lifeless fantasy world of Being, Nietzsche's goal is not only to affirm Becoming, but to celebrate it.

Resolving the Dispute: Being or Becoming?

Some of us are piercingly aware of transience. All we hold dear will soon pass away, and death is our certain end. The urge to seek refuge in what is permanent or beyond time should thus be easy to understand, even by those who think it is misguided. Psalm 18 of the Hebrew Bible gives voice to precisely this impulse:

> I love you, O Lord, my strength.
> The LORD is my *rock*, my fortress,
>   and my deliverer,
> my God, my rock in whom I take
>   refuge,
>   my shield, and the horn of my
>   salvation, my stronghold. (Psalm 18: 1–2)

The image is of solidity both indestructible and protective. God is a "rock" enduring without falter, precisely as we and everything else in this world do not. In His invincible "fortress," the psalmist urges us, we should take shelter, for only there can we be saved from the flux, the flow of time that sends everything in its wake to non-being.

To use a wonderful metaphor, on this view we can *count* on God, even as the world and all its inhabitants, especially ourselves, continually come-to-be and pass away. For just as "7 + 5 = 12" is universally, objectively, forever true, so too is God eternal and unfailingly present. This affinity between numbers and God is what makes Augustine and Pythagoras kindred spirits.[7] Both turn away from Becoming and toward Being, toward what just IS. Even if one does so by faith and the other by rational work, they both seek refuge from the tumult.

By contrast, Nietzsche and Heraclitus (as well as Lao-Tzu) champion Becoming. For them, water, not rock, is the symbol par excellence. They remind us that everything flows, that we cannot step into the same river twice.

Which is it? How to decide?

Perhaps you suspect that this dispute can be resolved empirically (scientifically). The sun looks like a permanent fixture in the sky, but the astronomers tell us that it is anything but. In fact, some predict that it is nearly halfway through its estimated life span of 10 billion years. The table on which my computer sits feels solid, but the physicists remind me that beneath its superficial veneer unimaginably small particles are flying around. My neighbor's dog seems to belong to a species that is a constant in the animal world. Darwin, however, taught us that this is not so. Thousands of years ago there were no dogs, only wolves. The scientists, then, seem to give the nod to Nietzschean Becoming by telling us that what seems to be stable is in fact in flux.

But both Darwinians and the astrophysicists face a challenge: how can they account for the fact that their own theories, which purport to explain the motion of physical things, are themselves neither physical nor in motion? Can they explain how the human mind seems able to transcend the flux by comprehending it? Augustine, the Pythagoreans, and Plato each have an answer to this question, but not ones that contemporary scientists are likely to favor.

A familiar philosophical move has just come into play. Recall the self-reference argument deployed against the relativists in Chapter 4. If they are to be consistent, then their motto, "all truth is relative," must apply to itself. This means that its truth must be taken as relative rather than as objective or universal. If this is the case, then they must count the competing statement, "some truths are not relative," as equally valid as their own, which of course they are reluctant to do. In short, it does not seem possible to maintain a coherent theory, at least one claiming to be objectively true, that espouses relativism.

The proponents of Becoming, from Nietzsche to the contemporary astronomer, face a similar dilemma. "Everything changes" is their motto. But if this is true, then this very sentence will also change and finally pass away. Therefore, the competing statement, "some things do not change," could someday have equal epistemic worth.

Let us apply this argumentative strategy to a passage written by Richard Dawkins and cited way back in Chapter 1:

> Darwinism encompasses all of life – human, animal, plant, bacterial ... extraterrestrial. It provides the only satisfying explanation for why we all exist, why we are the way that we are. It is the **bedrock** on which rest all the disciplines known as the humanities. (*The Blind Watchmaker*, p. x)

If Darwinism is true, as Dawkins so fervently believes it is, then the human animal is evolving. But doesn't this imply that the theory of natural selection itself, which is a human invention (a meme), is also subject to evolution and therefore not a "bedrock" at all? Just as the wolf became a dog, at some time in the future won't Darwin's theory morph into something new? Isn't it, like an organism, in flux? If so, then Dawkins has no business trucking in rock metaphors. Instead, he should invoke water.

Perhaps, then, a serious and consistent fluxist should follow the lead of Lao-Tzu and deploy a kind of language that is itself fluid, for only then would it be immune to the challenge of self-reference. Heraclitus embraces this strategy. He affirms the flux but does so in the language of paradox. Even as he asserts that "it is not possible to step twice into the same river," he also maintains that "we step into and we do not step into the same rivers. We are and we are not" (#41). And he says this: "changing it rests" (#55). And this: "the way up and the way down are one and the same" (#68). These utterances cannot be pinned down. Instead, they oscillate, which is what allows them to give proper voice to the intrinsically elusive idea of Becoming. On the other hand, it's also what makes them impossible to grasp.

The proponent of Being, the evangelist of Eternity, is vulnerable to an analogous challenge. He tells us that God is changeless and absolutely permanent. The Pythagorean says much the same about ratios and the Platonist about Forms. However, their saying so, their arguments and explanations of the Eternal, of Being, are not themselves eternal. Instead, they are strings of syllables that require time for articulation and comprehension. Language, then, does not seem capable of adequately capturing the nature of Being, since in attempting to do so it descends into Becoming. Is Being, then, as elusive as Becoming? Is it too beyond the reach of *logos*?

This impasse suggests that the truth of the matter lies somewhere in between the two extremes of Being and Becoming. Resolution of this debate will not be heralded by the triumph of one side, but instead will require the cooperation of both.

First, think of the Pythagorean. By his lights, even if all things in the physical world, including the sun and our brains, will pass away, it is nonetheless possible for the human mind to discover the timelessly true mathematical equations that govern their movements, and thus itself to participate in the timeless. Insofar as he studies the structure of the world he both resides in it, and is therefore no more than a temporary blip on the screen, but also moves beyond it to its permanent and intelligible structure. Next, think of the Platonist. He maintains that even if the two sticks he is holding in his hands are equal in length, they are only imperfectly equal. After all, the ruler he uses to measure them is imprecise, and the sticks are unequal in weight. From this he infers that the measurable or sensible equality of the two sticks is no more than a reminder of perfect and timeless equality: the Form of the Equal Itself. Although it is not itself sensible the Form is required for the equality of two sticks to be apprehended and measured by the senses. Finally, think of Augustine whose *Confessions* tells the story of his conversion; of how he became a Christian and thereby turned away from Becoming and toward Being. Because it is a story, one with a beginning, middle, and end, it unfolds over the course of time, even as its author proclaims that what is truly real is beyond time.

The point is this: to be human is to be *in between* Being and Becoming. Our capacity for *logos* – for language, reason, confession, argument, prayer, explanation – allows us to glimpse, however fleetingly, Being, even as our bodies continuously metabolize and move steadily toward non-being. Equally, however, does *logos* inhabit the sphere of Becoming. It takes time, goes through time, comes to an end, and is never complete.

As such, *logos* – which Aristotle identified as the defining characteristic of the human species – gives us a foot in two worlds: the permanent (numbers, Platonic Forms, God) and the continuously changing (hearts, lungs, neurons firing for a while). As a result, we are fractured beings. Neither simple animals nor gods, we will never be fully at rest. For us all is, and will continue to be, struggle. We ask questions, seek answers, long for what is beyond ourselves. As such, rather than being fixed or stable we are in between and on the way. Our nature is ever to strive. And so it is that we become questionable, especially to ourselves.

Notes

1   An enjoyable work of fiction that explores the human experience of time is Ben Lerner's novel, *10:04* (New York: Faber & Faber, 2014). The title refers to the time displayed on a large clock in the movie *Back to the Future*. It's when Marty's car takes off.
2   *The Hurt Locker* is a 2008 film directed by Kathryn Bigelow.
3   For a video on the contemporary version of mindfulness see: https://www.youtube.com/watch?v=01Pfs3VuizM.
4   Edmund Husserl, *On the Phenomenology of the Consciousness of Internal Time*, translated by John Brough (Dordrecht: Kluwer, 1991). This is an enormously technical book, and one that I have not myself studied.
5   Arthur Lovejoy's well-known book *The Great Chain of Being* (Cambridge, MA: Harvard University Press, 2001 [originally published in 1938]) is the standard work that describes the medieval *scala naturae* and its dismantling in the eighteenth century.
6   Citations of Heraclitus come from "Heraclitus," in *A Presocratics Reader*, edited by Patricia Curd (Indianapolis: Hackett, 2011).
7   A marvelous little book that describes the aesthetic and religious aspects of mathematics is G. H. Hardy's *A Mathematician's Apology* (Cambridge: Cambridge University Press, 2012 [first published in 1940]). It was the basis of an equally marvelous play by Simon McBurney, *The Disappearing Number*, which was first produced in 2007. I strongly recommend both.

Epilogue

This book ended just as it began: with the Socratic principle that, strange as it may seem, questions are somehow the answer. They tell us who we are. In between knowledge and ignorance, striving for answers, even if they are not forthcoming. Competitive.

Merely asking questions, though, is hardly enough. Someone who mutters, "What does it mean?" and then leaves it at that, is surely no philosopher. Instead, answers must be patiently formulated, reviewed for consistency, tested by considering the strongest possible objections that can be raised against them, and then revised. Furthermore, not all questions are equal. The Socratic injunction is to examine what he calls the "most important matters" (such as, why am I sitting here now?). Failure to do so – that is, to live an unexamined life – is a dangerous kind of negligence.

Still, the Socratic proposal is strange indeed. How in the world could questions rather than assertions represent intellectual achievement? Questions seek answers, and if the inquiry fails to turn one up, hasn't it failed altogether?

No. For just as not all questions are equal, neither are all answers. Even if no one of them succeeds completely or becomes invulnerable to criticism, some are still better than others. They explain more, even if not everything. For this reason, and as should be obvious by now, I have not been entirely neutral in the debates that I have staged in the previous chapters. So, for example, the kind of language I have used throughout this book to formulate these debates indicates that I do not finally side with Nietzsche, Heraclitus, or Lao-Tzu. This book has embraced a commitment to old-fashioned *logos*, to straightforward rational explanation, an

Thinking Philosophically: An Introduction to the Great Debates, First Edition. David Roochnik.
© 2016 John Wiley & Sons, Inc. Published 2016 by John Wiley & Sons, Inc.

enterprise these more paradoxical or poetic thinkers reject. Were I to defend them I would fail the test of self-reference.

Nor do I side with Rousseau on the question of whether we are by nature solitary. This book's epigraph speaks to that. For it expresses the hope that *together* we may strive and seek. On this issue, then, my deeper sympathy lies with Aristotle's conviction that we are essentially talkative, and therefore social and political, beings.

Even my Table of Contents, just by itself, expresses a conviction. Listing a variety of authors who hold competing views, it affirms the fecundity of philosophical diversity, a notion that Descartes would not abide. And the fact that only one chapter was devoted to the moral theories of Mill and Kant, while two addressed the conceptions of human excellence held by Aristotle, Nietzsche, Confucius, and Lao-Tzu speaks for itself.

And so, yes, I do take some of the answers reviewed in this book to be superior to others. Nonetheless, I do not simply dismiss any of the authors we have discussed. Thinkers of this magnitude are never just plain wrong. In fact, I have benefited from reading them all, even those with whom I am least sympathetic. For each has helped me to think harder about myself. So, for example, I often am reminded of Rousseau's riveting analysis of *amour propre*, that infectious need we have to compare ourselves with others, when I escape to the silence of the swimming pool. There, far from the pressure to promote myself in order to achieve professional recognition, I mindlessly go back and forth in the chlorinated water. Alone and glad to be so.

So too do I think about his story of the "state of nature," especially when I have to go to the doctor. The "savage" does not imagine future sufferings and then devise strategies to ward them off. Instead, he feels good when he's feeling good, and he hunkers down when he's in pain. He doesn't worry about cancer or death. Would that I could do the same.

Still, it does not occur to me that the spontaneity and solitude of the savage are more natural than my social bonds and responsibilities (and consequent worries). I'm too much of a Confucian to think that. Yes, society and its faithful attendant *amour propre* threaten to undermine our sense of authentic self, but without other people in my life – family, friends, students, colleagues, guys in the gym, fellow citizens – I would exhaust myself. My Aristotelian leanings are strong.

Augustine's analysis of time-consciousness, better than any I know, helps me to explain the restless energy that courses through, and too often distracts, both my body and mind. The future is not, the past is not, and the present, the only time-frame in which Being is available, is no more than an indivisible gateway of no magnitude. As such, the present, ever absent, does indeed cry out to me, just as Augustine says, and I long for it.

I'm itching to be elsewhere. For this reason, his argument on behalf of conversion, of turning away from Becoming and toward Being, makes terribly good sense. But when he declares that "our hearts are restless till they rest in Thee," when he tells me that salvation is available only through prayer and a loving relationship with a God who loves me in return, we part ways.

I cheerfully use a computer and have been grateful when doctors have healed either me or the ones I love. For this reason, I acknowledge my debt to Descartes, one of the great prophets of advanced technology. But unlike him, I fear that our unbounded confidence in, and enthusiastic (and often mindless) embrace of, technological progress may well generate disastrous consequences.

No, I am not neutral in the debates of this book. Nonetheless, I still affirm the entirety of the reading list. The great books sampled in the previous chapters, however divergent they may be, are like a team of superb teachers. Our job, as readers, is to become their students. This means that we must listen carefully to them, and allow them to provoke us. We must read and then reread. But we must also be critical, and not only affirm the positives, but jettison the negatives. And then we must reverse the process and once again challenge ourselves with views at odds with our own. So while my own allegiances are now with Plato and Aristotle, I look forward to once again confronting opponents like Rousseau, Kant, Descartes, Mill, Augustine, Nietzsche, and Lao-Tzu. Philosophy requires friction, and I thrive on competition. I hope you do the same.

Works Cited

Works are listed by chapter and annotations included where useful.

1 An Introduction to Philosophy

Dawkins, Richard. *The Blind Watchmaker*. New York: Norton, 1996.
Dawkins, Richard. *The Selfish Gene*. Oxford: Oxford University Press, 1989.
Descartes, René. *Discourse on Method and Meditations on First Philosophy*. Translated by Donald Cress. Indianapolis: Hackett, 1998.

> The *Discourse on Method*, and many other of his works, translated by Jonathan Bennett, is available at a site called "Early Modern Texts": http://www.earlymoderntexts.com/assets/pdfs/descartes1637.pdf.

Plato. *The Apology of Socrates*. In Five Dialogues: Euthyphro, Apology, Crito, Meno, Phaedo. Translated by G. Grube and revised by J. Cooper. Indianapolis: Hackett, 2002.

> An online translation is available at http://www.sjsu.edu/people/james.lindahl/courses/Phil70A/s3/apology.pdf.

Plato. *Euthyphro*. In Five Dialogues: Euthyphro, Apology, Crito, Meno, Phaedo. Translated by G. Grube and revised by J. Cooper. Indianapolis: Hackett, 2002.
Plato. *Phaedo*. In Five Dialogues: Euthyphro, Apology, Crito, Meno, Phaedo. Translated by G. Grube and revised by J. Cooper. Indianapolis: Hackett, 2002.

Thinking Philosophically: An Introduction to the Great Debates, First Edition. David Roochnik.
© 2016 John Wiley & Sons, Inc. Published 2016 by John Wiley & Sons, Inc.

Plato. *Phaedrus.* Translated by A. Nehamas and P. Woodruff. Indianapolis: Hackett, 1995.

> Translations of the Platonic dialogues typically use a standard pagination system called "Stephanus page numbers." These are what you see in parentheses following the quotation. An online translation, by Benjamin Jowett, which doesn't use Stephanus numbers, can be found at http://classics.mit.edu/Plato/phaedrus.html.
>
> The most comprehensive online resource for works in Greek and Latin is the Perseus Digital Library: http://www.perseus.tufts.edu/hopper/.

Plato. *Republic.* Translated by Allen Bloom. New York: Basic Books, 1972.

> The dialogue with Thrasymachus takes place in Book I.

2   Alone or With Others?

Aristotle. *The Physics.* Translated by Hippocrates Apostle. Grinnell, IA: Peripatetic Press, 1980.

> An online translation, by R. Hardie and R. Gay, is available at http://classics.mit.edu/Aristotle/physics.html.

Aristotle. *The Politics.* Translated by Carnes Lord. Chicago: University of Chicago Press, 1990.

> Aristotle's corpus has also been organized using a standard pagination system (called "Bekker numbers"). These are what appear in parentheses after my quotations. They should be found in any translation.
>
> An online translation, by Benjamin Jowett, is available at http://classics.mit.edu/Aristotle/politics.html. It does not use Bekker numbers, which make it difficult to coordinate with most other translations.

Darwin, Charles. *On the Origin of Species.* New York: Carlton House, 1934.

> The material cited is found on the first page of the "historical sketch," which does not appear in every edition of the book.

Landemore, Helene. "Democratic Reason: The Mechanisms of Collective Intelligence in Politics." 2011. http://papers.ssrn.com/sol3/papers.cfm?abstract_id=1845709.

Rousseau, Jean-Jacques. *Discourse on the Origin of Inequality.* Translated by Donald Cress. Indianapolis: Hackett, 1992.

An online version of this book, from an old (and unnamed translation) is available at http://www.gutenberg.org/cache/epub/11136/pg11136.html.

3 What Should We Do?

Mill, John Stuart. *Utilitarianism.* Indianapolis: Hackett, 1995.

An online version, which also includes Mill's book *On Liberty,* can be found at http://www.utilitarianism.com/jsmill.htm.

Kant, Immanuel. *Grounding for the Metaphysics of Morals.* Translated by James Ellington. (Indianapolis: Hackett, 1990).

An online version, translated by Jonathan Bennett, is available at http://www.earlymoderntexts.com/assets/pdfs/kant1785.pdf.
Another one, translated by Allan Wood, which contains several explanatory essays, is available at http://www.inp.uw.edu.pl/mdsie/Political_Thought/Kant%20-%20groundwork%20for%20the%20metaphysics%20of%20morals%20with%20essays.pdf.

4 Whom Should We Emulate? (1)

Aristotle. *Nicomachean* Ethics. Translated by Martin Ostwald. New York: Macmillan, 1990.

Ostwald's translation is quite readable, but at times is also inaccurate. For comparison consult Bartlett and Collins's *Aristotle's Nicomachean Ethics: A New Translation* (Chicago: University of Chicago Press, 2012), Broadie and Rowe's *Aristotle's Nicomachean Ethics: Translation, Introduction, Commentary* (Oxford: Oxford University Press, 2004), Crisp's *Aristotle's Nicomachean Ethics* (Cambridge: Cambridge University Press, 2000), and Irwin's *Aristotle's Nicomachean Ethics* (Indianapolis: Hackett Publishing Company, 1995).
A translation by W. D. Ross is available on the Internet Classics Archive: http://classics.mit.edu/Aristotle/nicomachaen.html.

Nietzsche, Friedrich. *A Genealogy of Morals.* Translated by Walter Kaufmann. New York: Vintage, 1990.

A translation (not clear by whom) is available at http://home.sandiego.edu/~janderso/360/genealogy1.htm.

5   Whom Should We Emulate? (2)

Confucius. *The Analects*. Translated by A. Waley. New York: Vintage Books, 1993.

> A translation of *The Analects* by A.C. Muller is available at http://
> www.acmuller.net/con-dao/analects.html.
>   A translation with some commentary by R. Eno is available at http://
> www.indiana.edu/%7Ep374/Analects_of_Confucius_(Eno-2015).pdf.

Lao-Tzu. *Tao Te Ching*. Translated by S. Addiss and S. Lombardo. Indianapolis:
Hackett, 1993.

> An online version is available at http://www.taoism.net/ttc/complete.
> htm.

6   What Do You Know?

Descartes, René. *Discourse on Method and Meditations on First Philosophy*.
Translated by Donald Cress. Indianapolis: Hackett, 1998.

> The *Discourse on Method*, and many other of his works, translated by
> Jonathan Bennett, is available at a site called "Early Modern Texts:
> http://www.earlymoderntexts.com/assets/pdfs/descartes1637.pdf.

Hume, David. *An Enquiry Concerning Human Understanding*. Indianapolis:
Hackett, 2005.

> An online version is available at http://www.earlymoderntexts.com/
> assets/pdfs/hume1748.pdf.

7   Being in Time

Dawkins, Richard. *The Blind Watchmaker*. New York: Norton, 1996.
Heraclitus. "Heraclitus." In A Presocratics Reader. Edited by Patricia Curd.
Indianapolis: Hackett, 2011.
Nietzsche, Friedrich. *Philosophy in the Tragic Age of the Greeks*. Translated by
Marianne Cowan. Chicago: Gateway Press, 1989.

> This translation is available at http://cnqzu.com/library/Philosophy/
> neoreaction/Friedrich%20Nietzsche/Friedrich_Nietzsche%20-
> %20Philosophy_in_the_Tragic_Age_of_the_Greeks_(tr._Marianne_
> Cowan_1996).pdf.

Nietzsche, Friedrich. *Thus Spoke Zarathustra*. In The Portable Nietzsche. Translated by Walter Kaufmann. New York: Viking, 1969.

A translation by Thomas Common is available at http://www.gutenberg.org/files/1998/1998-h/1998-h.htm.

Plato. Phaedo. In *Five Dialogues: Euthyphro, Apology, Crito, Meno, Phaedo*. Translated by G. Grube and revised by J. Cooper. Indianapolis: Hackett, 2002.

Pythagoras. "*Pythagoras and Early Pythagoreanism*." In A Presocratics Reader. Edited by Patricia Curd. Indianapolis: Hackett, 2011.

Saint Augustine. *The Confessions*. Translated by F.J. Sheed. Indianapolis: Hackett, 2003.

A rather old fashioned translation, by Edward Bouverie Pusey, is available at http://www.sacred-texts.com/chr/augconf/aug01.htm.

Saint Augustine. *On Free Choice of the Will*. Translated by Thomas Williams. Indianapolis: Hackett, 1993.

Index

Thinking Philosophically: An Introduction to the Great Debates, First Edition. David Roochnik.
© 2016 John Wiley & Sons, Inc. Published 2016 by John Wiley & Sons, Inc.